Professor Jean Héring, who died in February 1966, had been intimately connected with the Protestant Faculty of Theology at the University of Strasbourg for thirty years. In earlier years he had specialized in philology; for a time he had occupied a Chair of Ethics, prior to his Chair of Theology. Until his death he was joint Director of the internationally famous *Revue d'histoire et de philosophie religieuses*, to which he made frequent contributions.

His main interest for the greater part of his career was in New Testament studies. The three commentaries which he produced have been esteemed as amongst the best in the French language. The commentary on the *First Epistle of Saint Paul to the Corinthians* was made available in an English translation by Epworth Press in 1962. This was followed in 1967 by the translation of the commentary on the *Second Epistle to the Corinthians*. The trilogy is completed by the work here presented.

THE EPISTLE TO THE HEBREWS

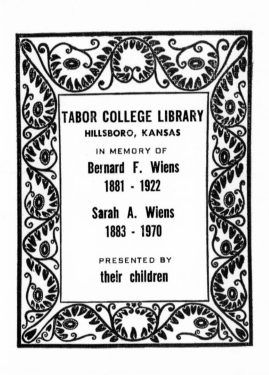

THE EPISTLE TO THE HEBREWS

JEAN HÉRING

*Sometime Professor in the Faculty of Protestant Theology
in the University of Strasbourg*

Translated from the First French Edition by
A. W. Heathcote and P. J. Allcock

LONDON
EPWORTH PRESS

FIRST PUBLISHED BY
DELACHAUX AND NIESTLÉ, NEUCHATEL AND PARIS

TRANSLATION © EPWORTH PRESS 1970

FIRST ENGLISH EDITION PUBLISHED BY
EPWORTH PRESS 1970

SBN 7162 0142 9

PRINTED AND BOUND IN ENGLAND BY
THE CAMELOT PRESS LTD,
LONDON AND SOUTHAMPTON

Dedicated to the memory

of

EUGÈNE MÉNÉGOZ (1838–1921)

and

ÉDOUARD RIGGENBACH (1861–1927)

'I have never known the application of the microscope to one phrase or one word of Holy Scripture which did not discover some thing not only interesting to the expositor, but profitable also spiritually to the student.'

C. J. VAUGHAN

PREFACE

THE PRINCIPLES which have guided us in the composition of this working commentary are the same as in that on the First Epistle to the Corinthians. Words in square brackets in the translation are added to facilitate an understanding of the text. We do not know whether the commentary has succeeded in making the Epistle loved, but we hope to have made it clear that the author 'ad Hebraeos' was a major theologian who knew how to give original and impressive expression to some of the fundamental truths of the Christian revelation.

J. H.

CONTENTS

CONTENTS

INTRODUCTION

ONE OFTEN hears of the enigma of the Epistle to the Hebrews. The expression is justified not only by our ignorance of the identity of the author and of its recipients and by the difficulty of determining its exact literary type (letter? sermon? dissertation?), but also by its contents. Its theology, or more precisely its Christology, though rooted in the soil of primitive Christianity, is of a quite unusual species and in some respects unique for the New Testament. Certainly, as the Epistles of Paul, it knows and makes use of such themes as the pre-existence of Christ as Son of God and Heavenly Man, His humiliation by His incarnation and passion, and His exaltation after death—which is much stressed. Yet in the exposition of these themes there is never discussion of His resurrection. Events unroll as though Jesus went up into heaven immediately after death. What we have is a Christology of ascension rather than of resurrection, and of an ascension which apparently takes no cognizance of the forty days which preceded it according to the Acts of the Apostles.

But it is particularly the fundamental theme of our Epistle, that of Jesus Christ as High Priest after the order of Melchizedek, which at the same time is the most important and most original element in its Christology. Seizing upon the figure of Melchizedek who appears only in Genesis 14 and later in Psalm 110, the author with remarkable wisdom has found the Archimedean point which enables him to lift from its hinges the entire Jewish cult going back by tradition to Moses and Aaron. This mysterious figure, hard to be understood (as the author himself says in 5[11]), by-passes in a sense the whole Jewish religion to link directly with Jesus Christ of whom he is the type. If some Christian theologians affirm that pre-Christian times knew only a solitary valid revelation, that granted to the Israelites, this is not the opinion of the Old Testament nor of our author, who on this point at least places on a higher plane than Judaism divine revelations granted to a pagan priest-king.

Nevertheless, the Epistle makes continual use of the Old Testament (in Greek), along with some rabbinical traditions, but employs an exegetical method which can sometimes seem strange to us. This exegesis is typological, and is not to be confused with allegorical exegesis, though this latter is not wholly absent from our Epistle. Typology, which is equally practised by the Apostle Paul, does not deny the literal meaning of the text, it sometimes even attaches great importance to it, but the events or persons spoken of in the Old Testament become pre-figurations of what takes place under the New Covenant, particularly at its beginning. Thus, Abraham the man of faith and pilgrim on the earth, becomes the type of the

Christian. Sometimes the inferiority of the type to the antitype is stressed, to the extent of creating opposition between them. In this way Sinai is opposed to Zion both by Paul and in our Epistle. Allegory, on the other hand, pays scant attention to the literal sense, which sometimes it completely rejects, in order to substitute for it a spiritual meaning. A classical example is 1 Corinthians 9⁹.

The difficulties we feel in following these interpretations are eased for us, however, by the parallels we find in a very prolix and often more explicit contemporary author who employs typological and allegorical exegesis—namely, the Jew Philo.[1] This statement implies a further one. Like Philo, our author accepts a kind of philosophical and cosmological framework which is more Platonic than biblical. Two successive aeons (the present age and the age to come), which is a classical concept in Judaism and in primitive Christianity, are replaced by two co-existent, superimposed planes—the suprasensible world and the phenomenal world. The former contains the eternal ideas, which the second one attempts to embody materially. The former is 'heaven' for Philo, as it is in our Epistle. For both authors this has an analogous consequence: they say very little about a bodily resurrection of the dead, since the ideal world is essentially incorporeal. Our author only mentions it once and in passing, as instruction given to beginners (6²), while his silence over the bodily resurrection of Jesus must be explained in the same way.

Nevertheless, the Christian sensibility of our author energetically reasserts itself against the Platonizing tendency whenever the Christian hope is at issue. To explain this briefly, as we must do, let us say that for a thorough-going Platonizer (as Philo often is) salvation can consist only in a return of the soul to the 'heavenly country' from which it came. The mystique of this return was a great theme of the Gnostics and later on of Christian mystics who were dependent on Plotinus. The terrestrial world is then only, at bottom, an unfortunate episode, a fall. But in our text the future homeland is something which had no existence before Christ founded it. It is, indeed, 'in heaven', but it is a result of the mission of the great High Priest. The Christian must ever look forward, never backward. The mystique of a return is replaced by the mystique of departure.[2]

This is why earthly life, although transient, is invested with a profound meaning unknown to consistent Platonism, and embodies positive values, as does the whole created order. And as the new homeland is described under the image of a city, as in the Book of Revelation, and not as a garden, this allows us to think that the values developed in human history (as we should say today) are not absent or nullified but transfigured there.

[1] One of the merits of the masterly book by E. Ménégoz (v. Bibliography) is to have brought clearly to light both the resemblances and differences between these two writers.

[2] The tension between Platonism as the framework of Alexandrine thought and biblical revelation has been well presented by J. CAMBIER in his study 'Eschatologie et hellénisme dans l'Epître aux Hébreux' in *Annales Louvanienses Biblicae*, II, 12.

We said at the beginning that this text, though often classed as an Epistle, is perhaps a different type of production. In fact, if we leave aside 13, which is only very slenderly linked to the main body of the book, we have rather the impression of a homily or of a series of homilies, in which doctrinal exposition is often interspersed with practical exhortations. But all these small exegetical or practical dissertations cluster round the central theme of the priesthood of Christ, which is developed in so complete and reflective a way that the work can be called the first essay in Christian dogmatics. We may, perhaps, approach the truth by regarding it as a sermon, but a sermon by a scholar who is not afraid of teaching his congregation theology, somewhat as the author of the so-called First Epistle of St John; and, it may be added, a theology intended for Christians who are already advanced, amongst whom elementary instruction can be taken for granted.

Who then is the author? He is not named, either at the beginning or at the end of 13.[3] Naturally a great number of suggestions have been made, of which we will mention only the most interesting. Pantaenus attributed the work to St Paul, as did his disciple Clement of Alexandria, though the latter with the reservation that Paul had written it in Hebrew and Luke translated it into Greek.[4] Origen, who cited the work yet more frequently than Clement, for his part abandoned the hypothesis of a Hebrew original, yet thought that the unknown author was a disciple of Paul.[5] In spite of these hesitations, direct Pauline authorship was asserted more and more in the East.

It was not the same in the West. If Eusebius classed the Epistle to the Hebrews amongst the disputed books it was because of western views. Clement of Rome, who knew it, does not speak of the author. Tertullian attributed it to Barnabas, a suggestion taken up occasionally by modern theologians, amongst whom are Franz Dibelius and Karl Bornhäuser,[6] who view the work as a letter written by Barnabas the Levite for some former Jerusalem priests. Nor does Jerome appear to consider it as of Pauline origin.[7] St Hilary of Poitiers appears to have been the first clearly to assert a Pauline origin.[8] In the Middle Ages this view became generally accepted. The Council of Trent was not, however, absolutely categorical on the subject. It referred to the fourteen Epistles of Paul as canonical, but refused to accept the proposition of one bishop (the meeting of 5th April 1546) who wanted to insert the formula 'by Paul the Apostle' in connection with the

---

[3] The question of *authenticity* has no relevance here, any more than it has for the so-called Johannine Epistles.

[4] In a lost text cited by Eusebius, *Ecclesiastical History*, VI, 14:1–4.

[5] *Ibidem*, VI, 25:11–14.

[6] FRANZ DIBELIUS, *Der Brief an die Hebräer*, 1910. KARL BORNHÄUSER, *Empfänger und Verfasser des Hebräerbriefes*, Gütersloh 1932.

[7] JEROME, 'But even unto this day [i.e. end of the 4th century] among the Romans it is not held as Paul the Apostle's', *De viris illustribus*, 59, *MPL* 23, col. 669. This judgement could be extended to the entire West.

[8] In particular see *De Trinitate*, IV, 11, *MPL* 10, col. 104.

Epistle to the Hebrews. The Biblical Commission (24th June 1914) energetically affirmed a Pauline origin, but added that it is not necessary to think that the Apostle who had inspired it had given it its form—'*salvo ulteriore Ecclesiae judicio*' ('without prejudice to the further judgement of the Church').

This decision is interpreted in a very wide sense by some contemporary Catholic scholars. In particular, Father Spicq thinks that the redactor was well acquainted with the Pauline Epistles, but that he had edited the Epistle to the Hebrews only after the death of the Apostle to the Gentiles, and he finds medieval witnesses in support of this hypothesis of an 'indirect Pauline origin'.

The Reformers, on their part, are quite negative on the question of the Pauline origin of the Epistle. If Luther in his lectures already expressed doubts on the subject, from 1522 he rejected it decisively in order to attribute the writing to Apollos.[9] Calvin, on the other hand, thinks of Luke or Clement of Rome (*Commentary*, p. 534). But a number of Protestant theologians from Theodore of Beza to T. W. Manson[10] also think of Apollos. Spicq, too, looks sympathetically on this suggestion. It is, indeed, an ingenious one, because Apollos admirably fulfils the required conditions. According to the Acts of the Apostles (18[24f.]) he was an Alexandrine and therefore could know Philonic exegesis; he was well versed in the Scriptures, and an excellent orator and apologist. What has also impressed modern theologians is the originality of style, of vocabulary, and of doctrine of the Epistle, and an ignorance of typically Pauline themes, including resurrection, justification by faith, and the opposition of faith and works. For these reasons the thesis of a Pauline origin has considerably lost ground. We may add that Harnack thought of Aquila, or rather Priscilla,[11] while William Manson (*v*. Bibliography) insists upon the dependence of the theology of our author upon Stephen.

The question of destination is just as hotly debated. Even assuming the identity of the author of the homily itself (**1-12**) with that of **13**, this is not to say that these two unequal parts were written or despatched at the same time. Hence the interpretation of the final remarks of **13** do nothing to settle the identity of the recipients or the auditors of the homily which runs through the first dozen chapters. In the greetings at the end of **13** 'people of Italy' ('*hoi apo Italias*') are mentioned, who send their greetings to the recipients. But this reference is ambiguous. It could signify Christians of Italian origin who

[9] 'The author of the Epistle to the Hebrews, whoever he is, whether Paul, or, as I judge, Apollos . . .' (W.A., 44, 709). 'This Apollos was a learned man. The Epistle to the Hebrews is certainly his' (1537) (*Ibid.*, 45,389).

[10] Bulletin of the J. Rylands Library, 1949, pt.I. For Apollos, cf. A. J. WALKER, *I am of Apollos*, London 1931.

[11] 'Probabilia über die Adresse und den Verfasser des Hebräerbriefs', *ZNW* 1900, pp. 16f.

are sending greetings to their compatriots still in Italy, to whom the Epistle is directed. But it can also be interpreted as Christians living in Italy (perhaps in Rome) who are sending greetings to another area.

Some have judged the work as addressed to Jerusalem or to Jerusalemites, whilst others think of Alexandria or Antioch. Indeed, there are few major cities of the Roman Empire which cannot contend for this honour, through the claim of some modern scholar or other.

We cannot even be absolutely certain that the title *ad Hebraeos*, so naturally added, was intended to denote Judaeo-Christians, though this is very probable—without our having to deduce that the recipients were Hebrew or Aramaic in speech and unable to read Greek.[12]

The date is equally much disputed. The receiving Church already has a past behind it, which is sometimes used as an example. Yet that does not force us to go beyond the year A.D. 70, as we know that Christianity spread rapidly in the lands around Palestine, and even in Rome. And though the destruction of the Temple did not hinder the Rabbis from continuing to discuss details of the cult, the absence of any reference to this catastrophe in our Epistle makes us incline nevertheless, along with E. REUSS, WESTCOTT, E. F. SCOTT, SPICQ and many others, to a date slightly before this.

Discussions of the canonicity of the Epistle generally run in parallel with those of its Pauline origin. It is therefore not surprising that the West was much slower in giving it canonical status than the East (whether Greek or Syriac speaking), and that moreover those who follow the decisions of the Council of Trent are eager to affirm at least its origin as indirectly Pauline.

In the Protestantism of the 16th century some tentative attempts were made to distinguish amongst the collection of New Testament writings those which were proto-canonical from those which were deutero-canonical, including the Epistle to the Hebrews among the latter, as in the first German edition of Luther's New Testament (1522). But this whim seems to have been of only short duration.

What is also most instructive is that the place of the Epistle in the Pauline corpus varies considerably in the manuscripts. S and A put it between 2 Thessalonians and 1 Timothy. B, which ends at 9^{14}, also puts it after 2 Thessalonians (the Pastoral Epistles and Philemon being lost). In C it is found after Colossians; in D after Philemon. Other manuscripts place it in still other positions, e.g. after Romans. This vacillation clearly reveals the relatively late entry of the work into the Pauline corpus.

---

[12] One of the writers who thought that the recipients were Gentile Christians was Hermann von Soden (*v.* Bibliography). VICTOR MONOD takes the title *ad Hebraeos* as allegorical, and as denoting Christians as pilgrims on the earth (' '*ābar*' = 'to travel'), v. *De titulo epistulae vulgo ad Hebraeos inscriptae*, Montauban, 1910.

So far as the form of the text goes, the text which is called Western —which in reality was the text universally read in the 2nd century— is represented by Dp, often denoted merely by D (Codex Clara-montanus, 6th century), as well as by the Latin and Syriac versions by and large. The Alexandrine text (4th century), which appears as a very careful editing of the foregoing, is given by S (4th century), B (4th century) and A (5th century), as well as by minuscule 33. The very incomplete papyrus p 13, and papyrus p 46 (one of the Chester Beatty papyri, 3rd century, and very important),[13] give a text which is a moderate re-editing of the Western text and which dates from the 3rd century. It shows analogies with the text which is otherwise called the Caesaraean text. As for C, this is already moving towards the Byzantine text, represented by L and the great majority of minuscules, and which forms the (insecure) basis of the Textus Receptus of Protestants.

The language and style of the Epistle, though influenced by the LXX, none the less approximates sensibly to classical Greek. Its literary qualities are equally apparent, but they must not be judged by the standards of modern logicality which would find the repetitive-ness rather surprising. The work unfolds rather as a musical com-position, sometimes taking up again a theme already announced or treated earlier, in order to vary it or develop it. Even the parenetic sections and the biblical quotations which at first glance interrupt their didactic context nevertheless fit very well into the whole, and the transitions are rather happily managed.

It is still true that it is difficult to set out the contents according to some precise academic plan. Generally speaking there is no doubt that we can distinguish a mainly didactic section (1–10) from another essentially parenetic (11–13). The former has for its dominant theme what today we should call an affirmation of the absoluteness of Christianity. It is demonstrated by the superiority of Christ with respect to the angels (1, 2), to Moses (3), to Joshua (4^{1-13}), to Aaron and to the Levites (4^{14}–10^{18}), and it is into this last part that there is inserted the familiar argument concerning the priesthood of Christ according to the order of Melchizedek and His decisive work (7–9).

The second section, which gives us some indications, though sum-marily it is true, about the recipients, exhorts them to persevere in the faith and in hope, following the example of the men of old (11), and puts them on guard against discouragement (12). 13 is probably a short letter added to the sermon, containing practical counsels and greetings.

---

[13] See the work of HOSKIER mentioned in the Bibliography.

BIBLIOGRAPHY

A. Lexicons and Grammars

JOHANN BUXTORF, *Lexicon Chaldaicum, Talmudicum et Rabbinicum*, Bâle 1639.

HENRY ESTIENNE, *Thesaurus Linguae Graecae*, 5 vols. 1572. We have used the edition by Didot in 1831.

BOISACQ, *Dictionnaire étymologique de la langue grecque*, 3rd edn, Paris 1938.

PREUSCHEN-BAUER, *Griechisch-deutsches Wörterbuch zu den Schriften des N.T.*, Berlin, 4th edn, 1952; ET (by Arndt-Gingrich) 1956.

G. KITTEL, *Theologisches Wörterbuch zum N.T.*, Stuttgart, in course of publication.

J. H. MOULTON and G. MILLIGAN, *The Vocabulary of the Greek N.T.*, London 1930.

H. L. STRACK and P. BILLERBECK, *Kommentar zum N.T. aus Talmud und Midrasch*, III, Munich 1926.

ALEXANDRE WESTPHAL, *Dictionnaire encyclopédique de la Bible*, vol. I, Paris 1932, vol. II, Valence 1935.

J. J. VON ALLMEN (ed.), *Vocabulary of the Bible*, ET London 1958. This important work appeared originally in French in 1954, too late to be cited in detail; so we draw the reader's attention to it here in a general way.

BLASS-DEBRUNNER, *A Greek Grammar of the N.T.*, ET (by Funk), Cambridge 1961.

J. H. MOULTON, *A Grammar of New Testament Greek*, II, ed. Howard, London 1930.

B. Editions of Texts

E. NESTLÉ, *Novum Testamentum Graece*, 21st edn, Stuttgart 1949.

A. RAHLFS, *Septuaginta*, 2 vols, Stuttgart 1935. Also contains the Apocrypha.

FRANÇOIS MARTIN, *Le livre d'Hénoch* (*Hénoch I, traduit de l'éthiopien*), Paris 1906.

A. VAILLANT, *Le livre des secrets d'Hénoch* (*Hénoch II, traduit du vieux slave*), Paris 1952. Texts published by the Institut d'etudes slaves, IV.

R. H. CHARLES, *Apocrypha and Pseudepigrapha*, 2 vols., Oxford 1913.

E. KAUTZSCH, *Apokryphen und Pseudepigraphen des A.T.*, Tubingen 1900.

L. GOLDSCHMIDT, *Der Babylonische Talmud*, small edn in 12 vols., Berlin 1930–36.

H. FREEDMANN, *Midrasch Rabba*, ET in 10 vols. Vols. 1 and 2 contain the important Midrash Bereshith Rabba.

BEH

L. Cohn and P. Wendland, *Philonis opera*: (a) *Editio major*, 6 vols. and 2 vols. of index (by H. Leisegang), 1896; (b) *Editio minor*, 6 vols., 1896ff.

B. Niese, *Opera Josephi*, 6 vols., 1885–95.

Salomon Reinach, *Les œuvres de Josèphe traduites en français*, 7 vols., Paris 1902–26.

Josephus, Text and translation by H. Thackeray and R. Marcus, Loeb Classical Library, 9 vols.

Migne, *Patrologia Graeca* (*MPG*).

Die griechischen christlichen Schriftsteller, pub. by the Academy of Berlin (*GCS*).

Migne, *Patrologia Latina* (*MPL*).

Corpus scriptorum ecclesiasticorum latinorum, pub. by the Academy of Vienna (*CSEL*).

Ascension of Isaiah, pub. in English by R. H. Charles (1900), and E. Hennecke, *New Testament Apocrypha*, ET London 1965, vol. 2, pp. 642ff.

The Odes of Solomon, in French by J. Labourt and P. Batifoll, Paris 1911.

C. Commentaries and Monographs on the Epistle to the Hebrews
   Works marked * contain a commentary.

* John Chrysostom, *Thirty-four Sermons on the Epistle to the Hebrews*, *MPG* 63, cols. 9–236.
* Theodoret of Cyrrhos, *Commentary on the Epistle to the Hebrews*, *MPG* 82, cols. 673–786.
* Herveus, *On the Epistle to the Hebrews*, *MPL* 181, cols. 1519–1692.
* Nicolas of Lyre, *Postillae perpetuae in Vetus ac Novum Testamentum*, 5 vols., Rome 1471–72. We have used the Bâle edition of 1506.
* Martin Luther, *Commentaire sous forme de cours sur l'Epître aux Hébreux de 1517–18*, edited by J. Ficker under the title: *Anfänge reformatorischer Bibelauslegung*, II, Leipzig 1929. Cf. Jean Baruzi, 'Le commentaire de Luther sur l'Epître aux Hébreux', *RHPR*, 1931, pp. 461–98.
* Desiderius Erasmus, *Annotationes in epistulam Pauli ad Hebreos*, Bâle 1521.
* Cajetanus (Thomas de Vio), *Epistolae Pauli enarratae*, Venice 1531.
* Jehan Calvin, *Commentaire sur l'Epître aux Hébreux*. We have used the Meyrueis edition, Paris 1855, vol. 4, pp. 357ff. The Latin text is found in the *Opera Calvini*, edited by Baum, Cunitz and E. Reuss, Brunswick 1896, vol. 55.
* Hugo Grotius, *Opera omnia theologica*, Amsterdam 1679, 4 vols. We have used the Bâle edition in 4 vols., 1732.
* Johann Albrecht Bengel, *Gnomon Novi Testamenti*, 1742, 3rd edn 1773. We have used an impression of the 3rd edn made in Berlin, 1855. The German edition should not be used.

* J. J. WETSTEIN, *H KAINE DIATHEKE*, II, pp. 383ff, Amsterdam 1752.

* FRIEDRICH BLEEK, *Der Brief an die Hebräer*, 3 vols., Berlin 1828, 1836, 1840.

J. H. R. BIESENTHAL, *Das Trostschreiben des Apostels Paulus an die Hebräer*, Leipzig 1878.

* EDOUARD REUSS, *L'Epître aux Hébreux*, Paris 1878 (in: La Bible, traduction nouvelle avec introduction et commentaire, Nouveau Testament, Part 6, pp. 8ff.).

EUGÈNE MÉNÉGOZ, *La théologie de l'Epître aux Hébreux*, Paris 1894. Annotated translation of the Epistle to the Hebrews in the Bible du Centenaire, pp. 363ff., 1928. This translation has been reprinted in 'The New Testament edited by Goguel and Monnier'.

* B. F. WESTCOTT, *The Epistle to the Hebrews*, London 1889, 3rd edn 1903.

* BERNHARD WEISS, *Der Brief an die Hebräer* (in the Meyer Kritisch-exegetischer Kommentar), 1897.

* HERMANN VON SODEN, *Der Brief an die Hebräer* (in the Kommentar zum N.T. edited by H. J. Holtzmann), Freiburg in Brisgau, 1899.

FR. BLASS, *Der Brief an die Hebräer*. Text mit Angabe der Rythmen, 1903.

W. WREDE, *Das literarische Rätsel des Hebräer-Briefs*. B.F.R.L.A.N.T., no. 8, Göttingen 1906.

A. NAIRNE, *The Epistle of Priesthood*, Edinburgh 1913.

* — *The Epistle to the Hebrews*, Cambridge 1921.

* H. WINDISCH, *Der Hebräerbrief* (in the H. Lietzmann Handbuch zum N.T.), Tübingen 1913, 2nd edn 1931.

* ED. RIGGENBACH, *Der Brief an die Hebräer* (in the Zahn Kommentar zum N.T.), Leipzig 1913, 2nd edn 1922.

* LÉON BOUILLON, *L'Eglise apostolique et les Juifs philosophes jusqu'à Philon*, 2 vols., Orthez 1914. The second volume contains an original translation and a commentary upon the Epistle to the Hebrews (pp. 743–875).

H. L. MACNEILL, *The Christology of the Epistle to the Hebrews*, Chicago 1914.

E. F. SCOTT, *The Epistle to the Hebrews, its Doctrine and Significance*, Edinburgh 1922.

* J. MOFFATT, *The Epistle to the Hebrews* (I.C.C.), Edinburgh 1924.

* T. H. ROBINSON, *The Epistle to the Hebrews* (Moffatt Commentary), London 1933.

V. BURCH, *The Epistle to the Hebrews, its sources and message*, London 1936.

* O. MICHEL, *Der Brief an die Hebräer* (in the Meyer Kritisch-exegetischer Kommentar), 1936, 2nd edn 1949.

H. C. HOSKIER, *A Commentary on the various readings in the Text of the Epistle to the Hebrews in the Chester Beatty Papyrus*, p 46, London 1938.

* J. BONSIRVEN, *Saint Paul. L'Epître aux Hebreux*, Paris 1943.

* J. S. JAVET, *Dieu nous parla*, Neuchâtel 1945.

T. W. MANSON, *The Problem of the Epistle to the Hebrews*, Bulletin of the J. Rylands Library, 1949, pp. 1ff.

WILLIAM MANSON, *The Epistle to the Hebrews. A Historical and Theological Reconsideration*, Edinburgh 1950.

* C. SPICQ, *L'Epître aux Hébreux*, 2 vols., I. *Introduction*; II. *Text and Commentary* (in the series Etudes Bibliques), Paris 1952; cf. our review in *RHPR*, 1954 (no. 2, pp. 169ff).

The works in this Bibliography are frequently referred to by abbreviated titles. Other publications are mentioned in the Introduction and the Commentary.

ABBREVIATIONS

ATANT	*Abhandlungen zur Theologie des Alten und Neuen Testaments*
ARW	*Archiv für Religionswissenschaft*
BZAW	*Beihefte zur Zeitschrift für die alttestamentliche Wissenschaft*
BZNW	*Beihefte zur Zeitschrift für die neutestamentliche Wissenschaft*
CTAP	*Cahiers theologiques de l'actualité protestante*
CSEL	*Corpus Scriptorum Ecclesiasticorum Latinorum*
DACL	*Dictionnaire d'archéologie chrétienne et de liturgie*
HDB	*Hastings Dictionary of the Bible*
DEB	*Dictionnaire encyclopédique de la Bible*
DTC	*Dictionnaire de théologie catholique*
EB	*Encyclopaedia Biblica*
EHPR	*Etudes d'histoire et de philosophie religieuses* (*Strasbourg*)
EJ	*Encyclopaedia Judaïca*
ERE	*Encyclopaedia of Religion and Ethics*
ETR	*Etudes théologiques et religieuses* (*Montpellier*)
ExT	*Expository Times*
GCS	*Die griechischen christlichen Schriftsteller der ersten drei Jahrhunderte*
HTR	*Harvard Theological Review*
JBL	*Journal of Biblical Literature*
JR	*Journal of Religion*
JTS	*Journal of Theological Studies*
Jud.	*Judaica*
MPG	*Migne, Patrology, Greek Series*
MPL	*Migne, Patrology, Latin Series*
RAC	*Reallexikon für Antike und Christentum*
RB	*Revue biblique*
RE	*Realenzyklopädie für protestantische Theologie und Kirche, 3rd edn*
RGG	*Die Religion in Geschichte und Gegenwart, 2nd edn*
REG	*Revue des études grecques*
REJ	*Revue des études juives*
RHPR	*Revue d'histoire et de philosophie religieuses* (*Strasbourg*)
RHR	*Revue de l'histoire des religions*
RKAW	*Realenzyklopädie der klassischen Altertumswissenschaften*
RTP	*Revue de théologie et de philosophie* (*Lausanne*)
SAB	*Sitzungsberichte der Preussischen Akademie der Wissenschaften zu Berlin* (*phil.-hist.Klasse*)

TB	*Theologische Blätter*
TLZ	*Theologische Literatur-Zeitung*
TR	*Theologische Rundschau*
TS	*Theologische Studien*
TSK	*Theologische Studien und Kritiken*
TWNT	*Theologisches Wörterbuch zum Neuen Testament*
TZ	*Theologische Zeitschrift*
TU	*Texte und Untersuchungen zur Geschichte der altchristlichen Literatur*
ZATW	*Zeitschrift für die alttestamentliche Wissenschaft*
ZKG	*Zeitschrift für Kirchengeschichte*
ZNTW	*Zeitschrift für die neutestamentliche Wissenschaft*
ZST	*Zeitschrift für systematische Theologie*
ZTK	*Zeitschrift für Theologie und Kirche*

CHAPTER I

(1) *On many occasions and in manifold ways God had [already] in past times spoken to the men of old by the prophets.* (2) *But at the end of time, in which we now are living, he has spoken to us by one who is the Son, whom He had appointed heir of the universe, and by whom also He had created the worlds.* (3) *He it is who faithfully reflects God's glory and who retains the exact imprint of His being. It is He also who maintains the universe by His powerful word, and who, after having through Himself effected the purification of sins, sat down at the right hand of the Majesty in the height of heaven.* (4) *And thus He became so much more powerful than the angels because He had inherited a more excellent name than they.*

1¹⁻⁴. This well-balanced passage recalls much less the style of the Apostle Paul or of the Greek Bible than that of classical authors. Nevertheless, we shall see that the Greek of the LXX was not without influence on our author. The passage gives a brief survey of some essential elements of the Christology of the Epistle, as well as of its concept of revelation.

1¹. The two adverbs *'polumerōs'* and *'polutropōs'* = 'on many occasions' and 'in many ways' are not exactly equivalent, as John Chrysostom imagined.[1] The first alludes to the many occasions in which God spoke under the old covenant. The second indicates the multiformity of the revelation, the variety of modes of revelation (visions, dreams, commands, promises, etc.) and varieties of content.[2] Only the revelation by the Son is complete and definitive.

In connection with *'en tois prophētais'* = 'by the prophets', Samuel Crell (1660–1747), a wise Socinian who wrote under the pseudonym of Artemonius, suggested reading *'anggelois'* = 'by the angels' instead of *'prophētais'*,[3] and this conjecture seemed so ingenious to Bengel, in general very sparing in his references, that he

---

[1] *'To gar polumerōs kai polutropōs tout' esti diaphorōs'* (the twofold expression means 'in a varied way').

[2] Severian (beginning of 5th century) explains that *'polumerōs'* = 'relating to differences of time', and *'polutropōs'* means that 'one command was given to Adam . . . and another through Moses, and other different ones through the prophets'—quoted from Staab, *Paulus-Katenen aus der Griechischen Kirche* (Munster in Westf., 1933), p. 346. Bengel: 'The very fact that there were so many prophets shows that they prophesied in part.' Cf. Ephesians 3¹⁰ and Wetstein, II, p. 387.

[3] In his now very rare work *Initium evangelii s.Johannis apostoli restitutum* (2 vols., 1726, without indication of place or printer), I, pp. 238f. The work is largely, though not entirely, devoted to the Johannine prologue. He regarded Luke as the author of the Epistle to the Hebrews because of its literary qualities.

mentioned it in his *Gnomon*. Later Friedrich Spitta, unaware of Artemonius, suggested the same thing,[4] with very similar arguments, of which the chief are these: (*a*) In the sequel (with the exception of **11**, which treats of other matters) there is no further reference to prophets but only to the Law of Moses and Aaron. It is this which is opposed by the Gospel. (*b*) It is precisely this Sinaitic legislation which is attributed to angels at the beginning of **2**.[5] (*c*) In the immediate context (**1** and **2**) the Christological argument vigorously insists upon the superiority of the Son to the angels.

What is to be thought of this view? The first argument loses something of its force when it is remembered that the Jewish scriptures call men of God 'prophets' who are much earlier than the written prophets and even than Elijah, in particular Abraham, Moses and Aaron.[6] The second and third arguments are more substantial. For it cannot be denied that the reading 'by the angels' provides a much more coherent and more suggestive text. The first verse of the Epistle would then announce at once the theme developed in the two first Chapters.[7] We have not adopted the conjecture, however, which is entirely unsupported by any textual evidence, although we mention it as interesting.[8]

Who are the '*pateres*' (lit. 'fathers', Hebrew, ''*āḇôṯ*')?[9] Not the patriarchs alone, but in a general sense 'men of old time', 'ancestors' (so Riggenbach). Cf. **3**[9]; **8**[9]; Matthew 23[30-32]; John 6[31,49,58]; Acts 7[19] and elsewhere. One must certainly not conclude from the use of this expression that the recipients must have been of Jewish origin. For the Christian Church, regarding itself as the heir of the promises of the Old Testament, could well also lay claim to the 'men of old time', and we know that the Apostle Paul did so quite expressly (Romans 4[1,11-18]; 9[10]; 1 Corinthians 10[1]).

1[2a]. '*Ep' eschatou tōn hēmerōn*' (lit. 'at the end of the days') is a faith-

---

[4] Cf. *TSK*, 1913, pp. 106–109. URBAN HOLTZMEISTER, S.J., has criticized Spitta in a conscientious but sometimes specious manner in *Zeitschrift f.kath. Wissenschaft* (Innsbruck), 1913, pp. 805f.

[5] 'The law-giving of Sinai . . . which is never ascribed to prophets but is ascribed in so many words to angels'—ARTEMONIUS, *loc. cit.*

[6] Deuteronomy 18[15] puts into the mouth of Moses this declaration directed at Joshua: 'The Lord your God will raise up for you a prophet *like me*.' Cf. Deuteronomy 18[18]; Ecclesiasticus 46[1] and Acts 3[22]; 7[37]. According to Exodus 7[1] Aaron is the 'prophet' of Moses. For Abraham, see Genesis 20[7].

[7] There is no need for uneasiness over the use of '*en*' instead of '*dia*'; as very frequently in Old Testament Greek and in the New Testament '*en*' is equivalent to '*dia*'. It is a Semitism, the use of '*en*' being modelled on that of the polyvalent Hebrew particle '*be*' (Aramaic: '*de*').

[8] If it is true that v. 1 contains deliberate alliteration (words commencing with 'p': '*polumerōs*', '*polutropōs*', '*palai*', '*patrasin*') this could be a reason for reading '*prophētais*'. Cf. 11[28]: '*pistei*,, '*pepoiēken*', '*pascha*', '*proschusin*', and the commentary by O. MICHEL on 1[1].

[9] p 46 reads '*patrasin hēmōn*' = 'our fathers'; also some other witnesses. But it is a pleonasm. John Chrysostom did not have '*hēmōn*', *v. MPG* 63, col. 13.

ful rendering of an Old Testament Hebrew expression,[10] a translation
attested by the LXX in Numbers 24[14]; Jeremiah 23[20]; Daniel 10[14],
and elsewhere. It is an equivalent of '*ep' eschatōn hēmerōn*' = 'in the
last days',[11] which is even more frequent in the LXX. In 9[26] we meet
the synonymous '*epi sunteleia tōn aiōnōn*' = 'at the consummation of
the ages'.

But what exactly does the pronoun '*toutōn*' mean, added to
'*hēmerōn*'? One might take '*hēmerai hautai*' = 'these days' as
synonymous with '*ho aiōn houtos*' = 'the present age', so common
with the Rabbis and with Paul. But it seems to us more likely that
the demonstrative pronoun is intended here to remind us that 'these
last days' are our days, i.e. the days of our generation. Then the
expression would underline the privilege of Christians living in
expectation of the imminent parousia. This eschatological hope was
not realized at the time. But it is none the less true that the time
between the ascension and the parousia represents in biblical
Christianity the final period of the old order, however long it may
last, and without our being under any obligation to insert Heidegger's
notion of an 'end' which impinges upon or threatens every moment
of our existence.

The use of '*huios*' = 'son' without the article is a little unusual.
We agree with Riggenbach and Spicq that the omission is deliberate.
The writer wishes to stress the exceptional excellence of the relationship of Christ to God, naturally without denying the uniqueness of
the Son, 'one who had the rank of Son' or 'one who was the Son'.

1[2b-4]. These verses give, as already mentioned, a résumé of the
author's Christology, in the form of subordinate clauses which it
is preferable not to render as such into English. First we are told that
the Son has been made 'heir of the Universe'[12] ('*klēronomon pantōn*').
It is this quality of being heir which distinguishes a son from a servant, as the Epistles to the Galatians (4[7]) and Romans (8[15]) explain
to us.

But when was the Son 'appointed' ('*tithenai*')? After His ascension
to heaven, as the Apostle Paul teaches, and as the quotation from
Psalm 110 in 1[13] suggests? Or from all eternity, as the mention of
inheritance before the reference to creation suggests? It must be
noted that '*ethēken*' can mean 'designate in advance' as a future heir.
The two explanations are therefore not mutually exclusive.

1[2b]. 'The worlds' were created by Him, i.e. by the Son. Many expositors here translate the plural by the singular, 'the world'—though

---

[10] '*Be' aharît hayyamîm.*'
[11] That is the reading given here by the Syriac and some other less important
witnesses. Cf. 1 Peter 1[20]: '*ep' eschatou tōn chronōn*' = 'at the end of the times'.
[12] '*Panta*' or '*ta panta*' is a normal expression for 'the universe' in the New
Testament (cf. German '*Das All*'). It should not be translated by 'all things', which
is maladroit and less pointed. Cf. John 1[3]; Colossians 1[16]; 1 Corinthians 8[6];
15[27f]; Ephesians 1[10, 23]; 3[9]; 4[6]; 1 Peter 4[7]; and elsewhere.

naturally with a twinge of conscience for no single text is found which would support this rendering. Then why not leave the plural with its normal meaning, remembering that an *'aiōn'* = 'world' is not necessarily a visible order of creation? The Enoch literature—not to mention Hellenistic ideas—recognizes seven superimposed worlds in the beyond, and it will be remembered that Paul speaks of a third heaven (2 Corinthians 12²). The notion that the Son created not only the visible world, but also the whole range of the others is not at all odd, as the Apostle Paul expressly says so.[13]

As in Paul and in the Johannine prologue, the Son is therefore the mediator (not the author) of the creation. Even in this form the doctrine is somewhat surprising in a type of Christianity which shows an immediate interest only in soteriology. Primitive Christianity had wider horizons. All the functions attributed to Wisdom (*'sophia'*, *'ḥokmāh'*), including that of being God's master-workman, in the Wisdom literature (and see especially Proverbs 8 and 9; Wisdom 7¹⁵–8¹), as well as to the Logos by Philo,[14] are carried over to Christ, who includes within Himself 'all the treasures of divine wisdom', as the Apostle Paul expressly affirms.[15]

In this connection it is not unprofitable to remark that behind this theological statement is hidden an important religious intuition which is specifically Christian—namely, that of the identity of the creative principle with the redemptive principle. It is no 'foreign' power which saves humanity (as with Marcion), but a power which we know intimately because we have been created by it. The Word comes 'to His own', as the Johannine prologue puts it. And this truth is not unconnected with another—that men have been created in 'the image of God', which image, according to Paul and to our Epistle (1³) is precisely the Son Himself.[16]

[13] See 1 Corinthians 8⁶; Colossians 1¹⁶; Tobit 13¹⁸, according to the text of the manuscripts A and B, *'pantas tous aiōnas'*. Cf. STRACK-BILLERBECK III, 671B.

[14] Cf. E. BRÉHIER, *Les idées philosophiques et religieuses de Philon d'Alexandrie*, Chap. 2, Paris, 2nd edn, 1925.

[15] As the Jewish Cabala affirms of the first or original Adam (*'aḏām ḳaḏmôn'*); for this see GINZBERG's good introduction, *The Cabbalah*, 2nd edn, London 1920. Cf. also Colossians 2³.

[16] Christian mystics of the Christocentric type who, in encountering Christ, claim to have experienced the feeling of rediscovering and of coming to know the ground of their own being, are therefore not outside the pale of the Gospel, whatever the objective value of their experience may be. Relating a vision of Christ, Sadhu Sundar Singh says: 'I felt when first I saw Him as if there were some old and forgotten connexion between us, as though He had said, but not in words, "I am He, through whom you were created" ' (B. H. STREETER and H. J. AP-PASAMY, *The Sadhu*, London 1921, p. 54). The theologian W. BOUSSET, while making some concessions to modern spiritual forms of expression, gives utterance to what is basically the same intuition when he ends his book on Jesus with the exclamation: 'When we strive to immerse ourselves in His life and person a cry of gladness echoes through our soul; for in truth we are encountering the basis of our existence as spiritual personalities.' *Jesus* (Religionsgeschichtliche Volks-bücher), 1907, p. 100.

1³. Here are outlined for us some of the characteristic aspects of the eternal essence of the Son. He is called *'apaugasma tēs doxēs'* and *'charaktēr tēs hupostaseōs autou'* (see the translation). To some extent the two expressions are synonymous. But while the first stresses in particular the majesty of the Son, the second is a reminder of His likeness to the Father. *'Apaugasma'* does not mean an emanation (this would rather be *'epaugasmos'*), but its result, i.e. the luminous reflection, as in Wisdom 7²⁶ (*'apaugasma gar estin phōtos aïdiou'*, 'she is a reflection of eternal light', meaning Wisdom). Is this explanation to be rejected on the grounds that a reflection would imply a mirror, and none can be found? If one thinks in this way, why not also challenge the translation of *'eikōn'* by 'image', because an image would require some support? Actually, the concern of the author is to make clear that the Son participates in a wholly special way in the glory of the Father. He is not merely like the Father, He is of the same essence,[17] although subordinate to the Father.

The meaning of *'charaktēr'* naturally has no relation here to the psychological significance of the word 'character' in modern languages. It denotes an 'imprint' which faithfully reproduces the original (from *'charassō'* = 'to engrave').[18] It is this which guarantees the absoluteness of Christianity, to use modern theological jargon.

'Pherōn ta panta tō rhēmati tēs dunameōs autou' (lit. 'carrying the universe by the word of His power'). This could mean that He maintains in existence the universe created by Himself (cf. Colossians 1¹⁷). But *'pherein'* (Heb. *'sābal'*) can also have the meaning of 'govern', 'be responsible for'. In which case this would be an allusion to His providential action in the world, an enormous privilege which the Old Testament reserves for God.[19] A third interpretation is

---

[17] Therefore He is *'homo-ousios'*, to use the word dear to the Valentinian Gnostics and to Athanasius. Philo uses *'hypostasis'* with a somewhat analogous meaning: a visible copy of an invisible reality. Cf. *De Plantatione*, §50 (Chap. 12), where the world is called 'an outshining of sanctity, a copy of the original' (*'hagiōn epaugasma, minēma architupou'*). On the other hand, in *De Somniis* I, §188 (Chap. 32), he uses the word in the same sense as in Greek philosophy (essence or substance): 'the world whose substance is discernible only by intellect' (*'ho noētēs hupostaseōs kosmos'*). With this connotation the term also entered the Wisdom literature; cf. for example Wisdom 16²¹, where the *'hypostasis'* of God is mentioned. Our Epistle uses the word in this sense later, in 11. The most recent monograph on the use of *'hupostasis'* in the theology of the Fathers is by M. RICHARD, 'L'introduction du mot "hupostasis" dans la théologie de l'incarnation', in *Mélanges de science religieuse*, Lille 1945.

[18] In *Quod Deterius Meliori Insidiari Soleat*, §83 (Chap. 23), PHILO calls the spirit (*'pneuma'*) 'an impression stamped by the divine power' (*'tupon kai charaktēra theias dunameōs'*). SÉBASTIEN CASTELLION, *Novum Jesu Christi Testamentum*, 1551, translates *'charaktēr'* by *'forma expressa substantiae'* ('the express form of the substance').

[19] This would be in harmony with the theology of the Midrash Lev. Rabba 4.8 (FREEDMANN, IV, p. 58), in which the soul carries the body and God carries His world (cf. STRACK-BILLERBECK, III, p. 673), and especially of Philo, who accords to the Logos the privilege of governing the world. See *De Cherubim* I, §36 (Chap. 11), where the *'logos theou'* is called *'diopos'* ('overseer'), or according to another reading, *'pēdaliouchos'* ('pilot') *kai kubernētēs* ('steersman') *tou pantos'*.

proposed by Gregory of Nyssa: *'pherō'* = 'call into existence',[20] a usage found similarly in Philo.[21] But then the remark would be somewhat of a repetition of v. 2b, 'by whom He created the universe'. *'Rhēma tēs dunameōs'* (lit. 'word of power') is clearly a Semitism for 'powerful word'.[22]

'Di' autou (or: *di' heatou*) *katharismon tōn harmatiōn poēsamenos'* = 'having through Himself effected the cleansing of sins'.[23] It goes without saying that the genitive *'tōn hamartiōn'* has the force of an ablative of separation in Latin; it is not the sins which are purified, but the world. This summary affirmation is made clear in the light of later developments in the Epistle—for the sacrifice of His life is plainly implied. So we can straightaway underline that 'purification' is a much more radical and mysterious operation than the simple forgiveness of sins, which God could freely grant (according to Luke 15[20f]), but which would not change the future of the world. The meaning of *'katharismos'* presupposed by the writer is attested also in the LXX (cf. especially Exodus 29[36]; 30[10]; Proverbs 14[9]). Our Epistle uses the noun *'athetēsis'* = 'abolition' (9[26]) in an analogous sense. Are we to think not only of the sins of humanity but of those also of the angels? The Christology of the Epistle does not completely exclude it, although Judaism, at least after the books of Enoch, rejects the idea of a re-instatement of the fallen angels.

'Ekathisen en dexia tēs megalōsunes' = 'He sat down at the right hand of the Majesty' (a current Jewish expression for God),[24] in the heavenly places. *'En hupsēlois'*, synonymous with *'en hupsistois'* (Luke 2[14]; Mark 11[10] par.) and with *'en tois epouraniois'* (8[1]) = 'in the high places', which here means: in the height of heaven. This implies the solemn enthronement spoken of in many Gospel texts and proclaimed likewise by the Apostle Paul (Philippians 2[11]). Note that according to Jewish conceptions, which at this point our

It is in this way that John Chrysostom has interpreted our verse: 'He says bearing the universe, that means guiding it' (*'pherōn te gar phēsi, ta panta, tout'* esti *kubernōn'*).

[20] *Contra Eunomium* II (MPL 45, col. 530), or III, §71, in Jaeger's edition, 1921 (vol. II, p. 324).
[21] Cf. *Quis Rerum Divinarum Heres*, §36 (Chap. 7), where God is called *'ta mē onta pherōn'*. This must mean 'He who brings into existence that which did not exist', for Philo continues *'kai ta panta gennōn'* = 'and generates the universe'. Cf. *De Mutatione Nominum*, §256 (Chap. 44). J. CHR. SCHÖTTGEN, *Horae Hebraicae et Talmudicae in universum N.T.* (1733, 2 vols.) draws attention to a passage in the Midrash Bereshit Rabbah 22.11, which he translates by: 'Thou bearest the upper and lower worlds (*"superna et inferna"*), but my sins thou bearest not' (God is, of course, the subject), vol. 1, p. 919; cf. FREEDMANN, I, p. 190.
[22] Like *'rhēma tēs hupomonēs'*, Revelation 3[10]. *'Apo'* is absent from p 46.
[23] The readings *'di' auto'*, attested by p 46, D, and *'di' heautou'* given by the Syriac and Byzantine texts, are entirely synonymous. S and B have neither; but the omission seems hardly justifiable. The lack of the article before *'katharismon'* is in no way surprising, because the noun is followed by a genitive. This is an imitation of the 'construct state' of Hebrew syntax.
[24] Cf. Mark 14[62] par.; Testament of Levi 3; Ascension of Isaiah 11[32]; 1 Enoch 14[20f].

(5) *Indeed, to which of the angels has He ever said 'You are my son, today I have begotten You'? And [concerning whom has He] again [said] 'I will be a Father to Him, and He will be a son to me'? (6) And, with a view to the time when He will bring again His firstborn*

author shares (*v.* infra, v. 13), even the most exalted angels could go no further than *stand* in God's presence.[25]

1[4]. This verse adds nothing new. It reaffirms the Son's superiority. But what is the 'name' which He inherited? We might imagine '*kurios*' = 'Lord', as in Philippians 2[11]. Yet our Epistle only uses this title when it occurs in an Old Testament passage, and without giving it prominence. It is preferable to think that the title 'Son' is in mind, which title is much in evidence in v. 5—at least, unless there is an allusion, as in Revelation 19[12], to an unknown name.

With 1[4] is brought to an end the general survey of the nature and rôle of Christ, in His pre-existence, His incarnation, and after His ascension. It emerges from this that the Son was already during His pre-existence divine by nature, and that His cosmological rôle has been of profound significance. On the other hand, the stress with which the writer speaks of His exaltation to the right hand of God seems to point to a supererogatory dignity conferred upon Him after His earthly mission (cf. '*huper-hupsōsen*' = 'He has super-exalted Him', Philippians 2[11]). It may be called the messianic dignity (Paul: '*kurios*'). Though our author will view it from a different angle: by His sacrifice the Son acquired a human perfection that He did not previously possess and which made Him the ideal High Priest, interceding for men and completing the work of salvation by a veritable renewal of humanity.

The second part of the first Chapter develops the theme of the superiority of the Son to the angels. 'Speculations' about angels seem to be void of interest for many contemporary Christians, who have ceased to believe in their existence. But Christian theology would be wrong to conform to the demands of our obscurantist age which denies everything that does not fall under sense-perception. The day is not far distant when only the New Testament doctrine of angels will form a barrier against certain gnostic or 'religious' movements which, intentionally or otherwise, run the risk of making many believers fall back into the cult of angels, dominions, and 'elements'. *Sapienti sat.*

1[5–13] presents us with a bouquet of quotations culled for the most part from the Psalter. Detailed exposition of their original meaning clearly belongs rather to Old Testament exegesis. Let us content

[25] On this matter see the observations in our article 'Un texte oublié: Mat. 18.10' in the miscellany presented to Maurice Goguel under the title *Aux origines de la tradition chrétienne*, Neuchâtel and Paris 1950, pp. 95–102, and the Enoch literature.

*into the world, He says 'Let all the angels of God worship Him'.
(7) And whereas on the subject of angels Scripture declares 'He makes
His messengers winds, and His ministers a flame of fire'—of the Son
it says:* (8) *'Your throne, O God, is established for eternity, and the
sceptre of equity is the sceptre of Your reign.* (9) *You have loved
justice and hated iniquity. Therefore, O God, your God has anointed
You with an oil that makes joy abound, distinguishing You thereby
from your companions'.* (10) *And, 'it is You, Lord, who at the beginning founded the earth, and the heavens are the work of your hands.*
(11) *They will perish, but You will remain; and all the heavens shall
become old as a garment.* (12) *You will roll them up like a cloak; as a
garment they shall be changed. But You, You remain the same, and
your years have no end.'* (13) *And to which of the angels has He ever
said 'Sit at my right hand, until I make your enemies your footstool'?*

ourselves with the observation that the writers of these passages were
thinking either of God (Psalm 102 [LXX 101], cited in v. 10, and
Isaiah, cited in v. 12), or of the king of Israel (Psalm 2 and 2 Samuel
cited in v. 5 and v. 6; Psalm 45 [LXX 44] cited in vv. 8, 9; Psalm 110
[LXX 109] cited in v. 13) or of the people of Israel (Deuteronomy
32[43] LXX, cited v. 6).

To all these texts the author *ad Hebraeos* boldly gives a Christological meaning, in conformity with the custom of the early Church
which sought—and found—in the Old Testament texts serviceable
for apologetics. Only in the case of Psalm 104[4] (LXX 103[4]) does he
retain the original meaning. It must be admitted frankly that this
sometimes rather forced interpretation of the Old Testament has
rather lost its value. The proof from prophecy was never, indeed, for
the Apostles and first disciples, the true cause of their faith. But it
goes without saying that this reservation deprives the themes themselves which the author develops of none of their value, nor the
instruction which in addition he succeeds in drawing from sacred
history. Similarly, the typological interpretation (which directly
implies a sense of history!) retains its value for the essential themes of
the Epistle, notably in all that concerns Melchizedek and the Israelite
cult. At all events, the shrewdness with which the writer succeeds in
culling from the Bible texts which suit his purpose, is to be admired.

1[5]. First this verse quotes Psalm 2[7], and in its exact form, as in Acts
13[33], and unlike Mark 1[11] par. and Matthew 17[5] where its purport is
modified.[26] Originally it referred to the enthronement of the king of
Israel; for our author it serves to demonstrate the sonship of Christ.
The same applies to the promise made to David concerning Solomon,
according to 2 Samuel 7[14] (LXX 2 Kings), quoted in v. 5b.

[26] See for this the commentaries on the Gospels which are appearing in the
Commentaire du nouveau testament (Neuchâtel and Paris). For rabbinical inter-
pretations, which sometimes relate this Psalm to the people of Israel, cf. STRACK-
BILLERBECK, III, pp. 673f.

1⁶. The verse of Deuteronomy 32⁴³ (blessing by Moses) reproduced here is not found in the Masoretic text. But it corresponds to the text of the Greek Bible, except that the majority of manuscripts of the LXX read '*huioi theou*' instead of '*anggeloi theou*',²⁷ which does not affect the sense, as the sons of God can only be the angels. Who is meant by '*autō*' (He before whom the angels must prostrate themselves)? In the context of Deuteronomy it can only be descendants of Moses; here, it is the Christ.²⁸ But the way in which this text is introduced raises difficulty. It is at the moment of bringing His first-born into the world that God is supposed to have uttered this word. It can only refer to the Parousia. Why, then, is the saying introduced by the present tense '*legei*' (= 'He says') and not by 'He will say'? There is only one explanation, it seems to us: God speaks now—through the Bible—but it is with a view to the return of Christ that the word is uttered and recorded. Another solution would be to attach '*palin*' to '*legei*', as Calvin, Bengel, Michel, Spicq and others do, and this would be a way of picking up again the '*palin*' of v. 5a, as continuing the series of quotations. One would then translate: 'and He says *again* . . .' But the position of '*palin*' between '*hotan de*' and '*eisagagē*' seems to us to make this explanation very difficult, and moreover it would compel us to see in this text an improbable allusion to the first coming of Christ (when He was subject to the angels, according to 2⁷!).

The preposition '*pros*' does not, indeed, necessarily imply that God addressed the angels directly. '*Pros tous anggelous*' can mean 'concerning angels' (like the '*pros*' at the beginning of v. 8 and often elsewhere). Furthermore, the imperative is in the third person ('*proskunēsatōsan*'), so the word has therefore been uttered long before the order becomes effective—which supports our interpretation.

'*Prōtotokos*' = 'first-born', as with Paul (Roman 8²⁹; Colossians 1¹⁸) and Revelation 1⁵, characterizes the Son as being heir, though it probably also alludes to his pre-existence before all creatures.²⁹

1⁷ quotes Psalm 104⁴ (LXX 103⁴). What interests our author is not merely that God bestows relatively elementary meteorological

---

²⁷ Nevertheless, '*anggeloi*' is attested by v. 43b of the LXX text, which expresses the same idea in conformity with the parallelism of Hebrew poetry.

²⁸ There are grounds for thinking, however, that Judaism already knew an interpretation of Deuteronomy 32⁴³ which was somewhat analogous to that of the Epistle to the Hebrews. According to the *Life of Adam and Eve*, §§12–17 (KAUTZSCH, p. 513) God ordered the angels to worship Adam. Those who refused were damned. Now for Paul as for our author, Christ is also an Adam, but a heavenly Adam.

²⁹ Philo sees in the '*logos*' the 'first-born' and sometimes also the 'eldest' '*nous*'. *De Confusione Linguarum*, §63 (Chap. 14), §146 (Chap. 28). Cf. *De Agricultura*, §51 (Chap. 12). In *De Somniis*, I, §215 (Chap. 37) we read: 'There are two temples of God: one of them this universe, in which there is also as High Priest His First-born, the divine Word, and the other the rational soul, whose Priest is the real Man ('*duo hiera theou, hen men hode ho kosmos, en hō kai archiereus ho prōtogonos autou theios logos, heteron de logikē psuchē, hēs hiereus ho pros alētheian anthrōpos*').

responsibilities on the angels,[30] but that He also uses them as servants and ministers (*'leitourgos'*).

1[8] quotes Psalm 45[7, 8] (LXX 44[7, 8]). *'Ho theos'* in the first line can only be vocative = 'O God'.[31] One might think God the Father was meant. But in what follows (v. 8 of the Psalm, cited here in v. 9) the vocative *'ho theos'* reappears alongside *'theos sou'* in the nominative: 'Thy God, O God, has anointed thee . . .' So there are two Gods. The use of the word 'God' for a king may seem surprising in the mouth of the Psalmist. But in Psalm 82 it seems that the gods are earthly kings (vv. 1 and 6), since they are threatened with death, which could hardly apply to angels. We have, then, hyperbolic language, in harmony with oriental etiquette. The king and his kingdom are idealized (just as the eternity of his 'throne' in v. 8a simply means the perpetuity of his dynasty).[32] This is a further reason for our author seeing there a reference to Christ, who (after His exaltation) fulfils these conditions.

1[9]. *'Elaoin agalliaseōs'* (lit. 'oil of joy') is clearly Hebraic; a genitive of quality used in a loose sense: the anointing is an occasion of joy. Who are the *'metochoi'* = 'companions', 'associates'? According to the Psalmist, certainly the brethren and friends of the king; for our author, probably the angels, an interpretation suggested by the general context of this chapter.

In sum, this section of the text (vv. 8, 9) is intended to stress: (*a*) that Christ is no usurper (like Zeus, who dethrones his father), but that He is anointed by God; and (*b*) that His reign is essentially defined as a reign of righteousness—in conformity with the most ardent and most legitimate of Jewish aspirations.[33]

1[10-12]. These verses are drawn from Psalm 102 (LXX 101)[26-28], which contrasts the power and eternity of God with the frailty and transiency of the creation. Our Epistle applies this to the Son,

[30] 'Angels' may then be lurking behind the winds. Mark 4[39] par. approximates to this.
[31] Indeed, in the LXX the form *'theos'* for the vocative is much more frequent than *'thee'*. *'Tou aiōnos'* following *'eis ton aiōna'* is absent from B (here and in the LXX). The sense remains the same, since the two expressions are used indifferently in the LXX and mean 'for all eternity' (cf. 13[21]).
[32] See MOWINCKEL, *The Psalms in Israel's Worship*, Oxford 1962. At the end of v. 8 some witnesses, and these not the least important (p. 46, S, B) read *'basileias autou'*. But the reading *'basileias sou'* which Nestlé adopts alone conforms to the syntax and to the text of the LXX.
[33] The use of the aorist by the LXX in Psalm 44[8], and here 1[9] (*'ēgapēsas . . . emisēsas'* = 'Thou didst love righteousness . . . Thou didst hate iniquity') is certainly due to a bad translation of the Hebrew imperfect of duration, which modern renderings give more accurately in the present tense ('Thou lovest . . . Thou hatest'), which alone is in harmony with the context. But we have no right to introduce this correction into the text of the Epistle. It is said that the verse was referred to by Pope Gregory VII before his death in exile: 'I have loved righteousness and have hated iniquity; for this reason I die in exile'.

harmonizing here with the Pauline terminology which calls Him Lord (*'kurios'*; cf. *'kurie'* at the beginning of v. 10).[34]

'Kat' archas' at the beginning of the same verse is reminiscent once again of the opening of Genesis: *'berēšît'* = 'in the beginning' (cf. *'en archē'* at the commencement of the Fourth Gospel).—God has founded (*'ethemeliōsas'*) the earth, in conformity with what comes later in Psalm 104 (LXX 103)—the beginning of which had been quoted in v. 7—where a most dramatic narrative of creation is unfolded (vv. 5–9): God had to struggle with the 'waters', which finally withdrew and allowed the establishment of the solid earth. The plural *'ouranoi'* = 'heavens' in v. 10b is current in the New Testament; it is to be explained not only on philological grounds (the Hebrew equivalent *'šāmayim'* being always in the plural), but also by the Jewish belief in a plurality of heavens.[35]

The affirmations in vv. 11 and 12a imply a condemnation of the belief, almost general in Graeco-Roman philosophies and religions, in the eternity of the world. But the comparison of the world with a cloak, which one casts away when it is too old, requires explanation. As Robert Eisler has shown in a most instructive study, a very widespread belief in Greece and the East thought of the star-bespangled sky as being really the cloak of one or other deity.[36] But apart from Judaism—and Mazdaism—no one had the idea of regarding it as perishable.

The words *'hōs himation'* = 'as a garment' in the second line of v. 11 are repeated at the beginning of the second line of v. 12 (before *'kai allagēsontai'*) in the majority of good manuscripts;[37] therefore we have no right to delete them, although they are not found in the text of the LXX. *'Himation'* and *'peribolaion'* are almost synonymous (= 'raiment'), except that *'peri-bolaion'* suggests rather an 'over'-garment. At the beginning of v. 12 we read with Nestlé *'helixeis'* = 'Thou shalt roll up', because the other reading, viz. *'allaxeis'* = 'Thou shalt change' was probably influenced by the use of the same verb (*'allagēsontai'*) in the following line.[38] The end of v. 12 is naturally also applied to the Son and must be put alongside **12⁸**.

---

[34] For the interpretation of Psalm 102 by the LXX and by our Epistle, see B. W. BACON, 'Hebrews 1.10–12 and the LXX rendering of Ps. 102.23', in *ZNW*, 1902, pp. 280ff.

[35] See our comment above on the 'aeons' mentioned in 1², as well as the article 'Heaven' in *The Vocabulary of the Bible*, ET London 1958, and STRACK-BILLER-BECK, III, p. 531f.

[36] R. EISLER, *Königsmantel und Himmelszelt*, Leipzig 1910. Hence the custom of the Byzantine emperors and those of the Holy Roman Empire of wearing robes adorned with stars as suited to their dignity as representatives of God on earth. Even in Catholicism are found icons of the Virgin in which, as Queen of Heaven, she wears a dress spangled with stars, which is not, perhaps, to be explained merely by the vision in Revelation 12¹. Details and illustrations in Eisler's book.

[37] Especially p 46, S, A, D.

[38] The reading *'allaxeis'* is attested by S, D, as well as by the old Latin.

(14) *Are not all the angels serving spirits sent forth to exercise a ministry on behalf of those who should inherit salvation?*

1^{13} = Psalm 110^1 (LXX 109^1) reminds us again that the angels never possessed the pre-eminent dignity of sitting at the right hand of the Father (see 1^3) and of triumphing over all enemies (cf. 1 Corinthians 15^{29}). The vanquished enemies are trodden under the victor's feet according to the eastern view which is attested in numerous epigraphic records.

1^{14}. The passage 1^{14} to 2^5 draws out conclusions from what has gone before, in the form of an exhortation. 1^{14} effects the transition by summarizing and focusing the rôle of the angels: the angelic world is not only at the service of God and of Christ, but to some extent also at the service of believers; not, of course, to receive orders from them, but to aid their progress towards salvation, in harmony with the providential will.[39]

---

[39] An excellent illustration of this assertion is given in the sympathetic little book of ERICH SCHICK on the rôle of angels according to the N.T.: *Die Botschaft der Engel im N.T.* (Stuttgart 1940). It deserves to be translated. For the Catholic conception of the providential rôle of angels, see JEAN DANIÉLOU, *Les Anges et leur mission*, Chevetogne 1951.

CHAPTER II

(1) *This is why we must pay the most particular attention to that which has been preached to us, for fear of going adrift.* (2) *For if the word spoken by angels was authoritative, and every transgression and disobedience [to it] received just retribution,* (3a) *how shall we ourselves escape if we disregard so exceptional an opportunity for salvation?*

(3b) *This salvation was first announced to us by the Lord, [then] it was confirmed to us by eyewitnesses,* (4) *and [finally] in addition God Himself reinforced this witness by signs and wonders and all other kinds of miracles, as well as by the gifts of the Holy Spirit, distributed according to His will.*

2^{1-3a} These verses present an argument *a minore ad maius*, so dear to the Rabbis, and in fact quite appropriate here. Transgression of the commandments of the old covenant, although they were but given by the mediation of angels (and here we are reminded again of Crell's conjecture in 1^1), were severely punished. How much more must the new covenant be respected, which was inaugurated through the Son.

In detail: *'perissoterōs'* in v. 1 could be a true comparative (= 'with more attention'). But as the points of comparison are mentioned only in the following sentence we shall give the adverb an elative sense = 'with most particular attention' (see the translation). *'Tois akoustheisin'* = 'to that which has been heard', viz. by Christians. *'Pararuōmen'* or *'pararrhuōmen'* is the second aorist passive of *'parareō'* and means 'to go adrift', 'to run into destruction' (cf. Proverbs 3^{21}).

That the Mosaic Law had been given through the mediation of angels (cf. the use of *'laleō'* in 1^1) is a view not peculiar to our author; see Galatians 3^{19} and Acts $7^{38, 53}$ (Stephen's speech).[1] *'Bebaios'* means 'valid', 'efficacious', 'authoritative'.

$2^{3b, 4}$ outline the history and stress the truth of the new revelation. It was preached by the Lord Himself; His proclamation was guaranteed and transmitted by witnesses; furthermore, God Himself in a way authenticated it by miracles and by the giving of the Holy Spirit, characteristic features of the history of the early Church. If we wish to distinguish *'sēmeia'*, *'terata'*, and *'poikilai dunameis'*, then for the first we think of cures, for the second marvels like that of

[1] Cf. JOSEPHUS, *Antiquities*, XV, §136 (5.3): 'we have learned the noblest of our doctrines and the holiest of our laws from the messengers sent by God' (*'di' anggelōn para tou theou'*). For the method of reasoning called *a minore ad maius* or *a fortiori* (used here, 2^{2-3}), *v.* BONSIRVEN, *Exégèse rabbinique et exégèse paulinienne*, Paris 1939, especially pp. 83ff.

(5) *For it is not to angels that He has subjected the world to come, of which we are speaking.* (6) *But someone has given a testimony somewhere [on this subject] in these words: 'What is man that you should remember him, or the son of man that you should interest yourself in him?* (7) *You have made him [it is true] for a little while lower than the angels, but you have crowned him with glory and honour. You have placed the whole universe in subjection under his feet.' Now, when he says: 'He has subjected the whole universe to him', nothing is excepted from that subjection. But at present, we do not yet see that everything is subject to him.* (9) *Yet we see Him who, for a little while, has been made lower than the angels—that is Jesus—crowned with glory and honour because of the death that He suffered, in order that, separated from God, He might taste death for the benefit of all mankind.* (10) *For it was fitting that God, because of whom and through whom the universe exists and who has begun to bring many sons to glory, should make the pioneer of their salvation perfect through sufferings.* (11) *Now, He who sanctifies and those who are sanctified all spring from one ancestor. This is why He [Jesus] is not ashamed to call them brothers* (12) *in the words 'I will proclaim your name to my brothers; in the midst of the assembly I will praise You'.* (13) *And again, 'As for Me, I will place my trust in Him', and then, 'Behold, Me and the little ones you have given Me'.*

Acts 12[7f], and for the third the various gifts of which the Apostle Paul speaks (glossolalia, prophecy, and the rest). The expression 'merismoi' = 'distributions' or 'apportioning' of the Holy Spirit likewise reminds us of 1 Corinthians 12[4f] and perhaps also of Acts 2[3] ('diamerizomenai glōssai hōsei puros' = 'dividing tongues as of fire'). The final remark, 'according to the will of God' ('kata tēn autou thelēsin') is a reminder that it is God who gives each his particular endowment, implying individual rights and duties.

2[5-13]. This passage takes up again the theme of the superiority of the Son to the angels, but adds to it a new note; namely, that of His abasement below the angels during His earthly life. It is true that the Hebrew text of the Psalm quoted in vv. 6-8 (= Psalm 8[5-7]) states: a little lower than 'Elohim',[2] which could mean: a little lower than God. But the LXX had already understood it as 'the elohim' (plural) and translated it by 'the angels'. The theme of abasement has also been developed in Philippians 2[5ff]. But while Paul (or his source) stresses particularly the ethical aspect of His rôle (voluntary obedience to the Father), our author characterizes it here particularly as submission to the laws of human existence as we might put it today, or, in terms of the theology of this Epistle, as abasement below the angels. That the angels are also the guardians of the cosmic and biological order (the two being inseparable, in any case, in ancient thought), is likewise the opinion of Paul, who sometimes elaborates

---

[2] '*Teḥasserēhû me'aṭ mē'elôhîm*' = 'Thou hast made him little less than God' RSV, RV (RV mg 'the angels').

very curious ideas about the 'powers' and 'elements' (*'archai'*, *'stoicheia'*, etc.), which even crucified the Lord according to 1 Corinthians 2⁸ (cf. Colossians 2¹⁵; Romans 8³⁸ᶠ; Galatians 4³, ⁹). The author reminds us first of all that the world to come will not be, or will no longer be, subject to angels—the expression *'hē oikoumenē hē mellousa'* = 'the world the come' obviously being synonymous with *'hē mellousa polis'* in 13¹⁴ (= 'the future city') and with *'aiōn mellōn'* = *'ha'ôlām habba''* (= 'the future world'). The parallel with the arguments in following chapters leads us to think that by this the final kingdom is meant, which elsewhere is called the kingdom of the Father, and not a messianic kingdom which is preparatory to this, like the messianic reign in apocalyptic,[3] or the kingdom of the Son in Paul's thought, extending from the resurrection to the Parousia.[4]

2⁶ brings in again the word of a Psalmist, viz. Psalm 8⁵⁻⁷.[5] *'Tis'* = 'someone', at the beginning of v. 6, shows that the identity of the Psalmist matters little to the author of Hebrews. Basically, it is always God or the Holy Spirit who speaks.[6]

The parallelism of members between the two lines of v. 6 (Psalm 8⁵) affords the proof—if we still need one—of the original equivalence of the terms *'anthrōpos'* (*''āḏām'*) and *'huios tou anthrōpou'* (*'ben-'āḏām'* in Hebrew = *'bar nāšā'* in Aramaic). Though the Psalmist was thinking of man in general, in our Epistle it is a case of man with a capital M, that is, of Christ, regarded in His capacity as 'Son of Man' in the technical and theological sense of the Gospels, or of the 'heavenly Adam' in the Apostle Paul's terminology (1 Corinthians 15⁴⁵ᶠ; cf. Romans 5, the 'second man'). And in fact, if this 'Man' was abased, it was by His incarnation; He was therefore already Man in

---

[3] E.g. Ezra Apocalypse (4 Esdras 7²⁸)—700 years; Revelation of John 20³—1,000 years.

[4] See our *Le Royaume de Dieu et sa venue*, 1938, pp. 171–183, and O. CULLMANN, *La royauté du Christ et l'Eglise dans le N.T.*, Foi et Vie, Christmas 1943. An excellent illustration of the morally disquieting nature of the 'powers' is given in the *Printemps olympien* of KARL SPITTELER. See the passages where he speaks of Ananke, Moira and Gorgo. Cf. our article on the theology of this eminent poet in *RHPR*, 1943, pp. 27ff.

[5] According to the Midrash Bereshit Rabba 8.6 (FREEDMANN, I, pp. 58f) it is angels who uttered the words reported in Psalm 8⁵ (*'tis estin'*, etc.) to express their astonishment that so much fuss should be made of Adam. But God put them in their place. So far as the form of the text itself is concerned the following observations must be made: (a) *'ti'* ('what is man?') is replaced by *'tis'* ('who is man?') by some witnesses, in particular by p 46 and C; but we do not think there are any grounds for following this reading. Luther thought that *'quid homo'* was a bad translation of the Hebrew. The sense should be *'quam homo'* = *'quam admirabilis homo'* (*Scholies*, p. 19). According to J. FICKER he may have followed Paul of Burgos († 1435). (b) Many witnesses, amongst them B, D, the Syriac and Latin versions, introduce at the beginning of v. 7 a phrase of the Psalm omitted by the other witnesses and by Nestlé: 'Thou hast set him over the works of Thy hands.' We could think that the addition of the words out of a concern to harmonize the text of the quotation with that of the Psalm is a simpler explanation than their omission, and we therefore follow Nestlé.

[6] PHILO sometimes introduces a biblical quotation in the same way; e.g *De Ebrietate*, §61 (Chap. 14): *'eipe gar pou tis'* ('for we find it said').

His pre-existent state.[7] '*Brachu*' in v. 7 could mean 'slightly', and this is no doubt its original sense; but here this adverb means 'for a little while' (cf. Acts 5[34]).

The elevation of the Man to heaven is represented under the figure of coronation, the crown being a sign of royal power and also of supernatural dignity. We are reminded of the crown of life in Revelation 2[10] and in Mandaean usage.[8] '*Doxa*' (= 'glory') and '*timē*' (= 'honour') are here almost synonymous (Windisch: '*Glanz und Ehre*'). The former places the stress somewhat on the supernatural dignity, and the latter rather on authority over all creatures.

2[8]. The beginning of v. 8, drawn also from Psalm 8, expresses the same assurance as Psalm 110[1] (LXX 109[1]) quoted in 1[13]. But in the Epistle a comment is added of the highest importance: it is not yet the case that all His enemies are subjected. The struggle therefore continues still, as in Pauline eschatology (1 Corinthians 15[23-28]). Although the text of the Psalm uses the aorist (rather like 1[9]) where the future would be expected, the author of Hebrews does not seem worried by the difficulty. Perhaps he thought of the Psalmist as a seer who was perceiving events to come as though they had already taken place (cf. the language of the Revelation of John). The first prediction ('*estephanōsas*' = 'you have crowned him') has already been realized by His glorious elevation. But this in turn presupposes the Passion ('*dia to pathēma*' = 'because of the suffering'). This is precisely Jesus' own thought, which could be summarized thus: it is necessary that the Son of Man suffer on earth, in order to reappear in heaven at the right hand of God. And strangely enough, what is true of the Man in the pre-eminent sense, applies to a certain extent also to men with a small 'm'. They must take up their cross and follow the Saviour, so that one day they can share in the future glory. This is the common teaching of early Christianity. But we notice also a radical difference between the two cases. For the heavenly Man, and for Him alone, the abasement is voluntary and unmerited.

The second part of 2[9], from '*hopōs*', presents several exegetical difficulties. The conjunction '*hopōs*' with the subjunctive has final force. But how can death be envisaged as the aim of the coronation which it precedes? All kinds of emendations have been proposed, including the simple deletion of the phrase. Some, on the other hand, wish to interpolate several words which are presumed to have dropped out before '*hopōs*'.[9] One particularly subtle interpretation which

---

[7] See our *Royaume de Dieu*, particularly Chap. 8, and TH. PREISS, 'Le Fils de l'Homme', *Etudes théol. et rel.*, 1951, no. 2 and 1953, no. 1, who has the distinction of showing the importance of this concept in Johannine theology.

[8] See in particular the Right Ginza, pp. 8–11, in Lidzbarski's translation, and many other passages in the same book. Likewise in the Odes of Solomon the elect receive a mystical crown: 1.1; 5.10; 9.8–13; 17.1.

[9] For deletion: Semler, according to BLEEK, II, p. 282. WINDISCH thinks some words have fallen out (*Comm.* 1913, p. 23).

may be be mentioned is the attempt to give the verb *'geusētai'* = 'that He may taste' a future perfect force: when He will be crowned His death will have become in consequence a genuine source of salvation.[10]

We can dispense with these *tours de force* if we connect the phrase introduced by *'hopōs'* to *'dia to pathēma tou thanatou'* = 'because of the death that He suffered', which it explains. The death was in fact necessary because, etc. Another difficulty arises over *'huper pantos'*. Is it masculine (= 'for all men') or neuter ('for all things')? Expositors are quite divided over the question. From the viewpoint of theology (and by this we naturally mean biblical theology), both interpretations can be defended. From the philological standpoint the expression is in any case rather odd. In the latter case (neuter) *'huper tōn pantōn'* would be expected; in the former (masculine) *'huper pantos anthropou'*. If with Riggenbach and Spicq we take the masculine, then it is because throughout the argument the writer seems to be thinking above all about mankind.[11] Use of the verb *'geuomai'* (= 'taste') does not necessarily suggest the brevity of His stay among the dead.[12] The LXX use of the term does not suggest this sense; see, for example, Psalm 34[9] (LXX 33[9]).

Finally, it must be emphasized that instead of *'chariti theou'* (Nestlé, = 'by the grace of God') a certain number of Fathers, and notably Origen, Theodoret of Cyrrhos, and Theodore of Mopsuestia, read *'chōris theou'* (= 'apart from God').[13] One can then think of

---

[10] See the discussion of the matter by Windisch and particularly by BLEEK, II, pp. 282ff.

[11] ORIGEN, who is the earliest witness for the neuter (*'sit venia verbo'*), thinks that the High Priest Himself sacrificed also for the angels: *'ouch huper anthrōpōn monon, alla kai huper tōn loipōn logikōn'* ('not for men only, but also for other rational beings'). See his *Commentary on John*, I, Chap. 35, ed. Preuschen (*GCS*), p. 45. In Paulinism one would think rather of the entire visible creation (*'ktisis'*) according to Romans 8[19f].

[12] See CHRYSOSTOM, *MPG* 63, col. 39: 'straightway he arose, having spent a brief interval in it [death]' (*'eutheōs anestē, mikron en autō (en thanatō) poiēsas diastēma'*).

[13] Origen, following the passage mentioned in note 11 *supra*, quotes *'chariti theou'*, but in the comment which he appends he speaks of *'chōris theou'*. We may therefore conclude that a copyist corrected Origen's text, but only the quotation itself. The reading *'chōris theou'* is found also in the same commentary, XXVIII, 18, p. 41, and XXXII, 28, p. 274. The commentary on the Epistle to the Romans, which we only have in translation, reads *'sine deo'*, III, 8; V, 7, *MPG* 14, col. 946A and 1036B. Theodoret (*MPG* 82, col. 692) likewise reads *'chōris theou'* and gives the explanation that everything, except for God, had need of redemption. Theodore of Mopsuestia (*MPG* 66, col. 956) mocks exegetes who read *'chariti tou theou'*: *'geloiotaton dē huparchousin entautha to chariti theou'* ('most laughably indeed they have here "by the grace of God" ') and he explains that there is an allusion to kenosis: the divine nature of Christ had no part in His passion. For other details, see RIGGENBACH, p. 43, note 13. HARNACK likewise thought that *'chōris theou'* is the best reading, corrected for dogmatic reasons to *'chariti theou'* ('Zwei alte dogmatische Korrekturen in Hebräerbrief', in *Studien zur Geschichte des N.T. und der alten Kirche*, *I.Neutestamt. Textkritik*, 1931, pp. 235f). BENGEL (*Gnomon*, 3rd edn, reprinted 1855, p. 566): 'the diligence of scribes, which is always looking for a clearer reading, would more easily change *'chōris'*

Matthew 27[46], when Jesus feels Himself abandoned by God at the
moment of death. It is true that this reading is only supported by a
very few Greek manuscripts, including M. But all things considered,
we think it merits preference, because it is the more original and more
difficult, and because the alteration of *'chariti'* to *'chōris'* is less
explicable than the reverse, as Bengel has already urged.

2[10]. *'Eprepen autō'* = 'it was fitting for Him'. Does the *'autō'*
refer to God or Christ? We accept the former interpretation, for if
the contrary were true the sentence should continue with *'heauton
teleiōsai'* = 'it was fitting for Him, to bring Himself to perfection'
and not *'ton archēgon . . . teleiōsai'* = 'to bring the leader . . . to
perfection'. The remark *'di' hon ta panta kai di'hou ta panta'* = 'because of whom and through whom the universe exists', therefore
applies here to God the Father, as in Romans 11[36] (cf. 1 Corinthians
8[6a], and the relevant commentaries in this series).

The idea that God had to bring the Son, by means of suffering, to a
perfection He did not previously have, is clear and will be taken up
again later. The crux for expositors is the participle *'agagonta'*
(aorist of *'agō'* = 'to bring'). Its object is clearly *'pollous huious'* =
'many sons', so that there is someone who brings many sons to
perfection. Is it God, or Christ? Against the former suggestion it is
urged that the correct construction would in this case require the
dative (*'agagonti'*). But the argument is not decisive,[14] and as
Christians are called sons and not brothers—as in vv. 12 and 17—
we judge that it is God who brings them to salvation. Why, then, the
aorist participle? Because the work of salvation did not finish at the
moment when Christ attained perfection (*'teleiōsis'*).[15] Windisch
thinks it is useless to want a definite decision ('we must leave the
time relationships indeterminate'). Moffatt has nothing to say.
Riggenbach holds that the aorist participle could have present
meaning. But that is no way out of the difficulty, because it is not
merely the first disciples who will be saved. We would take it as an

---

into *'chariti'* than *'chariti'* into *'chōris'*. Note further that the Peshitta, at least in
the London edition (1911) reads *'seṭar men 'alāhâ'*, which is precisely = *'chōris
theou'*.

[14] BLEEK (I, p. 294), who attaches *'agagonta'* to *'theō'*, quotes some analogous
constructions: Acts 15[22], *'edoxe tois apostolois . . . eklexamenous pempsai'*
('it seemed good to the apostles . . . to choose men to send'); Acts 25[27], *'alogon
moi dokei pemponta desmion'* ('it seems unreasonable to me to send a prisoner');
Luke 1[74] *'hēmin ek cheiros echthrōn rhusthentas'* ('to rescue us from enemy hands,
and grant us . . .'). He even claims to have found parallel incongruities in the
'best Greek authors'.
[15] The Vulgate translates *'agagonta'* by *'qui adduxerat'* ('who had brought'),
which is philologically correct. ERASMUS on the contrary: *'cum ille multos ad-
ducere vellet in gloriam'* ('since he wished to bring many to glory') (*N.T. cum
annotationibus*, Bâle 1535, p. 721). HUGO GROTIUS translates *'qui adduxerat'*,
but explains *'ut adduceret'* ('that he might bring') (*Opera Theologica*, Bâle 1732,
vol. 3, from p. 1010),

inceptive aorist.[16] The act of 'bringing' was already started before the *'teleiōsis'*, but it continues. So our interpretation approaches that of Spicq, who translates 'having to lead'. If this is rejected, it would be necessary to resort to strong measures and to emend *'agagonta'* to *'agonta'*.

2[11-13]. These verses stress the kinship between Christ (*'ho hagiazōn'* = 'He who sanctifies') and Christians (*'hoi hagiazomenoi'* = 'those who are sanctified'). Spicq justly observes that according to Jewish ideas a priest must be of the same race as the faithful. In harmony with the universalism of Paul and of our author, it is the humanity of the High Priest which is important. Angels could not therefore validly be priests amongst men. *'Pantes'* being separated from *'hagiazomenoi'* by *'ex henos'* must refer at once to the sanctifier and to the sanctified, for they form one whole.

But what does *'ex henos'* (lit. = 'from one') mean? If *'henos'* is taken as neuter, as Riggenbach wishes, the term would denote 'born of the same principle', which does not say very much. We would prefer to accept it as masculine ('from one man'), with the majority of scholars. Then who is this 'one'? Bleek, following John Chrysostom, explains *'ex henos'* by *'ex hou ta panta'* in v. 10, so that the 'one' is then God. But since the entire universe, comprising angels and all other creatures, owes its existence to God, this interpretation cannot explain the particular kinship between Christ and mankind. Therefore it must be admitted, with Bengel, that the *'heis'* is Adam.[17] So the Son, by His incarnation, became a descendant of Adam like all men.[18] The road to any form of docetism could not be more effectively barred.

2[12]. In support of its particular viewpoint ingenious use is made in our Epistle of Psalm 22[23] (LXX 21[23]), the Psalm to which Jesus Himself seems to have alluded according to John 17[6]. The Psalmist, who seeks to proclaim the name of God to his 'brothers', was no doubt thinking of his devout fellow-believers (the 'pious' in Israel). But according to our writer the reference is to men in general, and particularly to those who are converted.[19]

---

[16] BLASS-DEBRUNNER, §331 speaks of an ingressive or inceptive aorist, which denotes the commencement of an activity. An aorist participle does not necessarily refer to the past; *v. ibid.*, §339.

[17] For Chrysostom, see *MPG* 63, col. 40—cf. BLEEK, II, pp. 306f—BENGEL, *Gnomon, ad loc.* B. WEISS thinks Abraham; *v.* p. 78 of his Commentary.

[18] Naturally, even the virgin birth of the Saviour—which is not taught by our author—would not alter this.

[19] When Jesus speaks of His brothers, in Mark 3[34] par. and Matthew 25[40], He is thinking of a spiritual relationship, and this introduces a different slant. In so far as Matthew 28[10] and John 20[17] are concerned, it is possible that Jesus may have been speaking of His brothers by birth, namely, James, Joses, Jude and Simon; cf. 1 Corinthians 9[5]. On the other hand, the term *'adelphoi'* on its own finally became, as we know, a synonym for 'Christians'.

(14) Now since children have flesh and blood in common, He also, in a similar way, partook of the same nature, so that by His death He might conquer him who holds the power of death—that is, the devil— (15) and deliver those who were in lifelong slavery through fear of death.

2¹³. The next quotations are taken from Isaiah 8¹⁷ᶠ. The former, also found in Isaiah 12² and 2 Samuel (LXX 2 Kings) 22³, is here doubtless intended to express the faith of the man Jesus in God, a faith He shares with His brethren. The latter calls the brethren *'paidia'* = 'little children' stressing their feebleness; though it would be pressing overmuch to ask whether they are children of God or of Christ (the latter could be another way of speaking of His disciples).

2¹⁴ first reminds us that children of the same family are consanguineous (this is the meaning of *'kekoinōnēken haimatos kai sarkos'* = 'share the same flesh and blood'; no allusion to the Eucharist is to be sought here), and then adds a most interesting detail. For the first time we learn that salvation (*'sōtēria'*) consists not solely in the effacement of sins, but also in liberation from the power of the devil, who is expressly mentioned in v. 14b as the one who has 'the power of death'. This teaching is in accord with that of the Apostle Paul, for whom likewise Satan is the destroyer of life (1 Corinthians 5⁵; 10¹⁰), and death is one of the group of hostile powers (1 Corinthians 15²⁶); fundamentally, also, with Genesis 3, where the serpent (identified with the devil in Revelation 20²) leads Adam and Eve to throw themselves by their sin into the arms of death.²⁰ But the devil is not yet annihilated, since *'katargein'* means 'to reduce to impotency' or in a wider sense 'to conquer'.²¹ Christians, therefore, will themselves also die, but they have been delivered from the fear of death, which is a fearful slavery (v. 15) and poisons the whole of life. Death has lost its 'sting' (1 Corinthians 15⁵⁵); believers know that they live even if they die (John 11²⁵). We therefore attach *'douleias'* to *'enochoi'* = 'involved in' or 'subject to slavery' thanks to fear

²⁰ See also Wisdom 2²⁴, as well as the Bab. Talmud Baba bathra fol. 16a: 'Satan, the evil impulse, and the angel of death are identical' (GOLDSCHMIDT, VIII, p. 67). Other texts in STRACK-BILLERBECK, I, p. 815; III, pp. 155, 227.

²¹ Nevertheless, in 1 Corinthians 15²⁴, ²⁶, where the End is under consideration, we hold to the strong sense of *'katargein'* = 'reduce to non-existence' (see our commentary on *The First Epistle of Saint Paul to the Corinthians*, ET London 1962). In the Old Testament death is not always regarded as abnormal. Though there are texts which establish a relationship between sin and death on the one hand, and between death and the devil on the other, such as Genesis 3; Ecclesiasticus 25²⁴; 4 Esdras 3 *passim*, and 4 Esdras 7 §§116–126; and it is these ideas which led to the teaching of the New Testament. The modern reader must not let himself be seduced by a naturalistic philosophy which regards death as no more than a law of nature. The New Testament does not deny these laws; it presupposes them; but it views them from a theological angle and does not regard them as conforming in every case to the original intention of the Creator. 'The laws of nature are not natural,' said the elder BLUMHARDT, *Vom Reiche Gottes*, pub. Furche, n.d., p. 8.

(16) *For in fact it is not of angels that He takes care, but of the offspring of Abraham.* (17) *Accordingly, He had to become like His brothers in every respect, so that He might become a merciful and faithful High Priest, to officiate before God and to make expiation for the sins of the people.* (18) *For because He has Himself suffered temptation, He is able to come to the help of those who are tempted.*

(*'phobō'*). *'Douleias'* could naturally also be taken as the object of *'apallaxē'* = 'to free from bondage', with *'phobō'* dependent on *'enochoi'* = 'subject to fear', and this might be attractive grammatically, only *'douleias'* is definitely too far away from *'apallaxē'*—ten words separate them.[22] The construction *'dia pantos tou zēn'* = 'through the whole of life', is somewhat unusual, not because of the substantival use of the infinitive, which was current practice, but because the infinitive is linked with an adjective. Nevertheless, such constructions are not unknown.[23] That the fear of death is worse than death itself is affirmed also by Epictetus.[24]

In 2[16] angels are again under consideration, but the meaning of the statement is uncertain and depends upon the translation of *'epilambanō'*, translated by some as 'to take care of', and by others as 'to take up', 'to assume'. Early writers and Calvin adopted the second meaning and explained that the Son did not take upon Himself an angelic nature, but human nature. This interpretation has recently been defended by Spicq.[25] In general, modern scholars, resting upon Matthew 14[31] (Jesus touched him, *'epelabeto autou'*) and on Ecclesiasticus 4[11], prefer the other interpretation. What makes us adopt it is v. 17a, which would otherwise be a repetition of v. 16. Therefore we translate: 'take care of'. Why, then, does the writer specially mention the race of Abraham? Not in denial of the universalism taught elsewhere in his work, but doubtless as a reminder of Isaiah

[22] For *'enochos'* with the genitive, *v.* BLASS-DEBRUNNER, §182 n. 2, who refers to *Eranos* XI (1911), p. 232, where an epigraphic text is quoted, *'enochos mnēmēs'* (unfortunately the reading is doubtful). MOULTON-HOWARD, I, p. 39, say that this construction is not supported by the language of the papyri.

[23] BLASS-DEBRUNNER, §398 quotes *'dia pantos tou einai'*, Plato, *Parmenides*, 152 E. Cf. *'dia holou tou zēn'*, *Letter of Aristeas*, §130, 141, 168 (ed Teubner, pp. 36, 40, 47).

[24] Discourses, I, 17.25 (ed. Teubner, 1916, p. 65); II, 1.13f (*ibid.*, pp. 114f): 'For it is not death or hardship that is a fearful thing, but the fear of hardship or death.' In the face of death one needs 'confidence' (*'tharsos'*), and in the face of the fear of death, 'caution' (*'eulabeia'*). II, 18.30: 'take away the fear of death' (*'aron ton phobon tou thanatou'*).

[25] Chrysostom, *MPG* 63, col. 45. Theodoret (*MPG* 82, col. 906): 'for if He had taken the nature of angels, He would have been superior to death' (*'ei gar anggelōn aneilēphē phusin, kreittōn an egegonei thanatou'*). It is noticeable that this Father has *added* the word *'phusis'* which this interpretation requires. LUTHER on the contrary: 'He took hold of; He did not assume' (*'apprehendit, non suscepit'*, *Scholies*, p. 32). Likewise JAVET: 'He comes to the help of' (p. 30). For the old Latin see RIGGENBACH, p. 55, n. 43.

41⁸, 'the race of Abraham my friend', and also to prepare for the eulogy on Abraham as the prototype of all true believers of every race (see below, **11**; cf. Romans 4; Galatians 3).

2¹⁷, ¹⁸ take us a further step. The work of Christ comprises not only the atonement for sins through His passion, referred to in v. 17. He can be genuinely compassionate for human weaknesses, since He Himself has also been tempted. Therefore He can help us to overcome temptations and to pass victoriously through trials—a theme resumed in 4¹⁴ᶠ and 5⁷ᶠ.²⁶

'*Hilaskesthai*' = 'to make expiation'. We cannot here summarize the discussion provoked by this term, as well as by '*hilastērion*', and we therefore refer to *The Epistle to the Romans* by F. J. Leenhardt (ET London 1961), and to the article on '*hilaskomai*' in *TWNT*.²⁷ '*En hō*' = 'because', 'in that'.

---

²⁶ The writer does not explain why an angel would not likewise have been able by incarnation to assume human nature. But the answer to this is given implicitly in 1³ and 2⁶. The Son, as heavenly Man and perfect image of God, was thereby, as it were, predestined and was in any case alone qualified to become a man on earth, in order to save those who are made in His image. Angels are never said to be in the image of God. The rôle played by the heavenly Adam = image ('*eikōn*') theme in Paulinism also is familiar. Is there any need to say that none of the Greek gods ever decided to become fully human and to share the fate of mortals? As for Heracles, he was a man pure and simple, who was divinized only after his death (adoptionism!).

²⁷ p 46 reads '*pepothen*' for '*peponthen*' (v. 18), which can only be a slip. More interesting is the reading '*tais hamartiais*' in place of '*tas hamartias*' in v. 17, attested by A and 33. One might then translate 'to be merciful towards the sins'; but the variant is too weakly attested.

CHAPTER III

IN WHAT precedes our theological author has established the superiority of the Son to the angels, by the excellency of His supernatural nature, the superiority of His revelation, and the human perfection acquired by His earthly life.

In what follows he develops the theme of His superiority to Moses and Aaron, the organizers of the sacrificial cult of the old covenant, which was founded, moreover, upon a revelation given by angels, as we have already seen. As in the preceding chapters, theological exposition is interrupted by and linked with practical exhortation and biblical quotations.

(1) *Therefore, Christian brothers, who share in a heavenly calling, consider how Jesus, the representative and the High Priest of our religion, (2) is faithful to Him who appointed Him, as was Moses also in the administration of the house of God. (3) Yet Jesus has been favoured with a glory superior to Moses', inasmuch as the builder of a house receives more honour than the house itself. (4) Indeed, every house is constructed by somebody (and it is God who made the universe). (5) Moses, then, was faithful in all the administration of God's house, as a servant who gave the testimony which he had to proclaim. (6) But Christ, in virtue of His sonship, was overseer of His own house. And we ourselves are this house, if indeed we maintain without flinching the assurance and the hope which is our boast. (7) For this reason, as the Holy Spirit says, 'If today you hear my voice (8) do not harden your hearts, as at the time of the Exasperation, the day of testing in the wilderness, (9) when your fathers tried me by putting me to the test—(10) although they had seen my works for forty years. Therefore I conceived a loathing for this race and I said: Their heart is always going astray, and they have not known my ways. (11) So I swore in my wrath: Never shall they enter into my rest.' (12) Take care [therefore], brethren, that no one amongst you is refractory, becoming so unbelieving as to turn from the living God. (13) Rather than this, exhort one another day by day, so long as one can still speak of a 'Today', for fear lest any of you becomes hardened, deceived by sin. (14) For we are sharers in Christ, if indeed we maintain our faith as a firm basis—right to the end. (15) When it is said, 'If today you hear my voice, do not harden your hearts as at the time of the Exasperation', (16) [I ask you], Who were the embittered listeners? Were they not all those who had left Egypt under Moses? (17) Against whom did God show disgust for forty years? Was it not for the sinners, whose corpses fell in the wilderness? (18) And to whom did He swear that they should never enter into His rest, if not to those who were disobedient?*

(19) *And we see that* [*in fact*] *they were not able to enter it because of their unbelief.*

3¹. The '*hagioi*', as always in the New Testament, are those who are separated from others or 'set apart' (cf. the Latin '*sacer*', related to '*secerno*' = 'to separate'). They are therefore men who are consecrated through belonging to Christ, so that in many cases '*hagioi*' is synonymous with '*christianoi*', a term very little used in the New Testament.[1]

'*Metochos*' = 'participant'. But the expression 'participant in a calling' is hardly English, and so has been avoided in the translation. '*Katanoeō*' = 'consider with attention in a meditative attitude'. '*Apostolos*' applied to Jesus Christ is striking. But our author never uses this noun in the technical sense of 'apostle' and never so names the men of the first Christian generation. '*Apostolos*' therefore has here its etymological force of one who is 'sent out' (cf. Hebrew '*šālûaḥ*'). According to the Fourth Gospel, Jesus spoke of Himself in this way as the one sent by the Father. But in rabbinic literature '*šālûaḥ*' often denotes a 'representative of the community'.[2] This meaning fits very well here, for the High Priest represents believers before God.

'*Homologia*' not only means the act of 'confession' but also its object, though not implying a 'confession of faith' formulated as a stereotyped symbol. What is confessed is primarily the dignity of Jesus Christ and the efficacy of His mission. Up to a point the term is therefore a synonym for 'religion', and '*hē homologia hēmōn*' = 'our religion', of which Jesus is the High Priest ('*archiereus tēs homologias hēmōn*').

3². '*Piston onta*' = 'being faithful' has the force of a predicate: we must consider that (or to what extent) the High Priest is faithful. '*Piston*' has for object '*tō poiēsanti auton*' (lit. = 'to Him who made Him'). This could mean 'faithful to the one who created Him', which is the interpretation already admitted by the old Latin ('*creatori suo*'), as well as by a great number of scholars, including Herveus of Bourg-Dieu,[3] and more recently by Windisch and Michel. But '*poiein*' (cf. Latin '*facere*' and the Hebrew '*'āśāh*') can also be taken as synonymous with '*tithenai*' = 'to install', 'to appoint' (cf. 1²).

---

[1] See Acts 11²⁶. In JACKSON and LAKE's work (which needs no praise) on the Acts of the Apostles (*The Beginnings of Christianity*, I. *The Acts of the Apostles*, 1920f), H. J. CADBURY (vol. 5, pp. 354–375) studied all the terms used in the Acts for 'Christians' and 'Christianity'. Apart from '*hagioi*' he noted for 'Christians': '*adelphoi*', '*mathētai*', '*pistoi*', '*dikaioi*', '*Nazōraioi*', '*sōzomenoi*'; and for 'Christianity': '*hē hairesis*', '*hē hodos*', '*hē pistis*', or simply '*to euanggelion*'. This investigation should be extended to the other books of the New Testament.

[2] Mishnah Berakhoth 5.5 (GOLDSCHMIDT, I, p. 154) and STRACK-BILLERBECK, III, p. 683.

[3] 'Who is faithful to Him who made Him, that is to the Father who created Him as a human being' ('*qui fidelis est ei qui fecit illum, id est Patri qui secundum humanitatem creavit illum*'—Herveus, *MPL* 181, col. 1542 D).

This is the interpretation of Chrysostom and Theodoret, accepted for example by Westcott and Spicq. Chrysostom asks '*ti poiēsanti*' ('what has He made of Him? to what function has He appointed Him?') and he replies: '*apostolon kai archierea*' ('as envoy and High Priest'), and adds that the writer here speaks not of His essence ('*ousia*') nor of His divinity ('*theotēs*'), but only of His human rank ('*axiōmata anthrōpina*').[4] We are led to accept the second interpretation, not only by the immediate context, but also by the affirmations of 1[3] which do not favour ranking the Son as a 'creature'.

In 3[2b] the lawgiver is again expressly named.[5] '*En holō tō oikō autou*' = 'in all His house', i.e. in the administration of His house. This could refer to Jesus, if a comma were placed after '*Mōusēs*', but as there is probably an allusion to Numbers 12[7] (as in v. 5) where the same thing is said of Moses, it is he who is in question here.[6] Who is the proprietor of the house ('*oikos autou*')? Since Moses is regarded neither as master nor architect, we would think it is God, whose house comprises not merely the tabernacle but the entire community of the old covenant.

3[3]. '*Gar*' is surprising. We conjecture an ellipse: although Moses was faithful, Christ is superior to him, for He received superior status ('*pleionos doxēs ēxiōtai*'). Why? The reply is given in v. 3b: Jesus has Himself constructed a house, namely, the new covenant, whilst Moses was not even the architect of the old.

3[4a] presents no difficulty, but v. 4b disrupts the context. Why remind us that God is the creator of the universe? We cannot escape the impression that a gloss has been added by a reader who wished to emphasize the sovereignty of the Father.[7] In any case, the remark must be treated as a parenthesis.

3[5, 6a] develop the theme of the superior religious rôle played by Christ. Moses was only a servant of high rank ('*therapōn*' = 'servant' is much higher then '*doulos*' = 'slave'); Christ is overseer of the house of God ('*epi ton oikon*').

---

[4] CHRYSOSTOM, *MPG* 63, col. 49; THEODORET, *MPG* 82, col. 697 ('faithful to Him who appointed Him, that is as envoy ["*apostolon*"] and High Priest ["*archierea*"]').

[5] The orthography '*Mōusēs*' (as in the LXX) is interesting as showing that the Jews of the time, at least in Egypt, did not pronounce the name as Môschè but as Moüschè.

[6] In no circumstances must we translate '*with* all his house', for the Book of Numbers is insistent upon the unfaithfulness of the people, including also Aaron and Miriam. There are no grounds for deleting '*holō*' in v. 2, which is very well attested (p 13 and B are virtually the only ones which omit it). p 46 is here illegible.

[7] The attempt to refer '*ho kataskeuasas*' to the Son, and to translate 'the creator of the universe (cf. 1[2]) was divine', seems over-subtle. And even so this would not remove the difficulty created by the presence of the statement so ill-placed contextually.

Details in **3⁵**: '*Tōn lalēthēsomenōn*' = 'the words which will be spoken', naturally depends on '*marturion*' = 'testimony'. What words are these? Did Moses have to stand as guarantor for words uttered much later by Jesus and the apostles? This interpretation, apparently unknown to antiquity, has been upheld in the Middle Ages, as well as by Calvin, Westcott, and some contemporary scholars.[8] But in that case should not the dative have been used: '*tois lalēthēsomenois*'? It seems to us more natural, therefore, to take the genitive as explanatory: the words which Moses should himself utter constituted his testimony or message (so Riggenbach).

3⁶ᵇ adds a revealing statement for which we are already prepared. The house of Christ means the people of the new covenant, namely, ourselves.[9] This is precisely the idea developed by the Apostle Paul, see particularly 1 Corinthians 3¹⁶; 2 Corinthians 6¹⁹; cf. 1 Timothy 3¹⁵. Read '*eanper*' with p 46 and many other MSS, = 'if at all events', announcing a condition. We shall be God's house on condition we do not let go of the Christian faith, here spoken of as giving us a firm assurance ('*parrhēsia*', cf. **11¹**), and a hope of which we may boast ('*kauchēma tēs elpidos*'), i.e. one not to be ashamed of.[10]

The quotations in **3⁷⁻¹¹**, introduced by 'thus saith the Holy Spirit', come from Psalm 94⁷⁻¹¹ (LXX numeration and text), and allude to the unfortunate episodes in the wilderness related in Exodus 15²³ᶠ, that is, to the murmuring of the people at 'Marah', a Hebrew noun translated by '*parapikrasmos*' = 'bitterness' or 'exasperation' (Spicq). See Exodus 17³,⁷, where Massah and Meribah in the Hebrew text are translated by '*peirasmos*' = 'temptation'[11] (cf. also Numbers 20⁵). The point is, the ill-humour and murmuring of the people who hardened themselves and who went so far as to 'test God' by their unbelief.

These verses are a sequel to the warning given in v. 6b. If Christians harden themselves like the people in the wilderness they too will draw upon themselves the divine wrath, and will enter into the heavenly 'rest' no further than the wilderness generation entered the promised land. Details: '*mē sklērunēte*', v. 8 (= 'do not harden yourselves') follows upon the '*dio*' at the beginning of v. 7; the context is interrupted by v. 7b ('*sēmeron*', etc.) because the writer was

---

[8] See THOMAS AQUINAS, *Com. in Pauli Epistolas*, III, p. 230, Paris 1874: '*In testimonium eorum quae dicenda erant*' ('for a testimony of those things which were to be said'). CALVIN, Comm. IV, p 390, 'in testimony of the things which should be said'; WESTCOTT, *Comm. ad loc.*

[9] Even if, with Nestlé, we read '*hou oikos*', the sense is the same. But the reading of p 46, D, and of many Latin witnesses including the Vulgate, '*hos oikos esmen*' = 'and we are this house', seems the best and most original. Notice that PHILO also speaks sometimes of a 'house of God on earth'. But for him it is the human soul. See *De Cherubim*, §101 (Chap. 30).

[10] The three words '*mechri telous bebaian*' are absent from p 13, p 46 and some other witnesses. Perhaps they came into the text under the influence of 3¹⁴.

[11] These translations can be defended philologically. Psalm 95 (LXX 94) is, of course, chanted in Anglican churches every Sunday in the setting of the liturgy.

keen to quote this passage of the Psalm in its entirety. '*Dokimasia*' in v. 9 (= 'a test', lit. 'examination') reinforces the verb '*epeirasan*' = 'they tested', i.e. putting God and His patience to the test.

3¹⁰. The rhythm of the phrase shows that our expositor connects the mention of the forty years to what precedes; 'they saw (or: had seen) my works during forty years', and the text then adds a '*dio*'. The Psalm (of which we have no brief to give a detailed exposition here), on the contrary, attaches this little phrase to what follows: God [then] had a loathing for the people for forty years. But according to the Book of Numbers it also seems that Meribah (in the Kadesh region) was the last stage before Horeb, which is at the entrance to the promised land. In connection with '*planōntai tē kardia*' ('they err in their heart'; Spicq: 'they go astray'), it must be remembered that '*kardia*' (Heb. '*lēḇ*' = 'heart') in biblical speech has a wider meaning than 'heart' in English; it is the seat also of thought,¹² so that it can often be translated by 'thought', 'spirit', or 'head'.

3¹¹ᵇ. '*Ei*' introduces an oath and corresponds to the Hebrew "*im*'. But '*ei*' literally means 'if'. Thus, there is an ellipse: if such-and-such happens, then may God do so-and-so to me. Either the second part of the exclamation was forgotten, or it was found difficult to put it into the mouth of God Himself. Translate: 'never shall they enter'. The rest—which in the historical meaning was life in Palestine—was so called in contrast to the wearying journey through the wilderness. Naturally, for Christians, who are always pilgrims on the earth, the rest takes on another meaning. As for the wilderness generation, we know that with the exception of Joshua and Caleb they did not enter into the promised land. The misfortune of the people in the wilderness is a powerful reminder to Christians of the dangers of unfaithfulness, as the Apostle Paul also shows in 1 Corinthians 10. In both passages the fate of the people is a type of that of Christians, although happily only a hypothetical type, because it is not said that Christians will comport themselves in a way to merit punishment. They can still pull themselves together, in so far as they are in danger. This passage, with others like it, nevertheless shows that the writer is not too satisfied with the spiritual state of the Church which he is addressing.

3¹² reinforces this impression. It seems that there were some 'refractory persons' ('*kardia ponēra*') who wanted to get the better of God and who were not far from apostasy ('*apostēnai apo theou zōntos*'). The living God is He who may be called, with Pascal and the Bible,

¹² It is well known that the Jews localized psychological functions differently from ourselves. The head played no significant part. On the other hand, the kidneys also could be the seat of thought. With Pascal we find statements such as that the principles (i.e. fundamental categories, axioms) of geometry are known by the *heart*. See especially *Pensées*, no. 252, ed. Brunschvicg, in 16, p. 459. Cf. the expression used in Alsace: '*Was denkt dyn Herz?*'

DEH

'the God of Abraham, and of Isaac, and of Jacob'. He is living because He is active and bestows life.

3[13] is a reminder that exhortation and moral support (*'parakaleite'*)
is not a function reserved for Church leaders, but an obligation
resting on every Christian. *'Heautous'* here for *'allēlous'* = 'one
another'. *'Alla'* before *'parakaleite'* must have comparative force
here, as in John 16[2] and 2 Corinthians 1[9], and mean, 'but rather, on
the contrary'. *'Achris hou to sēmeron kaleitai'*, referring back to v. 7,
means 'while it is still today', that is, while there is yet 'time'. The
author is aware of two instances when it will be too late for amending
one's ways—the day of judgement, and the day of complete apostasy
(*v. infra* 6[6]). *'Hamartia'* = 'sin' at the end of v. 13 is slightly personified, as often in the Epistles of Paul. Sin deceives us by its deceitful-
ness and false promises; the paradigmatic instance is Genesis 3[5].

3[14] is a further reminder of the condition of salvation—the main-
tenance of faith. *'Hupostasis'* (= 'substance'?) presents some difficulty. The word cannot have the metaphysical and technical sense
here which it had in 1[2]. Doubtless it must be interpreted in the light
of 11[1]: faith anticipates the vision of supernatural realities. The
genitive *'tēs hupostaseōs'* could be partitive, 'the beginning of faith',
or again, 'the principle of faith'. But we prefer to take it as an explanatory genitive: 'the basis, which is faith', or, with Spicq, 'initial
faith'. The form *'bebaia'* (from *'bebaios'* = 'firm') is a solecism, as
the adjective does not like taking a feminine form. *'Metochoi
Christou'* = 'sharers in Christ' is introduced without further
explanation, but is illuminated by 2[10-14].

3[15] repeats vv. 7b–8a, and is introduced by *'en tō legesthai'* = 'with
reference to the above passage' (with 'I have this to say to you',
understood).

3[16]. The verb *'parapikrainō'* = 'to embitter' is not found in the LXX.
It comes from *'parapikrasmos'*; bitterness causes a deviation from the
right path (*'para'*!) and leads to revolt. The anaphora *'tines'* (v.
16), *'tisin'* (v. 17), *'tisin'* (v. 18) is to throw into relief the fact that
hardening is not only the doing of Pharaoh and of pagans in
general, but also and above all of the chosen people. Their election
did not preserve them from punishment.

3[17] quotes v. 10b of Psalm 95 (LXX 94) and **3**[18] v. 11b of the same
Psalm, whilst **3**[17b] (*'ta kōla . . .'*) is borrowed from Numbers 14[29]
(cf. 1 Corinthians 10[5]) and is a reminder that God struck the disobedient with death and this prevented them from entering into
'rest'.[13]

[13] In 3[17] A reads *'apeithēsasin'* for *'hamartēsasin'*, an error caused by conformity with *'apeithēsasin'* at the end of v. 18, where p 46 is alone in reading
'apistēsasin' (no doubt likewise a copyist's error).

CHAPTER IV

(1) Let us therefore take care lest any among us imagine that he has been denied entry into His rest, because the promise is slow to be realized. (2) For the good news has been addressed to us as to them [the Jews]. Yet the word which was heard did not profit the hearers, because they did not assimilate the word for themselves by faith. (3) For we Christians are on the way towards the [place of] rest which is referred to in this verse, 'As I swore in my wrath: Never shall they enter into my rest'—and this although the works were [already] ended with the creation of the world. (4) On the subject of the seventh day it has been said somewhere, 'And God rested on the seventh day from all His works.' (5) And the rest is specifically referred to again in the words 'Never shall they enter into my rest.' (6) Therefore, since the entry of some must yet take place, and on the other hand, those who first received the good news did not enter there because of their disobedience, (7) God fixed a new period, the day 'Today', speaking by the mouth of David after a long interval of time. It is this which is spoken of in the text already quoted, 'If you hear my voice today, do not harden your hearts.' (8) Indeed, if Joshua had led them into the rest, God would not have spoken much later on of another day.

4¹. This verse can be interpreted in two quite different ways. (a) 'Let us be afraid lest any of us, by neglecting the promise ('*kataleipomenēs epanggelias*') should be adjudged ('*dokē*') to have missed ('*husterēkenai*') entering into the rest.' (b) 'Let us be afraid lest—the promise not being actualized ('*kataleipomenēs*')—any of us should come to think ('*dokē*') that he has been denied ('*husterēkenai*') entry into the rest.'

Everything turns on the precise sense of the Greek words '*kataleipesthai*', '*dokein*' and '*husterein*'. '*Kataleipesthai*' can mean 'to be left on one side', 'to be scorned'. But its use as a synonym for '*apoleipesthai*' in v. 6 leads us to choose the translation 'to be in arrears', 'to be owing'. '*Dokein*' does not mean here 'to seem', since it is a matter of reality not appearance. We therefore have to choose between 'to be found' (a legal term, very rare in biblical usage), or, better, 'to think', 'to believe'. It is the second sense alone which is in accord with our translation of the first verb. '*Husterein*' certainly means 'to fall short of' an aim. Hence we arrive at the translation (b) above. The verse is no repetition; it introduces a fresh warning. As the 'end' is slow to arrive, some people might despair of the realization of the promises and regret being committed to an illusion (cf. 2 Peter 3⁴).

4² is a reminder that the promises were addressed not only to the Jews, but subsequently also to Christians. The Jews did not profit by them, as emerges from v. 2b. But the detailed explanation of the phrase from '*all*' *ouk*' to '*akousasin*' offers serious difficulties. Certainly the meaning of '*sungkerannumi*' is quite plain, viz. 'to mix with', 'be assimilated to'. But are we to read '*sungkekerasmenos*' (nom. sing.) or '*sungkekerasmenous*' (acc. pl.)?[1] In the former case the participle would be attached to '*logos*'; in the latter to '*ekeinous*'. If we choose the second construction this would mean: 'they are not united to what they have heard', and this would necessitate reading '*akoustheisin*'[2] (= 'to what has been heard') and not '*akousasin*' (= 'to those who have heard'). In the first case the translation would be that 'the word was not assimilated by those who heard it', and '*akousasin*' could be read, the dative being equivalent to '*hupo tōn akousantōn*' (= 'by those who heard').[3] We accept this, the first, interpretation, since it does not require the acceptance of the reading '*akoustheisin*', which is ill-attested and no doubt the result of emendation. Under no circumstances could the reading '*sungkekerasmenous*' followed by '*tois akousasin*' be accepted, for that would give no intelligible meaning. In translating, it is better to put the sentence into the active voice: the hearers did not assimilate the word for themselves by faith ('*pistei*'). Once again Israel's lack of faith is stigmatized and held up as a bad example.

4³⁻⁵. V. 3a is to encourage the readers. We believers, we Christians, shall enter[4] into the rest of God. Why, then, is the terrible oath of God referred to yet again (cf. 2¹¹) in v. 3b? No doubt to establish the

[1] The former reading ('*sungkekerasmenos*' or '*sungkekramenos*'), given by S, the old Latin and the Peshitta, was adopted by Nestlé. The alternative ('*sungkekerasmenous*' or '*sungkekramenous*') by the remaining witnesses including p 46.

[2] A reading attested only by Theodore of Mopsuestia, the Vulgate, and one solitary minuscule. One could also give the conjectural reading '*tois akousmasin*' following BLEEK (with the same meaning), and this would explain the origin of the reading '*akousasin*', which would then be an error. CHRYSOSTOM (*MPG* 63, col. 56) gives a quite different reading: '*ouk ōphelēsen ho logos tēs akoēs ekeinous, mē sungkekramenēs tē pistei tois akousasi*' ('the word did not profit those who heard, for the hearing was not united to the faith of those who heard'), the participle being in this case attached to '*akoēs*'. The meaning would be acceptable, but we have not found this reading anywhere else. The reading '*sungkekramenois*' has also been suggested. This would imply a dative absolute, and the verb would have to be taken as middle voice: 'those who heard not being united'. But the conjecture has had no success, since it is superfluous.

[3] For this use of the dative, see CH. JAEGER, 'A propos de deux passages du Sermon sur la montagne', *RHPR* 1938, pp. 415ff; J. HERING, 'Dieu, Moïse et les Anciens', *RHPR* 1942, pp. 192ff; BLASS-DEBRUNNER, §191.
For the meaning, cf. also Aboth Rabbi Nathan 24 (7a): 'When one learns the Torah daily it enters into the flesh and blood' (quoted from STRACK-BILLERBECK, III, p. 666).

[4] The subjunctive '*eiserchōmetha*', which would imply an exhortation, is much less well attested than the indicative. The only important witnesses for it are A, C, and the Vulgate.

(9) *But the Great Sabbath has not yet arrived for the people of God.*
(10) *For one who has entered into his rest, himself rests from his works,
as God did from His.*
(11) *Let us therefore apply ourselves eagerly to enter into this rest,
so that no one falls into disobedience of the same kind.*

existence of the 'rest' (*'katapausis'*) which is about to be discussed.
In v. 3c and what follows a somewhat specious argument is elaborated to show that the 'rest' already existed before the time of
Moses. Indeed, God's rest, the 'Great Sabbath' of the Rabbis (*v.*
end of note 9, p 32), existed from the creation (*'apo kataboles kosmou'*),
or, more exactly, from the seventh day (*'en tē hēmera tē hebdomē'*),
v. 4 (an allusion to Genesis 2²). But the Jews did not enter therein
(v. 5).

4⁶. The writer assumes here that all the same the peace is destined to
be enjoyed by some people (*'tinas'*, v. 6). In default of the Jews
(*'hoi proteron euanggelisthentes'* = 'the earlier recipients of the
good news'), it will be the Christians for whom God fixes a new
terminal date (*'palin horizei hēmeran'*, v. 7). Here again is the
significant *'sēmeron'* of Psalm 95⁷ (LXX 94⁷), cited in v. 7 and attributed here to David.[5]

4⁸ involves a contrast or parallelism which is lost in English translation. There are two *'Iēsous'*: Jesus the son of Nun (Joshua, in English)[6] mentioned in v. 8, and Jesus Christ. The first rest, into which
the first Jesus should have led the people is of no further significance.
All that matters now is the new *'katapausis'*.

4⁹⁻¹⁰ state the conclusion of the argument. It is for the people of
God, i.e. the Christian community, that there is reserved the privilege
of sharing in the sabbath of God (*'sabbatismos'*), which will be true
peace.

4¹¹ returns to exhortation. *'Spoudasōmen'* = 'let us apply ourselves'
(Moffatt: 'be eager to enter'). The meaning of 'to hasten' must not
be given to this verb, for the idea that by our behaviour we could
hasten the end is absent from the Epistle. V. 11b once more puts
believers on guard against disobedience. *'Hupodeigma'* could mean
'example'. But it would be difficult to render *'en hupodeigmati tēs*

---

[5] At the end of v. 6, p 46, supported by S and the Vulgate, reads *'apistian'*
instead of *'apeitheian'*. We have already noted confusions of this kind (*v.
supra*, note 13, p 28). In v. 7, p 46 suppresses *'hēmeran'* (not noted by Nestlé):
God fixes a new *'sēmeron'*. In fact, *'hēmeran sēmeron'* would be pleonastic
('the day today').
[6] The different transcriptions of the same Jewish proper names, as we meet them
in the Old Testament and the New Testament, e.g. Joshua-Jesus, Jacob-James,
Miriam-Mary, is very unfortunate, but is to be explained by differences between
their Hebrew and Greek forms.

(12) *For the word of God is living and active, and sharper than a two-edged sword. For it penetrates through the soul and through the spirit, reaching their very joints and marrow. By so doing it effects a judgement among the thoughts and desires of our heart.* (13) *No creature can hide before it, for all things are stripped and overwhelmed by its glance. To this* [*Word*] *it is that we must give account.*

apeitheias' by 'following the example of disobedience', since '*tō autō*' ('the same') is added to '*hupodeigmati*', and this would then involve a pleonasm: 'following the same example'.[7] Better, with Moffatt, take '*hupodeigma*' as meaning 'kind', 'sort' ('to fall into the same sort of disobedience'). What the author says, then, is 'do not fall in the same way as the wilderness generation did'. Then '*pesein*' ('to fall') clearly does not have the same meaning as in 3[17]. Throughout this passage the writer forgets that, although the company around Moses did not enter Palestine, their descendants nevertheless did so. He holds strictly to the text of the Psalm, which says nothing of this.

The glorification of '*katapausis*'[8] might create a measure of disquiet because is work, then, a misfortune? In this connexion it has to be remembered that it is not work itself that is regarded as a curse in Genesis 3[17-19]—a passage which throws its shadow over the whole question, even when not expressly cited—but toilsome drudgery done with sweat, and above all work dictated particularly by material needs. For before the fall Adam was not destined to a life of idleness, since he had to exercise dominion over all creatures, according to Genesis 1[28]. On the other hand, '*katapausis*' must not invoke merely the notion of repose, but also those of peace, joy and concord.[9]

4[12, 13] are striking but difficult verses. That '*logos*' is somewhat personified presents no problem; it is much less so than in the Fourth

---

[7] Nor can it be explained, with Riggenbach, that the Christians could give a new example of disobedience. For the example given by the Israelites alone is at issue.

[8] According to KÄSEMANN, *Das wandernde Gottesvolk* (Göttingen 1934), the Gnostics knew an Aeon called '*sabbatismos*'. But the only one among the texts to which he refers which strikes us as interesting is that from the pseudo-Clementine Homilies, in which a rest of the universe is spoken of: '*hē tōn holōn katapausis*' (*GCS*, p. 234).

[9] It goes without saying that a theology based on the New Testament cannot neglect such a verse as John 5[17], in which Jesus states that His Father is always at work. The idea of a God who ceased from creating after the appearance of man—i.e. at the end of the Tertiary epoch or at the beginning of the Quaternary— is perhaps more Jewish than Christian. In PHILO also the idea of a God ceaselessly at work occurs: 'For God never leaves off making, but even as it is the property of fire to burn and of snow to chill, so it is the property of God to make' (*Legum Allegoriae*, I, §5, Chap. 3). For the divine sabbath see Zechariah 14[7]; *Mechilta ad Exodum* 31.22 (Winter and Wünsche, 1909, p. 339), and BACHER, *Die Aggada der Tanaiten*, I, 1884, pp. 328f. Cf. Sanhedrin 97a (GOLDSCHMIDT, IX, p. 66). Gen. Rabba 10.9 and 11.10 (*ad* Genesis 2[2-3]; FREEDMANN, I, pp. 78 and 86) explain that God does not cease to reward the good and punish the wicked. The Mechilta passage just referred to maintains a similar view.

Gospel or Philo, and there is no hint that it is identified with Christ. The language is metaphorical. Comparison of the *word* of God with a sword is nothing new to the Old Testament (*v.* Isaiah 49[2]: 'my mouth is like a sharp sword', and Wisdom 7[22]; 18[15]), except that here the sword is two-edged (*'distomos'*) as in Revelation 1[16] (*'rhomphaia distomos'*; cf. also Revelation 19[15, 21] and Ephesians 6[17]). The word, moreover, is *living* (*'zōn'*) because life-giving, and *active* (*'energēs'*) because creative.[10]

What then does the rest of v. 12, from *'diïknoumenos'* to *'kardias'* mean? In spite of Bengel we do not hold that *'achri merismou psuchēs kai pneumatos'*, etc., means 'to the point of separating the soul from the spirit and the joints from the marrow' (!), but rather 'to make a separation within the soul and within the spirit, as well as passing through the joints and through the marrow', these parts being taken in a psychological sense—the joints and marrow of the soul. The justification for that interpretation—an interpretation found already in Calvin[11]—is in what follows: v. 12b assigns to the Word a 'critical' function, that is, of judging; it judges the desires (*'epithumēseis'*) and thoughts (*'ennoiai'*) of the heart, by separating what is good from what is bad. This interpretation is also in harmony with the Philonic view, according to which the Logos effects a separation within the human faculties.[12]

4[13] shows that nothing is hidden from the eyes of the Word, since all things are naked (*'gumna'*) before it. But with the participle *'tetrachēlismena'* we encounter a new and difficult exegetical crux. The verb *'trachēlizō'* is in fact a technical term used in wrestling and means to grip one's opponent by the neck; and since this hold is hard to break, the verb can extend its meaning to that of 'to throw an opponent' or 'to overthrow' (i.e. 'conquer') him. These are the only meanings attested.[13] But expositors who have fervently wished to

---

[10] *'Energēs'* is a rare form for *'energos'*, but it is found also in 1 Corinthians 16[9] and Philemon 6; B reads *'enargēs'* ('manifest'), which is no improvement of the text. Comparison of the Logos with a sword is found in PHILO: *v. De Cherubim*, §28 (Chap. 9) and *Quis Rerum Divinarum Heres*, §§130–133.

[11] 'Now . . . it is said that God's word *pierces*, or reaches to the dividing of soul and spirit, that is, it examines the whole soul of man; for it searches his thoughts and scrutinizes his will with all its desires. And then he adds *the joints and marrow*, intimating that there is nothing so hard or strong in man, nothing so hidden, that the powerful word cannot pervade it . . . Hence God's word is a *discerner* . . .' (*Comm. ad loc.*, trans. J. Owen, 1853).

[12] See *Quis Rerum Divinarum Heres*, §130 and particularly §132 (Chap. 26), where it is explained that the Logos divides each of the three faculties of man: the soul (*'psuchē'*) is divided into rational (*'logikon'*) and irrational (*'alogon'*); speech (*'logos'*) into true (*'alēthes'*) and false (*'pseudos'*); and sense perception (*'aisthēsis'*) into 'presentations where the object is real and apprehended ("*kataleptikē*"), and presentations where it is not ("*phantasia kai akatalēpton*")'.

[13] See especially PHILO, *Quod Omnis Probus Liber Sit*, §159 (Chap. 22), which speaks of a person overcome by wrath (*'trachēlizetai hup' orgēs'*) and *De Mutatione Nominum*, §81 (Chap. 12), where the philosopher is compared with a wrestler whom his opponents try to 'floor' by their arguments (*'trachēlizontas logismous'*).

34 HEBREWS

acrobatic feats to justify this meaning. Bleek lists a large number.
Thus, for instance, attempts are made to convince us that *'trachēlizō'*
can mean 'to lay bare the neck of one whose head is pushed back',
or that the writer may have been thinking of sacrificial animals the
skin of which is stripped back, thereby making them naked.[14] This

The author, in our view, seeks to teach that the word of God brings
down the adversary and strips him (*'gumna'*) by despoiling him of his
view is that it seems to involve something of an inversion, since dis-
arming should normally come after the victory. But the 'word' could
perfectly well first expose the thoughts of men and precisely by doing
so confound them (cf. 1 Corinthians 14[25], where it is said of the
spirit of prophets that it brings to light the thoughts of sinners with
houtōs pesōn'* etc., = 'the secrets of his heart become manifest, and

Finally, the closing phrase of v. 13 is obscure. If, with Grotius,
Bleek and Windisch[15] we translate *'pros hon hēmin ho logos'* by
'about whom we are speaking', we have a merely banal assertion;
so we prefer, with Spicq, to render it: 'to Him it is that we must give
with the context in which the 'word' is represented as our judge.[16]

It is nonetheless curious, in any case, that *'logos'* should be used
in two such different senses in v. 12 and v. 13, first as a theological
term and then in a secular sense. This is why we have to look not
could have been *'wehû' ba'al debārîm'* = 'and he [is] the master of

[14] An explanation promulgated, alas! by CHRYSOSTOM (*MPG* 63, col. 61)
*'tetrachēlismena eipen, apo metaphoras tōn dermatōn tōn apo tōn sphazomenōn
off sacrificial victims'). The Vulgate translates it *'aperta'* ('uncovered'). Similarly
other ancient translations, though this does not make us change our mind.
THEODORET (*MPG* 82, col. 705 C) likewise. Of course, emendations have also
been suggested, such as *'pephanerōmena'* ('made visible') or *'tetranōmena'* ('made
clear'). They are of no interest. The *Disputatio Theologico-Philologica* on 4[13] of
GUILIELMUS AB INHOVEN (Utrecht 1738) had already started on the right track
by translating *'trachēlizō'* as 'striking on the neck'. Cf. WETSTEIN, II, p. 398.
[15] GROTIUS, *'de quo nunc agimus'*, *op. cit.*, p. 1023.
[16] CHRYSOSTOM, *MPG* 63, col. 62.—The modern Greek version of the New
Testament, at all events that published under the auspices of the British and
Foreign Bible Society, correctly gives *'pros hon na dasōmen logon'*. Similarly
Cajetanus (= Thomas de Vio): *'ad quem referre debemus rationem'*. Similarly
LUTHER (*Gloses* 19–20). Calvin translates: 'with whom we have to do', but adds
'the meaning of the sentence is that it is God who addresses us . . . and for this
reason we must not trifle as with mortal man, but . . . must tremble' (p. 404).
Likewise JAVET, pp. 37f.
[17] JOHANN H. R. BIESENTHAL, *op. cit.*, pp. 141ff.

(14) *Having, therefore, a great High Priest who has passed through the heavens, Jesus the Son of God, let us hold fast to our religion.* (15) *For we do not have a High Priest who is unable to suffer with our weaknesses; on the contrary, He has been tempted in every way, because He resembled us—but without falling into sin.* (16) *Let us then boldly draw near to the throne of grace, so that we may obtain mercy and find grace, and be helped at the opportune time.*

words', i.e. the accuser, and the phrase reads as '*weh û'be' al debārîm*' = and he [is] the subject of [our] words'. Even so, and assuming that we grant that '*ba'al debārîm*' had the technical sense which is claimed, this would not be sufficient to make us think that the entire Epistle was first written in Hebrew, as Biesenthal holds. The author could very well have written directly in Greek and yet made use of Hebrew midrashim here and there.

4[14]. From this verse the author develops the main theme of his homily: Christ is the ideal High Priest. '*Archiereus megas*' (= 'great High Priest') is almost a pleonasm, yet it does not seem to have been coined by our author as it is found in Philo.[18]

Concerning the plurality of heavens nothing more need be said (*v. supra ad* **1**[2], **1**[10]). The theme of passing through the heavens is equally well known in Jewish literature. Enoch did it, guided by an angel, and he reported his journey; and the idea recurs in the Ascension of Isaiah and the Greek Apocalypse of Baruch.[19]

The figure of the heavenly High Priest is not unknown to Judaism, to judge from Enoch, the Talmud and Philo.[20] Was the narrative of the ascension, in the precise form related in Luke and Acts, known to the author of this Epistle? It is improbable, since he never mentions the forty days which separated the ascension from the resurrection. Some exegetes, including Calvin and Grotius,[21] and also the Synodale Version, have tried to take '*dielthein*' as simply meaning 'He entered' the heavens. But this interpretation is philologically unsound. Moreover, it is obvious that a High Priest must reach the highest heaven. For '*homologia*', *v. supra ad* **3**[1].

4[15]. '*Sumpathēsai*', a vulgar form of '*sumpathein*', must not be rendered 'have sympathy', because of the weakness of this term in

---

[18] In *De Somniis*, I, §219 (Chap. 38) the '*logos*' is called '*megas archiereus*' ('the great High Priest').

[19] Slav. Enoch Chaps. 1–20; Asc. Isaiah Chaps. 7–9; Greek Apocalypse of Baruch *passim*. See next note.

[20] According to Enoch 40.6 the voice of an angel intercedes for men. According to Talmud Chagiga 12b (GOLDSCHMIDT, IV, p. 272), Michael offers sacrifices. PHILO, *Quis Rerum Divinarum Heres*, §205 (Chap. 42): 'To His Word, His chief messenger, highest in age and honour, the Father of all has given the special prerogative, to stand on the border and separate the creature from the Creator. This same Word both pleads with the immortal as suppliant from afflicted mortality and acts as ambassador of the ruler to the subject.'

[21] GROTIUS, '*qui penetravit coelos*', *op. cit.*, p. 1023.

English. The passion of Christ was such that He suffered, and still does suffer, genuinely with men to the extent of understanding their weaknesses (*'astheneias'*), i.e. their physical and spiritual distresses. Furthermore, He was tempted as we are (*'kath' homoiotēta'*, i.e. 'in conformity with His likeness to us'—in this respect He was *'homo-ousios'*), and this enables Him to come to our aid in our trials (v. 16 *'boētheia'*). Yet He committed no sins (*'chōris hamartias'*). The sinlessness of Jesus therefore does not turn on the absence of human frailty, but in a constantly renewed victory over temptations.[22]

4[16]. This verse presents no particular difficulty. The difference between *'eleos'* and *'charis'* turns on this, that the former denotes the grace of mercifulness towards sinners, the latter the grace which intervenes in times of trial. The expression *'thronos tēs charitos'* (= 'throne of grace') is formed on the analogy of *'thronos tēs doxēs'* (= 'throne of glory': Ecclesiasticus 47[11]; Isaiah 22[23]; Jeremiah 14[21]; 17[12]; I Samuel [LXX 1 Kings] 2[8]).[23] It is the throne on which God sits to exercise His mercy (genitive of quality used in a very loose way as in Hebrew). The High Priest on the one hand obtains forgiveness, and on the other He comes to the aid (*'boētheō'*) of those who are a prey to trials and temptations.

---

[22] When our author speaks of *'hamartia'* he means what was later called actual sin. He did not ask himself whether Jesus, who shared human weaknesses, did not 'bear' original sin. Perhaps he would have replied in the affirmative, in order to show how radically Jesus was tempted and was victor over evil.

[23] According to rabbinical literature God has two thrones, the throne of justice and the throne of mercy. See Midrash Rabba ad Lev. 29[1] (FREEDMANN, IV, p. 390). In Philo the power of mercy (*'dunamis hileōs'*) is opposed to, and is an appendage of, legislative power (*'dunamis nomothetikē'*), which dictates the laws and impels their observance. It is the same in the Cabbala. See E. R. GOOD-ENOUGH, *By Light, Light*, New Haven, 1935, pp. 235f and 263f.

CHAPTER V

(1) *For every High Priest, chosen among men, has been appointed to represent them before God, that he may offer gifts and sacrifices for sins.* (2) *He may be indulgent toward the ignorant and erring, since he himself is afflicted by weakness,* (3) *for which reason he has to offer, not only for the people but for himself also, sacrifices for sins.*

5^{1–3}. These verses remind us first of all of some essential qualities of the Jewish High Priest. In the first place, he is chosen from among men ('*ex anthrōpōn*'). If the writer says nothing of his Jewish extraction this is because in the context it is only his humanity which matters. He is installed as man's representative in the relation of men to God ('*huper anthrōpōn ta pros ton theon*'). His chief duty is to offer '*dōra*' (= bloodless 'offerings', especially rendered in thanksgiving) and '*thusiai huper hamartiōn*' (= 'sacrifices for atonement of sins'). Further, his service is not regarded as an *opus operatum*. His heart must be in it. And he is capable of understanding the ignorance and errors of men ('*agnoousin kai planōmenois*'), for He Himself is subject to their weaknesses[1] ('*perikeitai astheneian*', where '*perikeitai*' with the accusative, as in Acts 28²⁰, means literally 'to be surrounded by'). The term '*metriopathein*' deserves some explanation. It seems to have been a technical term of certain philosophical schools of a Pythagorean or Platonic stamp, and is opposed to the Stoic term '*apatheia*' ('freedom from emotion', 'impassibility'). '*Metriopatheia*' is thus a more human virtue, denoting the well-regulated restraint of emotion. This is the sense in which '*metriopathein*' is used by Philo and Plutarch.[2] The sense which suits this context is 'to have an indulgent attitude'. If further proof were needed of the High Priest's participation in human weakness, it is the obligation to offer sacrifices on his own behalf, in conformity with Leviticus 4^{1–12}; 9^{7–8}; 16^{1–14}.[3]

[1] It is in place to remark here that the writer is not speaking of deliberate sins by those who are hardened. In harmony with Jewish ideas taken in the strict sense, the sacrificial cult was intended for the expiation of involuntary faults. Sinners who acted deliberately were threatened with extermination according to Numbers 15^{30f}; cf. 6⁸; 10²⁶. '*Agnoein*' is sometimes synonymous with '*hamartanein*', as '*ginōskō*' is with 'to be virtuous'. Generally, in the LXX and New Testament, '*ginōskō*', carries the impress of the Hebrew '*yāḍa*' ', which signifies knowledge gained and developed from practical contact with men or the laws.

[2] PHILO, *De Abrahamo*, §257 (Chap. 44) explains that the wise man experiences neither '*pathos*' nor '*apatheia*'; he must '*metriopathein*'. Cf. PLUTARCH, *De Cohibenda ira*, 10. (The excellent introduction to Plutarch's thought in DE FAYE, *Origène*, II, Chap. 8, 1927, is to be noted). JOSEPHUS, *Antiquities*, XII, §128 (3.2) attributes '*metriopatheia*' ('moderation') to Vespasian and Titus.

[3] We read '*di' autēn opheilei*' with all the ancient witnesses including p 46, and not '*dia tautēn opheilei*' with the Textus Receptus. According to PHILO, *Quis Rerum Divinarum Heres*, §174 (Chap. 36) the priests made vegetable offerings for themselves and offerings of lambs for the people.

(4) *And no High Priest arrogates this duty to himself, but only when he is called by God, as Aaron was.* (5) *So Christ did not usurp the glorious position of High Priest, but it was God who [gave it to Him, and who] uttered these words about it: 'You are my Son; today I have begotten you'.* (6) *Likewise, He says elsewhere: 'You will be a priest for ever, after the order of Melchizedek'.*

5[4]. *'Timē'* here does not mean honour given in virtue of a responsibility, but the responsibility itself. This meaning is the more justified as Josephus and Philo use precisely this term for the functions of the High Priest, historical or philosophical.[4] *'Lambanei'* means 'to take'. But after *'kaloumenos'* a second *'lambanei'* is understood, which in this case can only mean 'to accept'. He does not take the responsibility with egotistic aims (*'heautō'*), but he accepts the call of God.

Reference to Aaron, unmentioned up to this point, is somewhat surprising.[5] But after all, he and his descendants had been installed as priests by his brother, who himself was more of a legislator; and the Rabbis held that Aaron had been in some sense appointed by God Himself.[6]

5[5]. Do these features apply to the new High Priest? Perfectly, as we are going to be shown, with the exception of the sacrifices for His own sins; from these sacrifices He is obviously exempted. Yet Jesus does more. He not only fulfils in a perfect way the High Priestly functions on behalf of the people, He far surpasses them. But for the moment the stress is still upon the likeness between Aaron and Jesus.[7]

But what is meant by *'ouch heauton edoxasen genēthēnai archierea'*? At first glance: He did not extract any glory from the fact of having been appointed High Priest. But on second thoughts: He did not raise Himself to the glorious rank of High Priest (lit. 'He did not seek His own aggrandisement to the extent of making Himself a High Priest'). And this latter appears to fit the context better. Moreover, in Ecclesiasticus 45[23] and 2 Maccabees 14[7], *'doxa'* actually denotes 'the glorious responsibility' of the High Priest. 5[5] ends with the quotation of Psalm 2[7], encountered previously in 1[5].

The second quotation is taken from Psalm 110[4] (LXX 109), another verse of that Psalm having already been cited above (1[13]).

[4] JOSEPHUS, *Antiquities*, III, §190 (8.1) regards Moses as *'tēs timēs axion'* ('worthy of this honour'). PHILO, *Vita Mosis*, 11, §67 (Chap. 13): service of the true God (*'therapeuein to pros alētheian on'*) is a *'timē'* befitting a wise man (*'harmottousa tō sophō'*).

[5] The ending of the verse, i.e. *'kathōsper* [or: *kathaper] kai Aaron'* is absent from p 13.

[6] Midrash Rabba on Numbers 18[9] (FREEDMANN, V, p. 718) relates in connexion with Numbers 16[35], a speech of Moses to the people: 'If my brother Aaron had taken the priesthood himself, there would be grounds for being offended. But in fact it is God Himself, to whom is due majesty, power and dominion.'

[7] K suppresses *'houtōs kai ho Christos'*. One MS of the Old Latin (d) adds a 'not', which amounts to saying that Christ was not like Aaron, but superior to him. The correction is inspired by a concern with a theme which appears in v. 5 and is only elaborated later.

(7) *In the days of His incarnation He addressed prayers and supplications, accompanied by violent cries and tears, to the One who was able to save Him from death; and He was heard, by being delivered from His anguish.* (8) *By suffering He learned obedience, although He was the Son.* (9) *Having thereby attained perfection, He became for all who obey Him, the author of an eternal salvation,* (10) *being designated by God a High Priest after the order of Melchizedek.*

It is highly important because it is a prelude to elaborations concerning Melchizedek which extend to the end of 7. The Psalmist was perhaps thinking of a Hasmonean prince who in his own person would unite the functions of king and priest. But the present writer has truly seen that this announcement or prophecy, announcing a priesthood which is non-Aaronic and eternal, applies far better to Christ.[8]

5[7–9]. Let us first expound these verses, which are also most characteristic of the Christology of the Epistle. 5[7] sketches a moving picture of a terrible trial endured by Jesus. The reference to prayers and supplications, tears, and the danger of death (*'deēseis'*, *'hiketērias'*, *'meta dakruōn'*, *'ek thanatou'*) places this trial without any possibility of error at one precise moment in the earthly life (*'en tais hēmerais tēs sarkos'*) of the Saviour, namely in Gethsemane (Matthew 26[36–46] par.). But expositors disagree over the interpretation of the end of v. 7. Most, since John Chrysostom, take *'eisakoustheis apo tēs eulabeias'* as meaning that He was heard by reason of His 'fear of God' or 'piety'. So the Vulgate has *'pro sua reverentia'*, Luther's Bible *'darum dass er Gott in Ehren hatte'* ('because He reverenced God'), Riggenbach *'von wegen [sic] des Ehrerbietigkeit'* (same meaning), and similarly E. Reuss, E. Ménégoz (B. d. C.), Westcott, Moffatt.[9] It must be granted to this rendering that in Philo *'eulabeia'* often means 'piety'.[10] Why we feel driven to abandon it is that it leaves *'eisakoustheis'* (= 'heard') without a complement and even without an object. About what was Jesus heard? One of the clearest teachings in the Synoptics is precisely that the granting of His prayer did not occur, because Jesus withdrew His request that the cup should pass from Him. It is therefore understandable that Harnack[11] should have suggested the insertion of *'ouk'* before

[8] Nevertheless, our Epistle is perhaps not the first writing which may have interpreted the Psalm in a 'messianic' sense (to use common terminology). The Testament of Levi, in Chap. 18, speaks of a glorious priest of the future, though without citing Psalm 110. But this passage also shows that a priest of non-Levitic origin was unthinkable to Jews. Instead of *'hiereus'*, p 46 reads *'epeux'* (not noted by Nestlé); *v.* Hoskier, *op. cit.*, pp. 3f, who tries to make sense of this bizarre reading.

[9] See Ed. Reuss, *La Bible, N.T.*, V, 1878, p. 52, and Linden, *TSK* 1860, pp. 753f.

[10] See the concordance of Philo's works by H. Leisegang, which appeared as a supplement to the great edition by Cohn and Wendland.

[11] *Studien zur Geschichte des N.T. und der alten Kirche;* I. *Neustamentl. Textkritik* 1931, pp. 245f. This conjecture had been adopted by Windisch, *Comm. ad loc.*, and by Bultmann, *TWNT*, II, pp. 750f.

'*eisakoustheis*' (= 'He was not heard'); but this is a desperate solution.

Another most ingenious interpretation attaches '*apo tēs eulabeias*' to what follows ('*emathen*', etc.), i.e. 'because He feared God, He learned obedience from His sufferings'. This interpretation is presupposed by the Peshitta, of which Riggenbach[12] cites the Latin translation: '*et quavis esset filius, ex timore et passionibus, quas sustinuit, dicit oboedientiam*' ('and although He was a son, out of the fear and suffering which He sustained, He rendered obedience'). It has been adopted by Blass-Debrunner (§211). But here again '*eisakoustheis*' is left without an object.

Putting on one side other less significant explanations, a list of which may be found in Bleek, Riggenbach and Spicq, we adopt that of St Ambrose and Bengel, accepted by Holtzmann, Zahn, Michel and others,[13] which takes '*eulabeia*' in the sense of 'fear', 'anguish', a meaning lexographically well attested and in admirable accord with the context, which is stressing the fear of death—not the fear of death in general, but of that painful and ignominious death. In what respect, then, was His prayer heard? In His being delivered from fear. It is just this which the Synoptics also show us.

One other thing must be said about it being possible for God to save Him from death ('*pros ton dunamenon sōzein auton ek thanatou*'). It does not seem to us that this affirmation is given full weight unless it is seen as a genuine possibility: God would have saved Him if He had not Himself finally abandoned His insistence. For if there is one point on which the Gospels, the Pauline Epistles, and this Epistle, are in absolute agreement, it is on the *voluntary* nature of His death. In virtue of His sonship, Christ could have refused the cup; but the work of salvation would have been wrecked.[14]

5⁸. '*Kaiper ōn*' is a reminder of the privilege of the Son, which did not hinder Jesus from perfecting His humanity by obedience to the very limit. It was because He obeyed that the work of salvation was able to be carried through, as v. 9 explains.

---

[12] RIGGENBACH, *Comm.*, p. 131, n. 45.

[13] Ambrose, '*Exauditus ab illo metu*', *MPL* 1st edn, 14, col. 1169, or *CSEL*, vol. 64, p. 382 (Homily on Psalm 61). CALVIN thinks there is an allusion to the resurrection, which wrested Christ from the dead, so that in that sense He had been heard. This view is to be found already with PETER LOMBARD: 'He offered prayers and supplications to Him, that is God, who was able to deliver from death the one who besought Him, that is, to raise Him up'. See *Collectanea in epistulam ad Hebraeos*, MPL 192, col. 437.

[14] If the reader will forgive us a brief digression, we would observe that the Synoptics allow us to see how Jesus might have dispensed with the Cross. He could have asked the Father to take His soul to Himself there and then, in Gethsemane. It would have been a relatively easy death, rather like that of Gautama Buddha in the gardens of Kusinara. The reason for saying this is the words '*perilupos heōs thanatou*' = 'I am sorrowful to the extent of longing for death' (i.e. a peaceful death in Gethsemane, understood). Cf. Jonah 4⁹, where '*lelupēmai heōs thanatou*' ('I am sorrowful unto death') means exactly the same thing (cf. v. 8: '*kalon moi apothanein me ē zēn*' = 'it is better for me to die than to live').

(11) *On the subject of Melchizedek, we must give you some explanations, long and difficult to teach, because your mind is dull.* (12) *Indeed, you who ought [now] yourselves to be teachers after all the time which has passed, have [on the contrary] fresh need to be instructed in the first elements of theology. That is, you need milk instead of solid food.* (13) *Now, one who is fed on milk understands nothing of religious doctrine, for he is [still] a babe.* (14) *But solid food is suitable for grown men, by which I mean those who by their attitude have trained their faculties to distinguish good from evil.*

5⁹. This obedience He learnt not only in His sufferings but by them (*'aph' hōn epathen'*).[15] It is as if the writer had wished to imply that the succession of trials had driven Him more and more into the Father's arms. Yet a further idea must still underlie this text, namely, that by suffering He learnt to have compassion for His fellow men and to save them through His own submission to the designs of the divine providence.

5¹⁰⁻¹¹. The dominant theme of Psalm 110 occurs yet again, announcing the entry of Melchizedek, though he only appears in 6. Prior to this the writer speaks frankly. He is by no means satisfied with the progress of his recipients in the matter of theology, and he even asks if they will be in a fit condition to understand the profound significance of the figure of Melchizedek. He reminds them that the subject is a difficult one to treat (*'dusermēneutos'*) and that the explanations will inevitably be lengthy (*'polus hēmin ho logos'*), not only because of the difficulty inherent in every advanced subject, but also because of the sluggishness of understanding of his auditors (*'nōthroi tais akoais'*: Moffatt, 'dull of hearing'; Bouillon: 'their understanding dulled').[16] It would be easier if we could take *'akoais'* as the object of the hearing, but we are not sure whether such a translation is possible. Moreover, the phrase is paralleled in Ephesians 1¹⁸ where eyes are spoken of in connection with the mind (*'ophthalmoi tēs kardias'*).

In what follows (v. 12) the author treats them as babes who can only tolerate milk. This is reminiscent of Pauline sayings in which a distinction is similarly drawn between nurslings and adults, or the fleshly men (*'sarkinoi' or 'psuchikoi'*) and the perfect (*'teleioi'*) as here in v. 14.[17] But the content of the gnosis is not the same. For

---

[15] The expression *'emathen ho epathen'* is found in Philo, *De Fuga et Inventione*, §138 (Chap. 25); cf. the expression *'ho pathōn akribōs emathen'* ('the lesson which experience had taught him so fully'), *De Somniis*, II, §107 (Chap. 15). The article by J. Kögel, 'Der Begriff "*teleioun*" im Hebräer-Brief', *Theologische Studien, M. Kähler dargebracht*, Leipzig 1905, pp. 35ff, was not available to us.

[16] *'Nōthros'* might be derived from *'nosos'*, but it seems doubtful.

[17] 1 Corinthians 2⁶, ¹⁴⁻¹⁶; and particularly 3¹⁻². The distinction between beginners and mature men also plays a large part in Philo and especially in his greatest (indirect) disciple, Clement of Alexandria. While the Gnostics properly so called erect a barrier between 'fleshly' and 'spiritual' men, Paul and the author of Hebrews (like Clement later on) would desire all men to become *'teleioi'* or *'gnōstikoi'*.

Paul it concerns especially revelations of an eschatological character, but here teaching about the profound meaning of the new priesthood.

5¹². Amongst other important matters, this verse alludes to the long past of this Church ('*dia ton chronon*'), although the language is perhaps hyperbolic. The ideal would be that all Christians should make such progress in theology that in the end they themselves could teach ('*didaskaloi*') new-comers. But the recipients of the letter or auditors of the sermon, so far from progressing have gone back for they need someone to teach them afresh even the first elements of theology, that is, biblical theology ('*ta stoicheia tēs archēs tōn logiōn tou theou*').[18]

5¹³⁻¹⁴ insist on the opposition between '*nēpioi*' = 'babes' and '*teleioi*' (lit. = 'perfect'; here 'adults' or 'mature people').[19] 5¹⁴ᵇ gives a passing glimpse of the author's theory of intellectual and moral knowledge. There is a training which facilitates the development of special faculties ('*ta aisthētēria*') enabling us to distinguish good ('*kalon*') from bad ('*kakon*'). These two terms have so general a sense that they apply not only to the realm of the intellect but also to that of all values, and especially moral values. The ideal Christian should therefore possess as a cardinal virtue (on which 1 John 4¹ also insists) a perspicacity, developed by exercise ('*gegumnasmena*'), and resting not so much on reasoning as on the discernment of values. It is hardly necessary to draw attention to the great interest of this view.

The only real difficulty is the exact meaning of '*hexis*'. This is a technical philosophical term denoting a state or quality of soul or simply a 'capacity'. The capability is there when the faculties have been exercised.

---

[18] In the phrase '*logia tou theou*' we take '*tou theou*' as an objective genitive. It could also be taken as a subjective genitive, meaning then the words uttered by God which are found in the Bible. In any case it is a matter of biblical theology. What precisely does '*apeiroi*' mean? There seem to exist two homonymous adjectives '*apeiros*' : (a) = 'without limit' (from '*peras*'); (b) = 'without experience', 'ignorant of' (from '*peira*'). The second sense suits here: they are ignorant of the '*logou dikaiosunēs*'.

Now '*dikaiosunē*' is often a synonym for 'religion' (*v.* Matthew 5¹⁰). '*Logos dikaiosunēs*' is 'religious instruction', and this is a way of designating theology, as the word '*theologia*' did not then exist. For the various theological connotations of milk ('*gala*', v. 12), see the article by SCHLIER in *TWNT*, I, *sub voce*.

[19] It is to be remembered that in the New Testament '*teleios*' never bears the sense of 'divinized', as sometimes in the mystery religions, in spite of certain approximations occasionally to be detected; *v.* R. REITZENSTEIN, *Die hellenistischen Mysterienreligionen*, 3rd edn, pp. 133f and 338f; H. A. A. KENNEDY, *St Paul and the Mystery Religions*, 1913, pp. 130f; CH. GUIGNEBERT, *RHPR*, 1928, pp. 412ff; see also O. MICHEL, 'Die Lehre von der christlichen Vollkommenheit nach der Anschauung des Hebräer-Briefs', *TSK*, 1934/1935, pp. 333ff.

CHAPTER VI

THE AUTHOR seems to contradict himself somewhat. After having called his readers babes he nonetheless prepares to give higher instruction to them. No doubt he was trying to use a well-known pedagogic device to stir them to some exertion.

(1) *This is why we must go beyond elementary Christian instruction and tackle advanced teaching, without laying again the foundation, consisting of the doctrine of repentance from dead works, of faith in God, (2) of ablutions, of the laying-on of hands, of resurrection of the dead and of the last judgement. (3) This is precisely what we are going to do, God willing.*

6¹. '*Archē*' = 'the beginnings'; '*Christou logos*' could mean teaching given by Christ (= the Christian revelation), or teaching about Christ (= Christology). In the light of **7** the latter seems to give the better sense. '*Pherōmetha*' = 'let us carry ourselves', 'let us advance'; and the writer uses the first person because he will participate in the journey in the capacity of guide. '*Epi tēn teleiotēta*' = lit. 'towards perfection', though not the perfection of the recipients but of the teaching, that is, advanced teaching as opposed to the '*archē*'.

6¹ᵇ, ² give a curious list of headings for what is considered elementary theology and ethics. The 'dead works' ('*nekra erga*') which are mentioned could well apply to Jewish-Christians who may have practised the Law in a wrong way. But in any case these are works done without love or understanding, and which for that reason lack life and can lead to death. Abandonment of such legalism is one of the first demands laid upon beginners.

Faith in God also belongs evidently to the initial teaching; but as later with Clement of Alexandria there is the need for it to be clarified. Observe the choice of prepositions '*apo*' and '*epi*' in succession; there must be a turning *from* and a turning *towards*.

6². '*Didachē baptismōn*' = 'teaching about baptisms' or 'ablutions' is difficult because of the plural ('quite unique', says Spicq). For, contrary to the Mandaeans and Essenes, Christians knew only a single baptism which was not repeated. Should we think of a triple immersion in honour of the Trinity, which Tertullian knew?¹ Or of

---

¹ See *de Corona militis*, 3, where he says 'three times we are immersed' (*CSEL*, 70, p. 158). In other passages which are sometimes referred to in this connexion, namely *de baptismo*, 6, and *adversus Praxeam*, 26, the Trinity is mentioned in connexion with baptism, but not triple immersion.

the large number of baptisms already administered by the Church, as Theodoret believed,[2] or of some instruction in 'comparative religion' establishing the differences between Christian baptism, John the Baptist's baptism, and other rites of ablution practised by the Jews and in the mystery religions ([sic] Riggenbach and Moffatt)? There could be a great temptation to emend '*baptismōn*' to '*baptismou*', but we shall resist it. And unless we postulate that the Church also practised a feet-washing which could properly be called a '*baptisma*', we give partial acceptance to Riggenbach's view, that the difference between John's baptism and Christian baptism had to be explained to neophytes. If Apollos were the author of this Epistle, this concern could be well understood, in the light of what is said in the Acts of the Apostles (18[25]; 19[1ff]). It is surprising that this argument, so far as we know, has not been turned to account in support of the theory of Apollos' authorship.

'*Epitheseōs cheirōn*' (= 'the laying-on of hands') no doubt depends on '*didachēs*', as does what follows. This rite was practised, according to Acts 8[17-19] and 19[6], for communicating the Holy Spirit. When this endowment was definitively linked with baptism the laying-on of hands had normally to be done at the same time. The Pastoral Epistles also mention the act on the occasion of something like a consecration (cf. 1 Timothy 4[14]; 5[22]; 2 Timothy 1[6]), without its precise significance and scope being explained.[3]

'*Anastaseōs nekrōn*' (the doctrine of 'resurrection of the dead'),[4] which Paul presents as a revelation frequently ill-understood and needing extensive explanations (1 Corinthians 15), is here considered to belong to the first elements of doctrine. This is explicable if some years had elapsed and the recipients were Judaeo-Christians, less handicapped by Greek prejudices. On the other hand, we cannot escape the impression that the writer does not attach too much importance to bodily resurrection, which he mentions only here. It is the believer's access to heaven which interests him. '*Krima aiōnion*' = 'eternal judgement', that is the judgement which determines an eternal destiny, a concept common to Judaism and Christianity.

---

[2] *MPG* 82, col. 716, 'since many have the benefit of the grace of baptism'. ALFRED SEEBERG, *Der Katechismus der Urchristenheit*, 1903, p. 253, thinks of the duality of baptism by water and by the Spirit. But were the two baptisms not regarded as coincident? CALVIN's explanation is rather like Theodoret's: 'This doctrine does not mean that there are several baptisms. But he speaks of the accustomed ceremonies, and the public method of baptizing, or of the days appointed for baptizing, as baptisms' (*Comm.*, p. 418). J. SCHLICHTING, on the other hand: 'There is also the baptism of John' (*Comm. in Ep. ad Hebr.* [Racoviae 1634] *ad* 6[2]).

[3] See BEHM, *Die Handauflegung im Urchristentum*, 1911. J. COPPENS, *L'imposition des mains et les rites connexes dans le N.T.*, 1925. FR SPICQ, *Commentaire des Epîtres pastorales*, in the series 'Etudes bibliques', Paris, pp. 320ff.

[4] No more than the Apostle Paul, or the much later Creed of Nicaea, does our theologian speak of the resurrection of the *flesh*. For the distinction which St Paul drew between '*sōma*' and '*sarx*' see our commentary on *The First Epistle of Saint Paul to the Corinthians*, ET London 1962, particularly Chap. 15.

(4) *Imagine, now, that men who were once for all enlightened, who had sampled the heavenly gift, shared in the Holy Spirit* (5) *and tasted the good word of God and the powers of the future world,* (6) *[that these people] should fall once again—it would indeed then be impossible to lead them to repent afresh. They themselves are sharing in the crucifixion of the Son of God, exposing Him to insults.*

With this list in front of us we may ask whether our theologian was not inspired by a confession of faith known to his auditors and thought to summarize elementary instruction.

6³. *'Kai touto'* (= 'and this precisely') clearly refers, not to the basic instruction, but to the *'teleiotēs'* mentioned in v. 1, that is, to the advanced instruction, which, as for the Alexandrines, primarily consists in a penetrating study of the Bible, leading to a grasp of heavenly mysteries. The indicative *'poiēsousin'* agrees better with the sequel 'if God permits' (cf. James 4¹⁵) than the subjunctive *'poiēsōmen'*, read by a certain number of witnesses.[5]

But the execution of this promise is delayed yet again by the insertion of what amounts to a sermon (6³⁻²⁰), the essential purport of which is to highlight the beauty of a Christian life which takes account of the divine promises—and threats. Care must be taken not to draw from this over-precise inferences about the condition of the Church which was to receive the letter, for it is not absolutely certain that the exhortation was written for the occasion.

6⁴⁻⁶. These very important and much discussed verses teach the impossibility of repentance for apostates (*'parapesontas'*, v. 6), who had actually enjoyed previously the ineffable gifts of God. First we notice *'phōtismos'* = 'illumination', a term rare in the New Testament (see, however, Ephesians 1¹⁸; 3⁹; cf. 2 Corinthians 4⁶),[6] but one which will play some part in the thought of Ignatius of Antioch and of Justin. With the Fathers, we might think of baptism; but this was believed to coincide with the gift of the Holy Spirit, which is mentioned separately at the end of v. 4. It is a question, therefore, of the light spoken of by Jesus, Matthew 5¹⁴ ('you are the light of the world'); John 8¹² ('I am the light of the world'); 2 Peter 1¹⁹

[5] Namely, A, C, D and the Byzantine Text. The indicative is given chiefly by p 46, S, B and the Latin versions.
[6] *'Phōtizein'* seems to correspond to the Hebrew *'hôrāh'*, hiphil of *'yārāh'*. The chief LXX texts are Judges 13⁸; 4 Kings 12³; 17²⁷ᵗ; Psalm 12⁴; 118¹³⁰; Ecclesiasticus 45¹⁷. For IGNATIUS see the introduction to his Epistle to the Romans, where the Church is said to be 'enlightened through the will of Him who willed all things that are' (*'pephōtismenē en thelēmati tou thelēsantos ta panta ha estin'*). JUSTIN, *Apology*, §61, regards baptism as a *'phōtismos'* 'enlightening the mind of those who learn these things' (*'hōs phōtizomenon tēn dianoian tōn tauta manthanontōn'*). For the meaning of *'phōtizo'* in Hellenistic religions see REITZENSTEIN, *Hellenistische Mysterienreligionen*, 3rd edn, p. 292, and KENNEDY, *Saint Paul and the Mystery Religions*, 1913, *passim*, and also CH. GUIGNEBERT, *RHPR*, 1928, pp. 412ff.

('until the "*phōsphoros*"—the light-bringer—arises in your hearts'); 2
Corinthians 4⁶ ('the light which has shone in your hearts'). Then there
is mentioned the '*dōrea epourania*' (lit. 'the heavenly gift'); a gracious
gift which is compared with a food of which one has tasted the
savour ('*geusamenoi*'). If necessary we may think, with the majority
of the Church Fathers, of the Eucharist. The list proceeds with a
reference to sharing in the Holy Spirit (cf. 2⁴), and (in v. 5) to assimil-
ating the divine word, which is likewise compared with food and
envisaged somewhat as a sacrament.⁷ The list ends with reference to
the '*dunameis mellontos aiōnos*' (lit. 'powers of the world to come'),
which here evidently means the irruption of supernatural powers
from the new world-order, transitory and yet richly significant and
enheartening for believers (though disconcerting to others), shown
by miracles and other signs which presage the new order in which
matter will obey spirit (cf. 2⁴). One can have tasted the new order
through experience of these forces.

6⁶. A serious question now presents itself. Supposing someone has
been nourished by all these favours and then becomes an apostate,
what will happen to him?⁸ The reply is definite. He cannot be renewed
('*anakainizein*'), that is, brought back to repentance ('*eis metanoian*').
It is therefore the impossibility of *repenting* which is being affirmed,
and it is not a question of knowing whether fresh forgiveness can be
obtained if one does repent. Let us repeat, it is the repentance itself,
the turning round in one's tracks (Hebrew '*šûḇ*'), that has become
impossible. The point cannot be insisted upon too much or over-
stressed that the many discussions about the possibility of renewed
forgiveness⁹ are quite irrelevant to the question which is raised and
resolved in this passage.

Why the impossibility? 2¹⁴ together with what follows in the

---

⁷ Hebrew '*haddābāh haṭṭoḇ*', see Zechariah 1¹³; Joshua 21⁴⁵; 23¹⁵. p 46 omits
'*rhēma*' (not mentioned by Nestlé).
⁸ This question is clearly put. Yet the link between the passages 6¹⁻³ and
6⁴⁻⁶ is not always clearly seen. Why suddenly speak about the possibility of
apostasy? Perhaps the refusal to lay the foundation a second time—a foundation
involving amongst other things the repenting of dead works (6¹)—is a prelude to
the argument in 6⁴⁻⁶. But the situation is not the same, as we have already seen.
The one case concerns brethren who have made little progress; the other, Christians who have advanced along the way of grace but run the risk of abjuring everything. This observation supports our suggestion that the author has inserted here
a short address composed for another occasion.
⁹ Certainly HERMAS believes in a second pardon in principle, though not for
apostates (*Similitude* 8, Chap. 6). TERTULLIAN denies a second pardon for all
grave sins (see *De pudicitia*, 20, *CSEL*, 20, pp. 266ff)—to name only the two
oldest witnesses to these discussions. For this passage of our Epistle, as well as for
10²⁶ᶠᶠ, see M. GOGUEL, *La doctrine de l'impossibilité de la seconde conversion
dans l'Epître aux Hébreux et sa place dans l'evolution du christianisme* (Annuaire
de l'Ecole pratique des Hautes Etudes, section Sciences religieuses, 1931–32).
For the idea of '*metanoia*' in Christian piety in general, see HANS POHLMANN,
Die Metanoia als Zentralbegriff der christlichen Frömmighkeit (Untersuchungen
zum N.T., 25, 1938).

(7) *A field which drinks the rain that amply falls upon it, and produces vegetation acceptable to those for whose sake it is cultivated, receives the blessing of God.* (8) *But if [afterwards] it produces thorns and thistles, it is rejected. The curse is imminent and the end will be—'into the fire'!*

present passage (**6⁶ᵇ**) gives the answer. The apostate[10] has fallen again under the dominion of the devil from which the death of Christ had delivered him. But the passion of Christ cannot be repeated, and our writer places much stress on the fact that this event took place once for all. What then is the meaning of *'anastaurountas'*, etc. = 'those who crucify (or: crucify again) for themselves the Son of God'? Notice first of all that *'anastauroō'* does not necessarily mean 'crucify a second time', as the Vulgate (*'iterum crucifigentes'*) and the majority of ancient commentators thought as well as later on Bengel, Michel, and others.[11] For Josephus readily uses this verb as a synonym for *'stauroō'*,[12] the prepositional prefix *'ana'* stressing the lifting up on the cross. The notion of a second crucifixion, even of a purely subjective one, is outside our author's ken. The text quite simply accuses these fresh infidels of participating in some sense in the crime committed by the Jews who crucified and did outrage to (*'anastaurountas kai paradeigmatizontas'*) the Son of God. This is the worst that could be conceived.[13]

6⁷⁻⁸. The writer adds a parable intended not to demonstrate his argument rigorously but to illustrate it. If we put it into the language

[10] CALVIN has rightly discerned that it is not a question of any kind of crime, but of apostasy. 'The Apostle has nothing to say here about stealing or perjury or murder or drunkenness or adultery or any other such vice; but he is speaking about a universal revolt from the gospel in which the sinner does not offend God only in a part, but renounces totally His grace' (*Comm., ad loc.*).

[11] See TERTULLIAN, *'refigentes cruci . . . filium Dei'*, *De pudicitia*, 20; ORIGEN, *Comm. on John*, 20.12 (*GCS*), ed Preuschen, IV, pp. 341ff; CHRYSOSTOM: 'what is *"anastaurountas"*? It is to crucify yet again' (*'ti de estin anastaurountas; anōthen palin staurountas'*, *MPG* 63, col. 79).

[12] JOSEPHUS, *Antiquities*, II, §73 (5.3) uses *'anastauroō'* in speaking of the punishment of the chief baker whose dream Joseph interpreted; in *Antiquities*, IX, §246 (6, 10) there is reference to Mordecai whom it was desired to crucify (*'anastaurōsai'*); other Greek texts in ESTIENNE, *Thesaurus*, ed Didot, 1831ff, vol. I, 2, col. 562, and BLEEK, II, pp. 190ff. LIDDELL and SCOTT (1925–40) note both meanings, but for 'crucify afresh' they only cite a single text, viz. our 6⁶, which is precisely where the meaning is doubtful!

[13] How is such an impossibility psychologically conceivable? This is not within our present purview; but in an article in *RHPR*, 1950, pp. 31ff ('Serviteurs de Dieu') we have mentioned a situation which occurs sometimes at the present day in which it seems to us that repentance is at least extremely difficult if not impossible; namely, the case of those who do the works of the devil *with a completely good conscience*. If there is added to this perversion pride at having abandoned Christian teaching as outdated, superseded stuff, then we can seriously ask whether a 'turning back' remains possible.

of the Gospel parables we might give it the following form: Some
land was fortunate enough to benefit from ample rainfall, so that at
first it produced growth of good quality and was blessed (praised)
by God. But later on it bore only thorns and thistles, and it was
cursed and burned. Contrary to the majority of expositors we think
that it is the same field which is being referred to, and that a comma
should be placed after '*tou theou*' (end of v. 7), so that '*ekpherousa*'
(= 'bearing') follows on simply from '*tiktousa*' (= 'it produced').
In that way the parable becomes less banal and very relevant, since
it is an allusion to Christians who after having borne acceptable
fruits become reverted.[14] Details: '*piousa*', the earth 'drinks' the
rain, perhaps with a hint of the ancient personification of earth as a
mother; '*botanē*' is a general word for 'vegetation'; '*euthetos*' =
'well-placed', 'fit', 'usable'. The ground produces vegetables or corn
for the benefit of those for whose sake ('*di' hous*') it is cultivated, i.e.
the consumers. The translation 'by whom it is cultivated' (Vulgate,
Luther's Bible) seems faulty. '*Adokimos*' is the result given to someone who has failed to pass an examination, viz. 'failed', 'rejected'.
'*Kataras enggus*' = lit. 'near to a curse'.[15] The end of v. 8 is difficult,
not because in the first place it is the unprofitable growth which is
burned and the ground suffers only at one remove from this burning
—for we also talk of 'scorched earth'[16]—but because of the construction at the end of the sentence. We should expect '*hēs to telos
hē kausis*' = 'the end of which will be burning'.[17] '*Eis kausin*'
(= 'towards' or 'for burning') may be explained by an ellipse: 'the
end is that it will be rightly abandoned to fire'. But the '*eis kausin*'
must be put in inverted commas, with an exclamation mark: the
end is that it will be said 'into the fire!' The end of the wicked 'by
fire', which this comparison implies, is quite often predicted in the
New Testament (for example, see Mark 9[44-48]; Matthew 3[10-12];
25[41], and see the Commentaries on these texts).

---

[14] Cf. Ezekiel 19[10-14] in which a vine, fruitful to begin with, deteriorates, so
that its branches were broken off and devoured by fire.
[15] It is superfluous to point out that the theme of v. 8 re-echoes that of Genesis
3[17-18] (thorns, thistles, curse). But there is an inversion: contrary to the Genesis
narrative the unprofitable vegetation is the reason for the curse and not its
consequence.
[16] The custom of burning the ground is expressly attested for antiquity by the
ELDER PLINY, *Historia Naturalis*, XVII, 300, §72, 'some people also set fire to the
stubble in the field . . . their chief reason, however, for this plan is to burn up
the seed of weeds'.
[17] The difficulty in no way disappears if, with Calvin, we attach '*hēs*' to '*kataras*',
i.e. the end or the goal of the cursing will be, etc. In any case we have an ellipse.
For the '*kausis*' Riggenbach points out some Old Testament texts (Isaiah 40[16];
44[15]; Daniel 7[11]), but does not explain the construction of this verse 6[8].

(9) *But so far as you are concerned, dear brothers, although we have spoken as we have, we are persuaded that you have chosen the good way which assures salvation.* (10) *For God will not commit the injustice of forgetting your work and the love you have shown for His name, in having rendered service to other Christians and in continuing to do so.* (11) *What we desire for each of you is that you show right to the end the same zeal for the full expression of your religion,* (12) *that you may not become sluggish, but be imitators of those who by their faith and patience have entered into possession of the promised inheritance.* (13) *For God made a promise to Abraham. And as He could not take an oath in the name of one greater than Himself, He swore by Himself, saying,* (14) *'In truth, I will abundantly bless you, and will give you teeming posterity'.* (15) *So it was by his patience that he [Abraham] obtained the realization of this promise.*

6^{9-11}. Is the author afraid of having been too severe and too threatening? However that may be, what follows is designed to reassure his readers. He suddenly calls them *'agapētoi'* = 'my beloved',[18] and says in effect: but indeed we have a good opinion of you, although we have spoken in this way. *'Ta kreissona'*: as in Latin, the comparative sometimes, taking into account our grammatical habits, has the force of a positive, here = 'the good'; and *'pepeismetha ta kreissona'* is an abbreviated way of saying 'we are persuaded that you have chosen the right way, which reaches to salvation' (*'echomena sōtērias'*), i.e. which leads to it.

6^{10}. What impels the writer to this rather unexpected optimism is chiefly the goodness of God who, in spite of everything, will remember the deeds of charity of this congregation towards brother Christians (*'tois hagiois'*) past and present; *'ouk adikos'* = 'not unjust', but also 'not wicked'. 'For the name' of God means 'for the glory' of God.

6^{11}. Yet God imposes one condition. They must exercise all possible zeal for bringing forth in abundance the good fruits (*'pros tēn plērophorian'*) of their 'hope', i.e. of their religion, and that 'right to the end'.

6^{12}. *'Hina mē nōthroi genēsthe'* = 'that you may not become sluggish' or 'inert' (Riggenbach: *'schlaff'*, or vulgarly *'schlapp'*, i.e. 'slack', cf. 5^{11}); as though the author wanted to withdraw the opprobrious epithet which he had labelled them with in 5^{11}—unless 6^{9ff} originally formed part of another sermon. In any case, there must be followed the illustrious examples of those who have been faithful and have

---

[18] This reading is better attested than *'adelphoi'* which is supported only by S* and the Syriac versions. As often in such cases, one or two copyists can be found who amalgamated the two readings: *'agapētoi adelphoi'* (minuscule 257), or, better, *'adelphoi agapētoi'* (Codex r of the Old Latin).

(16) *For men swear by someone greater [than themselves], and an oath confirms beyond all possibility of contradiction.* (17) *God, for this reason, wanting to give the heirs of the promise additional proof of the immutability of His decision, guaranteed it with an oath,* (18) *so that by two immutable factors, in which God cannot lie, we refugees have powerful encouragement to seize the hope which is in front of us.* (19) *We have in this an anchor secure and firm [to which to attach] our life; it penetrates within the veil,* (20) *whither Jesus has entered as our forerunner, having become an eternal High Priest after the order of Melchizedek.*

endured even to death, a death leading them to heaven—'*klērono-mountōn tas epanggelias*' = 'those who have inherited the promises'. If the letter was sent to one of the communities at Rome this might be an allusion to the Neronian persecution, but we are on very insecure ground here. In 6^{10-12} we can observe the famous Pauline triad of love, hope and faith, though it is not thrown into relief, and here it is hope which surpasses the others so far as expressing the essence of Christianity is concerned.

6^{13-15}. The reference to divine promises leads our preacher to insist on their absolute value, by appealing again to the Old Testament. This time it is to a promise made to Abraham, in Genesis 22^{16f}, not so far mentioned but destined to play an important part much later, though not such a pre-eminent one as Melchizedek. It is the promise of an innumerable posterity, and it was realized because the patriarch gave proof of 'patience' ('*makrothumēsas*', v. 15). He had need of that patience because of the late birth of Isaac. But there is another point which our expositor urges. Although the divine promises are always valid, God insisted on binding Himself by an oath, presumably to overcome human incredulity. The oath is introduced by '*ei mēn*', according to the reading which establishes itself as the best attested. For the meaning of this '*ei*', *v. supra ad* 3^{11}.[19]

6^{16-18}. The general sense of the passage is clear: men swear by 'one greater' ('*meizonos*'), which is perhaps a euphemism for 'swear by God'; but God, at least the monotheistic God of the Bible, can swear only by Himself.[20] Detailed exegesis is not altogether easy. The oath ('*ho horkos*') is characterized as '*pasēs antilogias peras*' = 'beyond all possibility of contradiction' or 'dispute'. '*Eis bebaiōsin*' must be associated with an '*estin*', which is implicit. The oath is pronounced to make a promise authoritative (cf. '*bebaios*', 2^2).

[19] '*Ei mēn*' is read by p 46, S, A, B, D; '*ei mē*', in C and the Latin version, has a contrary sense; '*ē mēn*' is the Byzantine text. Manuscripts of the LXX vary from one to another (see Genesis 22^{17}).
[20] This does not hold for Greek polytheism, in which the gods swear by their grandparents: the Sky and the Earth! See, for example, Homer's quite frequent 'Let the earth and the wide heaven above know this' ('*istō nun tode gaia kai ouranos eurus huperthen*').

6¹⁷. *'Perissoteron'* must be attached to *'epideixai'*: God wanted 'to demonstrate' in a 'more abundant' manner, i.e. with an added guarantee. The complement of *'epideixai'* is *'to ametatheton tēs boulēs'* = 'the unalterable' or 'immutable character' of His will or decision. *'Emesiteusen horkō'* is a curious expression. *'Mesiteuō'* is unknown elsewhere in the Bible. Taken as intransitive, which is the only possibility the construction allows, it means 'to stand as a guarantor', and *'horkō'* is then an instrumental dative, i.e. 'by an oath'. In essence, then, God functions here in two ways, first as announcing a promise and then as guaranteeing it like a witness (*'mesitēs'*, from which *'mesiteuō'* is derived).

6¹⁸. The above explains the rather vague expression *'duo pragmatōn'* ('two facts') in this verse. Not two witnesses but two factors are meant, namely, the promise itself and the guarantee given by the oath. They are called *'ametathetoi'* ('immutable') by metonymy, because the content of the promise will suffer no change. This should provide us with strong encouragement.

6¹⁸ᵇ can be taken in two ways, according as we attach the last four words (from *'kratēsai'* to *'elpidos'*) to *'kataphugontes'* or to *'paraklēsin echōmen'*. In the former case the translation would be: 'we who have fled to lay hold of the hope', etc.; in the latter: 'we who have fled have the confidence which allows us to lay hold of the hope', etc. If we prefer the second construction it is because *'paraklēsin echōmen'* is more comprehensible with a complement, whilst *'kataphugontes'* can dispense with one, as meaning 'refugees', a notion akin to that of being foreigners—for are not Christians, the descendants of Abraham, strangers on the earth (*v.* **11**)? But it is appreciated that the other interpretation is likewise quite defensible.

6¹⁹. This verse contains the notable comparison of hope with an anchor, a familiar symbol and sometimes used today for publicity purposes.[21] Yet the figure is not a very happy one. True, it expresses quite well the idea that hope is our refuge, and that our vessel has ceased to be driven before the winds. It is called *'asphalēs'* because it does not drag along the bottom of the sea, and *'bebaia'* because it holds firm. But it is hard to imagine an anchor which 'enters into the sanctuary' (v. 19b).[22] Moreover, the word *'prokeimenē'* which qualifies *'elpis'*— the hope 'which is in front of us', i.e. whose object is in

---

[21] It is not necessarily to be thought that our Epistle invented the comparison. See a sentence in EPICTETUS (*Fragments*, 30, ed Teubner, 1916, p. 473): 'We ought neither to fasten our ship to one small anchor nor our life to a single hope' (*'oute naun ex henos angkuriou oute bion ek mias elpidos harmosteon'* [or: *'hormisteon'* ?]). The idea is certainly different from that in **6¹⁹** but the same figure is used. Cf. HELIODORUS, 7:25 (ed Teubner, p. 211).

[22] The turn of phrase *'eiserchomenēn'*, etc., could be reminiscent of Leviticus 16², but this is not certain. *'Echomen'* is replaced by *'echōmen'* in D, a useless emendation because the author was here intending to state a fact.

front of us, is inapplicable to an anchor. *'Psuchē'* = 'life', as almost always in the New Testament; our entire existence changes when once we are 'anchored' in hope. But who passes through the veil? Clearly, it is the High Priest, here meaning Christ. He, at least, is the first to pass through (*'prodromos'* = 'forerunner', v. 20); but that seems to imply that Christians themselves will also pass through it one day. Whilst waiting for this they are urged to glance behind the veil, by means of the gnosis which the writer after some hesitation will reveal to them.

Concerning *'katapetasma'* = 'veil', it is to be remembered that there were two curtains in the tabernacle. The first (in Hebrew: *'māsāḵ'*) separated the Holy Place from the outside, the second (in Hebrew *'pārōḵet'*) separated the Holy Place from the Holy of Holies, that is, from the most inward part (*'esōteron'*, etc., v. 19) where the deity was believed to dwell or at least to manifest Himself.[23]

In 7 Melchizedek will at last appear, announced once more by the *leitmotif*: Jesus, a High Priest after the order of Melchizedek (v. 20b).

---

[23] The Bible uses two terms for veil, *'kalumma'* and *'katapetasma'*. The first is used for a veil as a head-covering, and is a secular term. The second is used for the two curtains in the Temple. However, PHILO only uses it for the inner curtain, and calls the other *'kalumma'* (*De Vita Mosis*, II, §101, Chap. 21). In our passage *'katapetasma'* clearly refers only to the inner veil, and this is very probably the case in Mark 15[38] par.

CHAPTER VII

PRELIMINARY NOTE ON MELCHIZEDEK. The figure of Melchizedek and his rôle in Genesis 14 is entirely shrouded in mystery and it is understandable that much speculation has arisen about him. He appears in the chapter referred to from v. 18 onwards, right in the middle of a story in which, at first sight, he has no part.[1] His appearance is very brief. By v. 21, he has already disappeared without further trace in the Old Testament other than the mention 'after the order of Melchizedek' in Psalm 110 (LXX 109).[2]

How then is it that this Canaanite king, who lived only on the fringe of sacred history, as this history was conceived by the Israelites, could have had any knowledge of the true God, could have offered worship to Him and played a part which makes him Abraham's superior?[3] It is understandable that the Rabbis tried to explain— and to attenuate—this mystery. In some traditions, not at all widespread be it said, Melchizedek was identified with the Archangel Michael, which is one way of explaining his illustrious rôle. More frequently,[4] at any rate during the period when anti-Christian polemics did not yet play a big part, he was identified with Shem, the son of Noah, who was supposed to have received priestly status from

---

[1] Genesis 14 as a whole, in which the Melchizedek episode seems to be an interpolation and which tells of the battle of Chedorlaomer against the 'kings' of the lower Jordan, as well of Abraham's intervention, is the despair of source-seeking scholars, because it can be linked with none of the classical sources of the Pentateuch. It is like an erratic block of unknown origin. See MEINHOLD, *Erster Mosis* 14, *Eine kritisch-historische Untersuchung* (Supp. vol. 22 to *ZATW* 1911). Note also the text of Genesis 14[18-20]: 'And Melchizedek king of Salem brought forth loaves and wine; and he was the priest of the most high God (*'tou theou tou hupsistou'*). And he blessed Abram, and said, Blessed be Abram of the most high God, who made heaven and earth, and blessed be the most high God who delivered thine enemies into thy hands. And Abram gave him the tenth part of everything'.

[2] Outside the canon, he is briefly mentioned in Slavonic Enoch; see note 11, p. 55.

[3] If some Protestant theologians have sought to take up afresh the thesis that there was no divine revelation outside the religion of Israel and Judah, this is a personal opinion and in contradiction to the Old Testament. Remember the texts in Isaiah in which God calls the king of the Persians 'my anointed', etc. (Isaiah 44[28]; 45[1]) as well as the way in which the Arab Job is presented as a model of piety. See our article 'Le christianisme et les grandes religions', in *Les problèmes de la pensée chrétienne*, 1, Paris 1945, p. 110.

[4] Cf. LUEKEN, *Michael*, Göttingen 1898, first part, §3 and the texts which he cites; also the article by NAGEL, 'Ueber die Bedeutung Melchisedekhs im Hebräerbrief', *TSK.*, 1849, vol. 2. In another tradition, recorded by the Midrash *ad Canticum* 2.13, §4 (FREEDMANN, IX, p. 125), Melchizedek was alleged to be one of the four anonymous smiths of Zechariah 1[20] (Heb. 2[3], Vulgate 1[20]).

his father and, by the chronology of the Priestly Code, was still alive at the time of Abraham, whom indeed he outlived.[5] It was a way of incorporating Melchizedek if not among the Jews, at any rate in the succession of the Patriarchs.

But from the time when the Rabbis had to oppose the Christology of the Epistle to the Hebrews and in general the use being made of Melchizedek by Christian apologetics, another tendency made its appearance, namely that of playing down the figure and rôle of this priest-king.[6] There is general agreement about the honour which Melchizedek (whether identified with Shem or not) bestowed on Abraham. Sometimes writers go a step further: Melchizedek is alleged to have been stripped of honour and forced to relinquish his priesthood 'for ever' to Abraham because he had (Genesis 14[19-20]) named Abraham before God.[7] Other traditions say that Abraham discovered Melchizedek in hiding in the mountains to which he had withdrawn because of his revulsion from the idolatry of his fellow-citizens, and that Abraham instructed him in the truth.[8]

As for Psalm 110, it was, according to the majority of present-day specialists, composed during the Maccabean period, in honour of a Jewish king who was also High Priest; and it was this union of the two offices in one person which was to find expression in the turn of phrase 'after the order of Melchizedek'. But the Rabbis sometimes attributed the Psalm to Melchizedek, who was supposed to have

---

[5] See P. BEER, *Das Leben Abrahams nach Auffassung der jüdischen Sage*, Leipzig 1859, and the Targum Onkelos on Jeremiah (trans. ETHERIDGE, II, 1865, p. 199). LUTHER (*Vorlesung, Gloses*, p. 28) also accepts the identification of Melchizedek with Shem. CALVIN declares it 'quite improbable' (*Comm.*, p. 432). On the point of chronology: Shem lived 600 years in all and at the age of 100 had a son named Arpachshad. Between this birth and that of Abraham is a period of 290 years. Shem was then 390 years old. As Abraham lived only 175 years, Shem survived him by 35 years. See Genesis 11[10-26] and 25[7], following the Masoretic text (not the text of the LXX!). For the identification of Melchizedek with Shem, see also the Midrash Bereshit Rabba 44.7 (FREEDMANN, I, p. 365).

[6] See the important article by MARCEL SIMON, 'Melchisédekh dans la polémique entre juifs et chrétiens et dans la légende', *RHPR* 1937, pp. 58 ff. Perhaps—but it is rather doubtful—the synagogue also had to defend itself against a Jewish Gnostic sect which gave great importance to Melchizedek (and which may have been perpetuated in the Melchizedekian Christians), as was supposed by MORITZ FRIEDLÄNDER. See his thought-provoking book, *Der vorchristliche jüdische Gnostizismus*, Göttingen 1898; cf. his article in the *Revue des Etudes juives*, 1882 (vols. 5 and 6) entitled 'La secte des Melchisédékhiens et l'Epître aux Hébreux'. Friedländer's opinion is opposed by G. BARDY, *RB* 1926, pp. 496ff, and 1927, pp. 25ff. Some information about the Melchizedekians has been preserved for us by Mark the Hermit (5th century?), in his polemical writing '*eis ton Melchisedek*', which is also called '*kata Melchisedekianōn*' (*MPG* 65, col. 1117–1140). According to him, this sect looked on Melchizedek as the Logos.

[7] Midrash Levit. Rabba, Chap. 43, §6 (FREEDMANN, IV, pp. 319ff). Cf. Midrash Ber. Rabba 55.6 and 7 (FREEDMANN, I, pp. 486–488); *ibidem* 46.5 (FREEDMANN, I, p. 392); Midrash Deut. Rabba 2.7 (FREEDMANN, VII, p. 35).

[8] See the anonymous writing preserved among the works of ATHANASIUS which has brought together a collection of Jewish legends about Melchizedek (*MPG* 28, pp. 523ff).

glorified Abraham as the vanquisher of God's enemies and to have appointed him a priest for ever (cf. note 7, p. 54). Sometimes also it was thought that David was the one in question;[9] but most often an eschatological figure was envisaged, either Elijah redivivus, or a king of the end time.[10] It is also understandable that Christians were interested in Psalm 110. Jesus quotes it (Mark 12[36-37] par.) to refute the idea of His being a 'son of David', that is a political king. St Paul also refers to it (1 Corinthians 15[26-28]). But the writer *ad Hebraeos* is the first to make use of Genesis 14 also and to declare clearly that the priesthood of Melchizedek is a prefiguration of a cult superior to that of Aaron. Melchizedek at once becomes the 'type' of Christ. This does not mean that our theologian seeks to deny the historicity of Melchizedek. Quite the contrary—he presumes it. But some details only interest him as teaching allegorically certain points about Christ. 'It is sufficient that we see in him the features of Christ', says Calvin.

As for the sect of the Melchizedekians, it cannot be proved that the writer knew it, even if it were already in existence in his day. But later, it caused much vexation to the Church Fathers. For it exalted Melchizedek to a point of placing him higher than Christ.[11]

[9] Midrash on Psalm 110 (WÜNSCHE, *Midrash Tehillim*, Trier 1892, II, pp. 138–139).

[10] The Jerusalem Targum on Deuteronomy 30[4] (ETHERIDGE, II, p. 653); cf. STRACK-BILLERBECK, IV, 1, p. 462. We have deliberately avoided speaking of any *messianic* interpretation, because in Christian literature and in post-Christian Jewish writings the term Messiah took on a very wide extension of meaning which was unknown in the pre-Christian period. See our *Royaume de Dieu*, Chap. 2. According to E. R. HARDY, 'The date of Psalm 110', *JBL* 1945, pp. 385ff, this Psalm dates back to the days of the kings of Israel who are glorified as the legitimate successors of Melchizedek, but became popular only in Maccabean times.

[11] See CHRYSOSTOM's homily on Melchizedek, *MPG* 56, col. 257–262. See EPIPHANIUS, *Haereses* 55.6, §1 (ed Karl Holl, II, *GCS* p. 331). This Father also thinks that the identification of Melchizedek with Shem is chronologically impossible. This is correct so far as the chronology of the LXX is concerned, in distinction from that of the Hebrew text, as we have already indicated.
    Other works on Melchizedek not previously quoted: HARNACK, the article 'Monarchianismus', in *RE*, XIII, from p. 315; G. WUTTKE, *Melchisedekh der Priesterkönig von Salem* (Supp. vol. to *ZNTW*, no. 5, 1927); *Jewish Encyclopaedia*, art. 'Melchizedek'.
    STRACK-BILLERBECK, IV, pp. 452ff. 'Der 110te Psalm in der altrabbinischen Literatur'. W. HERTZBERG, 'Die Melchisedek-Traditionen', *Journal of the Palestinian Oriental Society*, vol. 8, 1928, pp. 169ff. Cf. JOACHIM JEREMIAS, *TB*, 1937, p. 308.
    On Jewish legends concerning this subject consult LOUIS GINZBERG, *The Legends of the Jews*, V, pp. 225ff, and also E. A. W. BUDGE, *The Book of the Cave of Treasures*, London 1927. This was a book written in Syriac by a Christian who had made a collection of Jewish legends, but who attributed to Shem the distinction of having buried Adam at Golgotha, and having installed Melchizedek as priest at Jerusalem to officiate at Golgotha. Finally, there are in Slavonic Enoch some curious texts on Melchizedek, who is spoken of as Noah's nephew (see Appendix).

(1) *Now this Melchizedek was king of Salem, priest of the most high God. He went out to meet Abraham, who was returning from the destruction of the kings, and blessed him. It was to him that Abraham gave the tenth part of everything.* (2) *And on translating [his name], we find first that he was called King of Righteousness; but also King of Salem, which means: King of Peace.* (3) *He is without father and without mother and appears in no genealogy. The days of his life have neither beginning nor end. He is like the Son of God. And he remains a priest for ever.*

7$^{1-3}$ comprises a single sentence with the verb *'menei'* (at the end), v. 1b (from *'ho sunantēsas'*) and v. 2a (as far as *'emerisen Abraam'*) forming a sort of long parenthesis. The translator must break this sentence down and understand an *'estin'* before *'ho sunantēsas'*.[12]

Let us first examine the name *'Melchisedek'*, bearing in mind the importance which the Hebrew attached to names. In v. 2 it is translated by *'ho basileus dikaiosunēs'* = 'the king of righteousness'; but it would be better rendered as 'my king is righteous' = *'malkî ṣeḏek'*[13] (cf. Adonizedek, 'My Lord is righteous' Joshua 10^{1}). We already have the hint that he is the type of Christ, the one who dispenses righteousness. He is also called king of Salem (v. 1), as in Genesis 14. The majority of the Fathers identified this Salem with Jerusalem, which is indeed called Salem in Psalm 76^{3} (LXX 75^{3}). This was perhaps too hasty. Our Epistle—just like Philo—shows no knowledge of such an identification; otherwise it would certainly have insisted on this strange coincidence: Melchizedek officiating at the very place where the new High Priest sacrificed Himself. In fact, Jerome mentions a tradition which identifies our Salem with the Salim of John 3^{23}.[14] In the event, like Philo, he explains Salem etymologically as signifying 'peace', although *'šālēm'* is an adjective (the noun would be *'šālôm'*)—a further qualifier which reinforces the prefigurative function of this king.

To return to the text. Melchizedek is also called the priest of *'theos hupsistos'* (= 'the supreme God' or 'the most high God'). This divine name is the translation used by the LXX for the Hebrew *"ēl 'elyôn'*. That this term originally indicated a polytheistic idea,

---

[12] We read *'ho sunantēsas'* with p 46, C* and the Textus Receptus. The alternative reading, viz. *'hos sunantēsas'*, would require a fresh finite verb, and such cannot be found.

[13] It could also be interpreted as 'my king is righteousness'. But Philo and Josephus call him *'basileus dikaios'* which amounts to the same thing as the rendering given in this Epistle. See JOSEPHUS, *Antiquities*, I, §180 (10.2); *Jewish War*, VI, §438 (10.1); PHILO, *Legum Allegoriae*, III, 79 (Chap. 25): *'basileus eirēnēs kai basileus dikaois'* ('king of peace and righteous king').

[14] JEROME, Epistle 126, *ad Evagrium* (or better: *ad Evangelium*): 'Salem is not Jerusalem . . . but a town near Scythopolis, which still today is called Salem, and Melchizedek's palace is pointed out there', *MPL* 22, col. 680. JOSEPHUS on the other hand calls Melchizedek *'ho tēs Soluma basileus'* ('king of Solyma'), v. *Antiquities*, I, §180 (10.2). Calvin makes no reference to Jerusalem.

there can be no doubt. What is more interesting is that when it is used in the Bible, we often find ourselves on the fringe of Judaism. Apart from the story of Melchizedek, see also that of Balaam (Numbers 24[16]), the orders of Cyrus (cf. 1 Esdras 6[30] LXX) or of Artaxerxes (1 Esdras 8[19, 21] LXX) or the exclamation of the Gerasene demoniac (Mark 5[7] par.).[15]

Then, still following the text of Genesis, the writer recalls the meeting of Melchizedek and Abraham after the patriarch's victory over the kings who carried Lot away. This interview is characterized by two very curious facts: Melchizedek blesses Abraham, and the latter pays to him a tithe of 'all', presumably of all the spoils. On the other hand he does not exploit the fact that Melchizedek brings bread and wine, because he seems to have little interest in the Eucharist.

7[3]. In this verse the writer uses a curious argument *e silentio*. As Genesis, contrary to its usual practice, speaks neither of the forebears nor of the descendants of Melchizedek (*'agenealogētos'*), the bold conclusion is drawn that he had no father or mother (*'apatōr kai amētōr'*),[16] which favours the idea that he is a supernatural being; it is understandable that the Rabbis saw in him an angel, and notably the Archangel Michael. Our writer does not make himself clear on this point; but he does recall that Melchizedek has neither beginning nor end. He probably relies somewhat on Psalm 110[4] (LXX 109[4]), quoted above at 5[6] and 6[20]; but one can sense that much speculation has already been at work in Judaism. On the other hand, it is not certain that he really looked on the historical Melchizedek as immortal. What interests him is the eternal nature of Christ and of His priesthood, of which Melchizedek is a prefiguration: *'aphōmoiōmenos tō huiō tou theou'* = lit. 'made like', i.e. an image of 'the Son of God'. Apparently typology here slips into allegory. What is said of Melchizedek really refers to Christ.

---

[15] There were in the Greek world also some sects who venerated a *'theos hupsistos'*, v. FRANZ CUMONT, *The Oriental Religions in Roman Paganism* (Dover Books, New York 1956; originally Chicago 1911) p. 62, pp. 128ff. The term Hypsistarians does not seem to occur in ancient Greek literature. But *'hupistarioi'* can be found in Gregory Nazianzus (*MPG* 35, col. 990) and *'hupistianoi'* in Gregory of Nyssa (*MPG* 45, col. 482). It is known that Goethe would have liked to be a Hypsistarian.

[16] Among the Greeks *'apatōr kai amētōr'* could refer to an orphan. But *'apatōr'* is also used in connexion with the supernatural birth of a god (e.g. Hephaestos), similarly *'amētōr'* (e.g. for Pallas Athene or the goddess of Victory), according to PHILO, *De Opificio Mundi*, §100 (Chap. 33). Philo himself speaks thus of the Divine Word (*'logos theios'*), who is at the same time the heavenly High Priest. He is *'apatōr kai amētōr'* because he has God as his father and Wisdom as his mother (*De Fuga*, §109, Chap. 20). He also alludes to an *'amētōr archē'* (*De Ebrietate*, §61, Chap. 14). So far as Philonic thought is concerned, its influence on 7 of this Epistle does not seem to have been decisive. See V. BURCH, *The Epistle to the Hebrews*, 1936, in particular Chap. 5.

(4) *Consider how extraordinary this man is: Abraham, himself a Patriarch, gives him the choicest share of the spoils!* (5) [*We know that*] *the descendants of Levi, on receiving the priesthood, obtain by the Law the right to ask for tithes from the people, that is from their brothers, although they too are descendants of Abraham.* (6) *But yet this man who figures in no genealogy asked Abraham for tithes. And it was he who blessed the receiver of the promises!* (7) *Now, without any dispute, it is the inferior who is blessed by the superior.* (8) *And whilst here it is mortal men who receive the tithes, there it is someone of whom it is testified that he lives.* (9) *And to give the real point: through the intermediary of Abraham Levi himself, who receives tithes, paid them.* (10) *For he was still in the loins of his ancestor when Melchizedek came to meet him.*

7[4-10]. The writer now has a fine hand to play. From what precedes he deduces the superiority of Melchizedek over Abraham, and the superiority of his priesthood over Aaron's.

7[4]. '*Pēlikos*' signifies greatness and quality at the same time (Bengel: '*quantus qualisque*'). '*Akrothinia*' = 'the top of the heap' ('*akros*' = 'peak, summit'; '*this*' = 'heap'), that is to say the best of the booty, the 'pick of the basket' in some degree. The noun '*patriarchēs*' = 'patriarch' is found elsewhere only in the Books of Chronicles and 4 Maccabees 7[19], as well as Acts 2[29]; 7[8-9].[17]

7[5, 6]. It is true that the descendants of Levi (from the time of Moses and Aaron is the implication) levy taxes from the descendants of Abraham according to the Law. But here we see Melchizedek, who is not even a Jew, levying tax from the patriarch; that is the startling thing.

7[7, 8]. Not only does the part played by Melchizedek testify to his superiority, but also the fact that he is immortal ('*hoti zē*'). There again no precise information is given about the import of that life. Could he have been transported to heaven like Enoch and Elijah? Might he be an appearance of Christ? We cannot be sure. Obviously when the author wrote these lines, he was already thinking about the new High Priest.[18]

7[9, 10] return to the receipt of the tithe by Melchizedek and draw a specious conclusion: in Abraham all his descendants were taxed

---

[17] The word '*patriarchēs*' seems to be unknown in Hellenistic literature.

[18] That a '*tupos*' of Christ might also incarnate Him in some degree, was not unthinkable at the time. For the Apostle Paul, for instance, the rock in the desert is at the same time a type of Christ and Christ Himself (1 Corinthians 10[4]). According to A. AUBERLEN, *Melchisedeks ewiges Leben und Priestertum* (*TSK*, 1857, vol. 3) '*zē*' (v. 8) means eternal life in the Johannine sense (p. 494). He is a priest to all eternity like 'all blessed spirits' ('*alle seligen Geister*', p. 497). A view hard to maintain.

(11) *Now if the Levitical cult had achieved its purpose—the people had indeed received laws on this point—what need was there for the appearance of another priest after the order of Melchizedek, reputed not to be of the order of Aaron?* (12) *Indeed, change the priest-hood, and there will necessarily follow also a change of law.* (13) *For the one who is brought to notice by this proclamation belonged to another tribe, no member of which had done duty at the altar.* (14) *Indeed, it was from Judah that our Lord manifestly appeared. And Moses had said nothing concerning priests in connexion with this tribe.*

by Melchizedek, including Levi, the ancestor of Aaron. It is as if the ancestor and his descendants formed a single organism. The lot of the ancestors falls upon their descendants and vice-versa (cf. Rachel, long dead, weeping for her children, Jeremiah 31[15] = LXX 38[15]; Matthew 2[18]). '*Hōs epos eipein*', in v. 9, could mean 'so to speak', and this is the sense which would perhaps suit *our* way of viewing the matter. But the writer has no reason to attenuate his claim. In fact, '*hōs epos eipein*' can also mean 'in a word', 'to give the real point' (many examples in all good lexicons from the *Thesaurus* of Henry Estienne downwards); this is the sense which seems most suitable here.[19]

7[10]. It follows from the whole of this discussion that the priesthood of Christ must be superior to that of Aaron.

7[11–14]. These verses take us another step forward. After proving this superiority in an abstract way, the writer now sets forth details to prove it more concretely. It might be believed from what has gone before that the new priesthood would be the final issue or the per-fecting of the other. It is no such thing. The heterogeneous character of the two offices becomes clear, if an important fact is taken into account: Christ did not come from the tribe of Levi, but from the tribe of Judah.[20] Why then this transfer of the priesthood from one tribe to another, which had never held office ('*aph' hēs oudeis pro-seschēken tō thusiastēriō*', lit. 'of which no member has approached the altar', v. 13)? It would not have been necessary if the Levitic cult had been fully satisfactory. But already v. 11 announces that this

[19] The Fathers of the Church, who did not flinch before any problem, wondered whether in Abraham Jesus Himself had not also been taxed. St Augustine tries to resolve the question by explaining that unlike Levi, Jesus was a descendant of Abraham only after the flesh, not after the spirit ('*secundum carnem, non secun-dum animam*', *De Genesi ad litteram*, X, Chaps. 19, 20, in *MPL* 34, col. 423ff).

[20] Does our Epistle rely solely on the prophecies of Isaiah and Micah who proclaim a king of Davidic descent? Or did the writer have acquaintance with the genealogies of Jesus reproduced by Matthew and Luke? We do not know. Perhaps the Epistle merely reiterates an opinion which was universally accepted at that time ('*prodēlon*', v. 14), see Romans 1[3]; Luke 1[69]; Matthew 9[27]; 15[22]; 20[30–31]; 2 Timothy 2[8]; Revelation 5[5]; 22[16], as well as the genealogies of Matthew 1[1ff] and Luke 3[23ff]. As for the High Priest of Levitic descent announced by the Testament of Levi, Chap. 18, he does not figure in the New Testament; nor does the Messiah from the tribe of Ephraim mentioned in the Talmud.

(15) *And this becomes more than obvious, if this fact is taken into account: the other priest who arose is like Melchizedek;* (16) *and He was appointed not according to the ritual observance of laws of the flesh, but according to the power of an indestructible life.*

(17) *For this testimony is given concerning Him: You shall be a priest for ever after the order of Melchizedek.* (18) *Indeed the point at issue is the abolition of an earlier command, because of its lack of power and efficacy.* (19) *For the Law accomplished nothing; but now there is the advent of a higher religion, through which we draw near to God.* (20a) *And inasmuch as this was done with the support of an oath,* (22) *the covenant of which Jesus is the mediator was by this token superior.* (20b) *The former ones became priests without any oath,* (21) *but He did so with the support of an oath, given by the one who said of Him: The Lord has sworn and He will not repent of it,* '*You shall be a priest for ever*'.

was not the case. '*Teleiōsis*' (= 'perfection') still remains a little imprecise: was it merely the cult that was imperfect, or was it unable to ensure the reinstatement of the faithful, that is the pardon of their sins? Precision will be given by what follows.

The parenthesis '*ho laos . . . nenomothetētai*' (lit. = 'the people were furnished with laws') naturally contains the idea that the Law imposed obligations on the people. But what is the exact meaning of '*ep' autēs*'? The reading '*peri autēs*' = 'about it' (which is without textual support), or else '*ep' autēn*' = 'for it' (a badly attested reading) would be preferable. For lack of better, we must resign ourselves to take '*epi*' with the genitive in the sense of '*peri*', although this is rare.

7[15], [16] bring some enlightenment about the shortcomings of the Jewish cult. We are reminded that the former priesthood was '*kata nomon entolēs sarkinēs*' (lit. = 'according to the Law of a fleshly command'). In the eyes of the Jews, that was its justification; for our writer it is a sign of inferiority. It only has the support of the Law. Against it is placed '*kata dunamin zōēs akatalutou*' ('the power of an indestructible life'). Christian dynamism is set against Jewish legalism and the author is clearly aware of it. Philologically speaking, '*kata entolēn nomou*' = 'according to a prescription of the Torah' would be more to be expected. The genitive '*entolēs*' after '*kata nomon*' obviously cannot have the sense of a *genitive causae*, but rather of a *genitivus qualitatis*; it is the Law which contains a requirement or from which a requirement derives. But immediately we shall be slightly at a loss in translating '*kata dunamin zōēs*', etc. For here '*zōēs*' seems to be a genitive of cause or a subjective genitive; but a genitive of quality is not out of order: a force 'full of life' or 'giving life'.

7[16]. This '*entolē*' is termed '*sarkinē*' (= 'fleshly') in addition; we do not think that the word has as bad a sense as when used by

(23) *And they were made up of a multitude of priests because death prevented them from enduring;* (24) *He on the other hand holds the priestly office in a form which cannot end, because He endures to eternity.* (25) *Therefore He can utterly save those who draw near to God through Him; for He is alive for ever, in order to intercede for them.* (26) *And such a High Priest was necessary for us; holy, innocent, pure, untouched by compromise with sinners, exalted higher than the heavens.* (27) *He is not obliged, like [other] High Priests, to offer sacrifices day after day, first for His own sins and then for the people. He did that once for all by offering Himself.* (28) *Indeed, the Law appoints as High Priests men who are subject to shortcomings. But the Word supported by an oath, aimed at the period after the Law, appoints for all eternity the Son, who has attained perfection.*

St Paul, for in his writing '*sarx*' almost always carries the idea of sin. It must, however, characterize the Levitical cult as inferior, because it has earthly functions only.

7[18, 19] in some degree dot the i's. The old order is abolished ('*athetēsis*'), a new and superior religion ('*kreittōn elpis*'), has been introduced ('*eisagōgē*', a '*ginetai*' is understood).[21] The old religion has been abolished, because it was weak and ineffective ('*asthenes kai anōpheles*'), characteristics which will be explained further on.

7[20–22] add a new argument which is based on a theme already used in **4**, that of the oath. It was not only to Abraham that God made a promise under oath, but also to Melchizedek, as is shown in Psalm 110[4] (LXX 109[4]), quoted at the end of v. 21. 7[20–22] form a single sentence, v. 20b (from '*hoi men gar*') and v. 21 being in parenthesis. For our purpose, in order to bring out the reasoning, it is better to separate v. 20a from v. 22. That is why we have placed v. 22 before v. 20b and v. 21. The new order of things is all the better for having been established with the support of an oath uttered by God. Vv. 20b and 21 recall that the institution of the Aaronic priesthood was not accompanied by any oath (see the consecration of Aaron, Exodus 28[1ff]; cf. Jubilees 32[1]; Testament of Levi 8), in contrast with the priesthood in the manner of Melchizedek concerning which God has sworn and will not repent.[22]

Now, the new religion is called '*diathēkē*' (= 'covenant'? 'testament'?). It is the first time that the term is used. In opposition to the

---

[21] After what has been read above at **3**[6] and **6**[11, 18] the reader will not be too surprised to find '*elpis*' translated as 'religion'. Greek did not have a word which corresponded exactly to the latter, and New Testament writers use '*pistis*', '*elpis*', '*latreia*', and other nouns besides. Everyone is agreed on this point, so why not take the fact into account in translations?

[22] Can God 'repent' of a decision, that is rescind it? Such a thing is clearly supposed in Psalm 110[4]. Cf. perhaps 1 Samuel 15[11]; 2 Samuel 24[16]; Jeremiah 42[10] (LXX 49[10]); Joel 2[13]; Amos 7[3]; Jonah 4[2].

authority of the Preuschen-Bauer lexicon, and in agreement with
E. F. Scott (Chap. 5 of his book listed in the Bibliography), we think
that the translation 'testament' is nearly always incorrect. In the
LXX, '*diathēkē*' is the translation of '*berît*' = 'covenant', concluded
by means of a sacrifice; moreover, how could God make a testament? It is only in special circumstances such as perhaps the occasion
of the Last Supper or in certain verses of our Epistle that the sense of
'testament' is fitting.[23] The author is probably already thinking of
the text of Jeremiah, which he will be quoting all the way through **8**
and in which '*diathēkē*' means 'covenant' without a shadow of doubt.

But our theologian does not lose sight of the *person* of the new
High Priest. He is called '*engguos*' ('surety'? 'mediator'?) of the new
covenant. One cannot see in what way a covenant or disposition
ordained by God under oath would still need a surety. So here we
must translate this noun as 'mediator', for in the new order of
things it is Jesus who is the mediator, to the exclusion of any other
priest.

The final pericope of **7** (vv. 23-28) gives no further details of the
covenant, but forms a brief study of the person of the new priest.
The Levitical priests were mortal, a fact which prevented them from
'enduring' ('*paramenein*'); so a multitude ('*pleiones*') of them was
necessary to ensure the continuity of the cult. This was evidently one
reason, though not the only one, since in any case the Temple cult
required a vast number of priests all the time. But the new High
Priest endures for ever ('*menei eis ton aiōna*') (*v.* Psalm 110) and will
never need a substitute (v. 24); His priesthood is therefore not
transferable ('*aparabatos*').

Furthermore, (v. 25) He saves '*eis to panteles*', i.e. 'totally, for
good and all', those who come to God through His mediation
('*di' autou*'), and He can always intercede ('*entungchanein*') for them.
This point deserves to be underlined; for according to the Rabbis,
intercession was the prerogative of the angels, in particular of the
Archangel Michael.[24] In any case, here there is involved the only
sacerdos in aeternum known to the New Testament.

7[26]. Further, the new High Priest is distinguished from the old ones
by His holiness. '*Toioutos*' at the beginning announces the qualities
listed in what follows. 'He is like this: namely . . .', and it was fitting
('*eprepen*') that He should be like this. '*Kai*' before '*eprepen*', which
in any case is too well attested to be struck out,[25] attaches the whole

---

[23] Literature on '*diathēkē*': J. BEHM, *Der Begriff der Diatheke im N.T.*, 1912.
E. LOHMEYER, *Diatheke*, 1913; J. BEHM and G. QUELL, *sub voce*, in *TWNT*, II,
pp. 105ff. But the best treatment of this subject is without doubt that of L. G.
DA FONSECA, ' "*Diathēkē*," Foedus an testamentum?', *Biblica*, Rome 1927 and
1928. RIGGENBACH's article on 'Diatheke' (in *Theologische Studien Th. Zahn
dargebracht*, 1908) was not available to us. The Excursus on the two covenants in
SPICQ, *Comment.*, pp. 285-299, must not be forgotten.

[24] STRACK-BILLERBECK, III, p. 532.

[25] '*Kai*' is read by p 46, B, A, D and the Syriac versions.

sentence to what precedes it. He is *'hosios'*, which stresses most of all His holiness. In the LXX *'hosios'* is in fact the translation of *'hāsîd'* ('holy'; cf. *'hosios'*, Titus 1⁸; 1 Timothy 2⁸—whilst *'hagios'*, as we have already emphasised, does not necessarily have this sense).²⁶ *'Akakos'* (lit. = 'without evil') emphasizes His moral purity (Bengel: ' "*hosios*" with respect to God, "*akakos*" in His own nature').²⁷ It is more difficult to distinguish *'amiantos'* from *'akakos'*; perhaps *'amiantos'* is meant to stress the absence of original sin; but this is doubtful.

The end of the verse reminds us that Christ is even now above the heavens (*'hupsēloteros tōn ouranōn'*), and all the more above our world defiled by sinners (*'kechōrismenos apo tōn hamartōlōn'*, lit. = 'separated from sinners'; 'untouched by compromise with sinners', Bouillon. Cf. Ephesians 4¹⁰: *'ho anabas huperanō pantōn tōn ouranōn'* = 'He who has ascended above all the heavens').

7²⁷ states two facts: firstly, the sacrifice of Christ is unique; secondly Christ has no need to offer any atonement sacrifice for Himself, as was necessary for Jewish High Priests. But *'kath' hēmeran'* (= 'every day'?) is a stumbling-block for expositors. For the Jewish High Priest, as our Epistle expressly states in 9 (vv. 7 and 25), entered the Holy of Holies only once a year, not once a day, to make an atonement sacrifice first for himself and then for the people, according to Leviticus 16⁶, ¹¹. Some have wished to render *'kath' hēmeran'* by 'on the appointed day', but this is difficult to support. Biesenthal suggests that it is a mistaken rendering of the Hebrew *'yôm yôm'* or of the Aramaic *'yômā' yômā' '*, which could mean: one day each year, namely the Day of Atonement, which is in fact bluntly called *Yôma* by the Talmud.²⁸ But it seems highly improbable to us that this Epistle, which always quotes the Greek Bible, was first written in Hebrew or Aramaic. As for the occasional use of a Jewish text in a Semitic language, this is not absolutely ruled out *a priori*, but it is much less plausible in this very Christian pericope than at the end of 4.

Unless we postulate a quite deplorable lapse by our author, we must suppose therefore that the great Day of Atonement did not enter his mind, but that he was thinking about other sacrifices offered by the High Priest in the Holy Place and not in the Holy of

²⁶ The Corinthians, for example, were *'hagioi'*, but not all were *'hosioi'*.
²⁷ CHRYSOSTOM recalls at this point the verse of Isaiah 53⁹: *'oude heurethē dolos en tō stomati autou'* ('nor was deceit found in his mouth'), *MPG* 63, col. 106.
²⁸ See his work already quoted in connexion with 4¹³. In fact, Biesenthal found no parallel for *'yôm yôm'*; he thinks that the expression may have been coined by analogy with *'šenā' šenā' '* = 'each year'. *'Yôm yôm'* would then mean 'each Day of Atonement'. But all this presupposes an underlying Semitic text. The situation would be different, if the LXX used *'kath' hēmeran'* in the absolute sense for the Day of Atonement as the Talmud used Yôma; then one might be able to think that *'kath' hēmeran'* had the suggested sense. But the LXX does not know this usage.

Holies. Josephus states that the daily sacrifice was sometimes offered by the High Priest, and Ecclesiasticus 45[14] praises Aaron for having offered each day a *'thusia'*.[29] The importance of the word *'ephapax'* can hardly be exaggerated (see the remark further on concerning 9[26]).[30] The end of the verse introduces an idea which had only been hinted at earlier: the new High Priest sacrificed Himself. So in some degree He was at the same time the sacrificer and the victim, and it can now be better understood why He had to be 'without defilement' (*'amiantos'*, v. 26).

7[28] sums up this argument, by tersely contrasting the Law with the words of God pronounced under oath. The former institutes High Priests who are tainted with 'sickness' (*'astheneia'*), that is defiled by sin; the latter establishes the Son, who has attained perfection (*'teteleiōmenos'*) and who has 'achieved the full realization of His potentialities' (Bouillon). *'Eis ton aiōna'* is added, which could be linked with *'teteleiōmenon'*, but the allusion to Psalm 110 forces us to regard it as depending on *'kathistēsin'*, according to which the Son is established 'to eternity'. It is a curious detail that there seems to be some insistence on the fact that the oath was apparently pronounced after the Law. Or might we have an ellipsis to consider: the oath which concerns the new state of things succeeding the reign of the Law? We find the second explanation preferable because theologically speaking it is less banal.

---

[29] The manuscript D* does have at this point *'ho hiereus'* instead of *'hoi archiereis'*, which would settle the matter quite well. But this variant gives us the impression of being an emendation intended to remove a stumbling block for exegetes.

[30] Cf. also G. BALDENSPERGER, *RHPR* 1939, pp. 217ff.

CHAPTER VIII

(1) *But here is the crowning point of our argument: we have, indeed, such a High Priest who has taken His seat at the right hand of the Majesty in the heavens.* (2) *He is the minister of the sanctuary and of the true Tent, the one which the Lord erected and not man.* (3) *Now, every High Priest is appointed to present offerings and sacrifices. That is why He also must have something to offer.* (4) *Yet if He were on earth, He would not even be a priest, since there are [already] others who present offerings, in accordance with the Law.* (5) *And these administer a cult which is only a pale copy of the heavenly cult. This is attested by the order given to Moses at the time when he had to set up the Tent. For 'See', he was told, 'that you make everything in accordance with the model which has been shown to you on the mountain.'* (6) *But now Christ has obtained a more exalted ministry because He is the mediator of a superior covenant, which has received the force of law as a consequence of better promises.* (7) *Indeed, if the first covenant were beyond all criticism, there would have been no cause for seeking a second.* (8) *For it is while reproaching them that it is said [in Scripture]: 'Behold, the days will come, says the Lord, when I will bring about a new covenant with the house of Israel and the house of Judah.* (9) *It will not be of the same kind as the covenant which I concluded with your fathers, on the day when I took them by the hand to lead them out of the land of Egypt. Indeed, they did not persevere in my covenant; and so I lost interest in them.* (10) *For this is the covenant which I will establish with the house of Israel after those days, says the Lord. I will put my laws in their conscience and I will write them in their heart, and I shall be God for them, and they shall be a people for me.* (11) *And there shall no longer be any question of each one teaching his fellow-citizen, and each his brother, saying: Know the Lord. For all shall know me, from the least of them to the greatest.* (12) *For I shall be indulgent towards their iniquities; and I shall completely forget their sins'.* (13) *Now, by speaking of a new covenant, He declared the old one obsolete. And that which is touched by old age and senility is on the point of passing away.*

8[1]. '*Kephalaion*' basically means 'the essential matter' or 'the capital point', and this is the sense most fitting here.[1] '*Epi*' with the dative could be translated 'in addition to', that is 'in addition to what we have said'; but the present participle does not suit this at all well. It is better to take '*epi*' = 'about', 'concerning'. '*Toiouton . . . hos*' = 'such a one who'. '*Megalōsunē*' = 'majesty', as in **1**[3]; it is a way of

---

[1] Derived sense: 'argument' at the head of a chapter, where the main points are summarized; finally, the chapter itself (in Latin: '*capitulum*').

speaking of God without using His name, a device much favoured by the Jews, who will often replace God by one of His attributes or influences ('the glory', 'the name', etc.). With *'en tois ouranois'* (= 'in the heavens'), the author, who elsewhere places God above all heavens (see 4^{14} and 7^{26}), reverts to a more popular turn of phrase.

8^2. *'Leitourgos'* (cf. *'leitourgein'*) is 'one who administers a cult'; *'to hagion'* = 'the holy thing' in general; but here a synonym for *'skēnē'* (= 'tent').[2] The adjective *'alēthinē'* (= 'the true') added to *'skēnē'* shows that the heavenly tabernacle is involved; it is to reappear in v. 5.[3]

'Epēxe' (normal aorist of *'pēgnumi'* = 'to erect') recalls Numbers 24^6 in which *'kurios'* is really God, but this may not have prevented our expositor from thinking of Christ. In any event, these two verses teach us that the new High Priest, after sacrificing Himself on earth, now officiates in heaven in the supernatural tabernacle. It is this heavenly service that is now solely under discussion.

$8^{3, 4}$. Offerings and sacrifices involving blood (in the usual sense) were not presented by Christ on earth. There could be no question of this, because there were priests already for the purpose. Otherwise these two verses present no difficulties and put forward no new idea.

8^5 is more curious. The opposition between 'heavenly' and 'earthly' things is used to denigrate the Levitical cult, which is only a copy (*'hupodeigma'*) and shadow (*'skia'*) of the true cult.[4] This judgement is to be firmly held. The inefficacy of the old cult is not due solely to the sabotage of unbelieving Jews, but is inherent in it. And here, consciously or otherwise, the author is a true disciple of Stephen.[5]

___

[2] We have not found the expression *'leitourgos tōn hagiōn'* in the LXX, but it is used by PHILO, v. *Legum Allegoriae*, III, §135 (Chap. 46), where the *'logos'* is the one 'who attends to and ministers in holy things' (*'therapeutēs kai leitourgos tōn hagiōn'*).

[3] *'Alēthinē'* is rather reminiscent of Johannine language: v. John 15^1, *'hē ampelos hē alēthinē'* ('the true vine'). But the sense is not the same. The Fourth Gospel contrasts the true with the false. Here the model is being distinguished from the copy, as in PHILO, who also speaks of the *'skēnē alēthinē'* ('true tent', *Vita Mosis*, II, §74, Chap. 15).

In Platonism, the suprasensible ideas are the only 'true' realities. It is known that Philo sometimes identifies Plato's ideas with heavenly things or beings, e.g. with the angels. For all questions concerning the spiritualization of cultic concepts in some Jewish milieux, see HANS WENSCHKEWITZ, 'Die Spiritualisierung der Kultusbegriffe', *Angelos*, Supp. 4, 1932.

[4] This sense of *'hupodeigma'* recurs in 9^{23} (but not 4^{11}). Cf. PHILO, *Legum Allegoriae*, III, §96 (Chap. 31) in which he uses *'paradeigma'* and *'skia'* as synonyms (although the context is not very clear) and especially *De Confusione Linguarum*, §190 (Chap. 38), where he declares that literal exegesis gives only the shadow (*'skia'*) of the truth. Cf. also JOSEPHUS, *Jewish War*, II, §28 (2.5), where he distinguishes between the shadow (*'skia'*) and substance (*'sōma'*) of royalty.

[5] WILLIAM MANSON was right to insist afresh on this relationship in the book listed in the Bibliography. See Stephen's speech, Acts 7^{1-53}.

Certainly our Epistle does not go as far as the so-called Epistle of Barnabas, which is hostile to the Jews for daring to countenance an interpretation of the Law other than its own, which is purely allegorical. For our writer, there was evidently a time when the first covenant was not yet obsolete and senile (v. 13). Nevertheless, its inferiority is inherent.

Further, our expositor turns a text from Exodus to his advantage. According to Exodus 25[40], Moses in fact made the tabernacle in accordance with a heavenly pattern which God showed him on the mountain. This revelation is first qualified as an oracle. For the text says '*kathōs kechrēmatistai*' (lit. 'as it was oracled', i.e. conforming to an oracle which he received). But later there is reference to a vision ('*hora*'), the oracle containing the order to conform to the vision.[6] The heavenly tent which appeared to him was therefore the archetype (here: '*tupos*') which he copied (cf. Wisdom 9[8], where the Temple is likewise qualified as a copy of a heavenly model).[7]

8[6]. Once more we meet the construction dear to the writer, which is characterized by a comparative followed (or preceded) by a '*hosō*' or '*kath*' *hoson*', to express a compared judgement (see 3[3]; 7[20, 22]). What the author wished to remind us of is this, that the divine service celebrated in heaven is superior not only by its very nature; it rests also upon a covenant of an unusual kind, itself founded on excellent promises; '*diaphoros*'—what distinguishes itself is 'distinguished', as in English. Christ is called '*mesitēs*' (= 'mediator') of this better covenant ('*kreittonos diathēkēs*') which confirms our translation of '*engguos*' (7[22]) as 'mediator'. He was mediator on sealing this covenant, and He continues to be so as intercessor in heaven. As for the promises concerning the new covenant, they will be dealt with at length from v. 8 onwards. The verb '*nomothetein*' (= 'to fix by a law'), makes no allusion to the Torah. '*Nomos*' here has the wide sense of 'divine decree'. The verb has already been encountered in

[6] The verb '*chrēmatizo*' in the passive (and with a passive sense) is found here, in 11[7], and also in Matthew 2[12, 22]; Acts 10[22], and in Hellenistic literature. Yet p 46 reads '*Mōusē*', which must be the dative. Then the verb is impersonal: 'it was indicated to Moses' (a reading not shown by Nestlé).

[7] Rabbi Levi (*c.* A.D. 300) declares that on the mountain Moses saw a tabernacle in four colours 'of fire': black, red, green, white. See BACHER, *Die Aggada der palästinensischen Amoräer*, II, Strasbourg 1896, p. 367. Rabbi Akiba (died A.D. 135) taught that models 'of fire' of the ark, of the table and of the candlestick descended from heaven so that Moses could copy them. See BACHER, *Die Aggada der Tanaiten*, II, Strasbourg 1890, p. 419.

It is worth pointing out that the construction of a religious building through inspiration or following a vision is not an idea peculiar to the Jews. It is recorded among the Chaldaeans of Lagash in the 3rd millennium B.C. See ALFRED JEREMIAS, *Babylonisches im N.T.*, Leipzig 1905, Chap. 4, especially pp. 64ff. What is true for religious architecture, may also be valid for the fine arts in general in the ancient world. We may wonder who would have had the idea of carving the strange creatures in Assyrian palaces, if no one had ever 'seen' them, if only in a dream.

the passive in 7[11]; a Semitism may be involved (the hophal of *'yārāh'*?).

8[7a] contains one of those gems of expression which it is a joy to meet after arguments which are not free from wordiness and repetition. If the first covenant had been 'without reproach', it would have been out of 'place' (*'topos'*) to create a new one.

8[8]. And now we have the prophet Jeremiah quoted as accuser (*'memphomenos'* = 'blaming') of the old rite. But this time, there is less censure for the old law itself than for the Jews, who made it null and void by their disobedience; in comparison with v. 7 therefore the stress has shifted. The text quoted is from Jeremiah 38[31-34] (LXX), or 31[30-33] (Hebrew). It is one of the finest passages in the prophet's book. In fact the censure of the people has only a minor place in it. The essential point is the revelation of the divine mercy (*'hileōs esomai'*, v. 12) which will forgive the lack of gratitude and faithfulness (He will remember their sin no more, end of v. 12), and what is more important, announces a new covenant. This will be characterized by two innovations: (1) it will not be inscribed on tables of stone, but in the mind (*'dianoia'*) and heart (*'kardia'*) of believers, which amounts to saying that the religion of the Spirit will have replaced the religion of authority, to use the words of Auguste Sabatier; (2) and following as a consequence of the first point—every one will have a direct knowledge of God. The prophet probably thought that this promise would come to fruition after the return from the Exile. But as this was not the case, Christian theologians could hardly be prohibited from seeing in it a prophecy of something more extraordinary, namely what the Synoptic Gospels call the Kingdom of God, and the Apocalypse of John the New Jerusalem, and our writer: access to the highest sanctuary; an ideal situation, of which the Christian Church will itself be only a very imperfect foreshadowing, in conformity with the eschatological dualism inherent in Christianity, which views the new covenant as already concluded, but as unable to reach full flowering except in the world to come.

Details: *'Epilambanomai tēs cheiros'* in v. 9 (= 'to take by the hand') is a touching expression, which reminds us of a father or mother taking a child by the hand. The departure from Egypt, so long before, had been a manifestation of the divine goodness, but the people repaid it with ingratitude. On the fourth line of v. 9 *'hoti autoi'* = 'because they . . .' must justify the ending of the old covenant (see the first line of v. 9), but could well have the sense of a relative pronoun = *'hoi'*, 'who'. It is the more probable in that the Hebrew text uses ' *'ašer'* here (v. 31).

In 8[11] (first line) some witnesses, the Vulgate among them, read *'plēsion'* (= 'neighbour') instead of *'politēn'* (= 'fellow-citizen').

It is a banal reading without interest. The text of the quotation, which moreover presents no difficulty of interpretation, is very close to that of the LXX.

8¹³ dots the i's again, straining the point a little: if a new covenant can be spoken about, it means that the old one is decrepit and senile.[8]

---

[8] After the destruction of the Temple, certain Rabbis taught that the practice of ethics can replace the cult. But the cult as such is never devalued. See HANS WENSCHKEWITZ, *op. cit.* p. 76, n. 2.

CHAPTER IX

(1) *Now the first covenant required cultic observances and the material sanctuary.* (2) *For a Tent had been erected, the first Tent; in it were the candlestick and the table used for displaying the loaves, and it is called the Holy Place.* (3) *But behind the second curtain was the Tent called the Holy of Holies.* (4) *It contained an altar made of gold for the incense, and the Ark of the covenant, which was completely overlaid with gold. In it was a vessel of gold containing the manna, as well as the staff of Aaron which had blossomed, and the tablets of the covenant.* (5) *And above the Ark were cherubim, the seat of the Glory, overshadowing the mercy-seat—objects about which this is not the place to go into detail.* (6) *With this arrangement thus made, the priests go continually into the first Tent, in the performance of their duty.* (7) *But into the second, only the High Priest goes, and that but once a year. And he does not go in without [taking the precaution of offering] blood for himself and for the involuntary sins of the people.* (8) *Thus the Holy Spirit showed that the way to the sanctuary was not yet open, as long as the old sanctuary remained standing.* (9) *And this was [only] a sign pointing to the present time. In accordance with the ordering of this sanctuary offerings and gifts were presented which were incapable of giving a perfect conscience to the worshipper.* (10) *And the ritual laws dealt only with food, drink and various ablutions. They were commandments for the flesh, in force until the time of reform.*

9¹. '*He prōtē*', with '*diathēkē*' understood (= 'the new [covenant]') as in 8¹³. '*Latreias*' (from '*latreia*' = 'cultic service') can be either an accusative plural or genitive singular (*sic* Luther and Calvin). In the first case, we have a list of three items: '*dikaiōmata*' (= 'observances'), '*latreias*' (= 'services'), and '*to hagion kosmikon*' (= 'the material sanctuary'). In the second case we must translate: 'observances concerning the cult as well as the sanctuary', etc. We have opted for the second rendering, because '*latreia*' is little used in the plural; but the other remains perfectly possible. '*Kosmikos*' = 'what is in the world', that is 'earthly', in contrast to what is in heaven. Bengel: '*sanctuarium mundale et carnale*'.[1]

[1] See JOSPHUS, *Jewish War*, IV, §324 (5.2) who speaks in a similar vein of a '*kosmikē thrēskeia*' = 'ceremonies of world-wide [cosmosial] significance'.

Theodoret's contention that the tabernacle was a type of the universe contains an idea interesting in itself, but it does not come into the reckoning here. For our author, the earthly tabernacle is the type of the celestial sanctuary, that is of the supernatural one. See *MPG* 82, col. 737: ' "*to de hagion kosmikon*". *Tēn skēnēn houtōs ekalese, tupon epechousan tou kosmou pantos*' ('the tabernacle so called is a type of the entire cosmos'). According to GALLING, *ZNTW*, 1950/51, pp. 263ff, the curtain, by its figurings represented the cosmos.

The use of the imperfect *'eiche'* (= 'it had') at the beginning of the verse is not conclusive proof that the Temple at Jerusalem had already been destroyed. The author considers the old covenant as outworn and belonging consequently to the past. Moreover Herod's Temple is of little interest to him, like the two earlier Temples. His interest is concentrated on the Tent of Meeting of the wilderness.

9[2]. *'Hē prōtē'* here refers to the exterior part of the sanctuary called the Holy Place, and contrasted with the Holy of Holies (v. 4).[2] In the Holy Place was the seven-branched candlestick, according to Exodus 25[31–39] and 37[17–24] [3] (LXX 38[13–17]), and the table for the loaves of the Presence. We could expect to find *'hoi artoi tēs protheseōs'* ('the loaves of the presence'). *'Hē prothesis tōn artōn'* ('the display of the loaves') is somewhat incorrect (Bengel: *'metonymia abstracta'*); concerning the table, cf. Exodus 25[23–30]; 37[10–16] (LXX 38[9–12]). Concerning the loaves, cf. also Leviticus 24[5–9]; Numbers 4[7] (*'hoi artoi hoi dia pantos'* = 'the perpetual loaves'). Up to that point everything is in agreement with the text of the Pentateuch.

9[3]. The Holy Place is separated from the Holy of Holies by a curtain, which is called the second one here. Yet 6[19] speaks of only one curtain (the one at the entrance to the Holy of Holies); this is in agreement with Exodus 26[31]. The author is following here a rabbinical tradition which also occurs in the Mishnah and in Philo.[4] *'Meta'* at the beginning of v. 3 can mean only 'behind', a rare sense, but not unknown in Greek. The awkward point is that our text places the *'thumiatērion'* (= 'altar of incense'?) in the Holy of Holies. This contradicts Exodus 30[1–10] and in all probability Exodus 26[35] also, where this altar is placed in front of the curtain of the Holy of Holies. Lengthy discussion of this point has taken place among scholars. Some have thought that the word might refer to something else, namely something like a censer containing burning incense which

---

[2] *'Hagia'* at the end of v. 2, seems to be the plural of *'hagion'* (v. 1) = 'the collection of holy things'. But this word can also be taken as feminine singular ([sic] Vulgate) with *'skēnē'* understood. This seems less probable. But the sense would be the same. For the expression *'hagia tōn hagiōn'*, cf. Numbers 4[19]; 1 Kings (LXX 3 Kings) 8[6]; 2 Chronicles 4[22]; 5[7]. Instead of *'hagia hagiōn'* p 46 simply reads ΑΝΑ, a copyist's error for ΑΓΙΑ according to Kenyon. According to Hoskier (pp. 6ff) this could be a Semitic word synonymous with *'hagion'*.

[3] In Solomon's Temple there were ten candlesticks (v. 1 Kings 7[49] in the Masoretic text, or 3 Kings 7[35] in the LXX), in the Temple of Herod only one. Josephus, *Jewish War*, V, §217 (5.5), speaks of a candlestick with seven lamps which he compares to the seven planets. We have few details about the Temple of Zerubbabel. If 1 Maccabees 1[21] and 4[49] can be relied upon, this Temple also contained one candlestick only. Josephus, *Antiquities*, XI, §64–78 (3.9 to 4.1) gives a few details about this sanctuary, but does not speak of the candlestick.

[4] See Yôma, V, 1.2–3 (Goldschmidt, III, pp. 140ff). In Philo the *De Vita Mosis*, II, §101 (Chap. 9) must be consulted; two veils are mentioned there: the inner (*'endon'*) 'called the veil' (*'ho kaleitai katapetasma'*), and the outer (*'ektos'*) 'called the covering' (*'ho prosagoreuetai kalumma'*). Later Philo speaks of the seven-branched candlestick.

was then to be spread on the altar of incense. Indeed, in Ezekiel 8[11]; 2 Chronicles 26[19] and 4 Maccabees 7[11], the noun is used for something of this sort. This does not solve the problem however. For why would such a utensil be kept in the Holy of Holies, if the altar was not there? The Mishnah, which speaks of the censer, seems to suppose that is was to be found in an adjoining room.[5] It must be supposed then either that the writer was following another tradition,[6] or that he made a mistake—something which would somewhat weaken the theory of his having a Levitical origin.

9[4]. What in fact did stand in this most sacred part of the tabernacle was the Ark. But at this point new difficulties have beset commentators. First of all the author makes no reference whatever to the fact that the Ark had long since vanished, at the latest when Jerusalem was sacked by the Babylonians. This is attested by Jeremiah (3[14-17]), who speaks of the distress over the vanished Ark. 'In those days, says the Lord, they shall no more say, "The ark of the covenant of the Lord." It shall not come to mind, or be remembered, or missed; it shall not be made again.'[7]

This silence can once more be explained by the fact that our theologian like the Rabbis was still speculating on the non-existent Ark; what interests him here is the theory which is to be found in the Pentateuch and which, it is claimed, was put into practice in the wilderness. For the same reason, our Epistle fails to take into account the fact that in the Temple of Solomon the Ark contained only the tables of the Law (v. 1 Kings (LXX 3 Kings) 8[9], two tables).[8]

What is more serious is that according to the Pentateuch itself, the jar containing the manna was placed in front of the Ark (v. Exodus 16[33f]). Similarly for Aaron's staff (v. Numbers 17[10] = LXX 17[25]). Again the author is following a rabbinical tradition, analogies of which can also be found in the Apocalypse of Baruch.[9]

---

[5] Yôma, V, 1.3 (GOLDSCHMIDT, III, p. 142).

[6] Cf. the Syriac Apocalypse of Baruch 6.7, which places in the Holy of Holies the altar of incense and several other objects which were never there. OLAF MOE, *TZ*, 1953, pp. 23ff, reminds us of Revelation 8[3], where the altar of incense is found before the throne of God. But does this remark resolve the difficulty?

[7] It was this that gave rise to the legend that Jeremiah hid the Ark in a secret place in order to keep it from the Chaldeans; and that it would reappear at the end of time (v. 2 Maccabees 2[4]). JOSEPHUS categorically declares that the Holy of Holies in Herod's Temple was empty (*'ouden holōs en autō'*), v. *Jewish War*, V, §219 (5.5). According to Yôma Mishna 5.2 and Gemara 53b (GOLDSCHMIDT, III, p. 147) the Ark had been carried off to Babylon and a stone stood in its place. According to the same Gemara, 54 (*ibid.*, p. 149), the Ark had been hidden. Cf. the Syriac Apocalypse of Baruch, Chap. 6 (KAUTZSCH, p. 414).

[8] The texts which speak of the Temple of Solomon mention neither the vessel nor the staff in the Ark. The hypothesis has been put forward that these objects were lost in the Philistine wars. Yet Yôma 52b (GOLDSCHMIDT, III, p. 142) states that they were hidden with the Ark.

[9] Cf. CYRIL, *MPG* 74, col. 980: 'Paul, perhaps from tradition, included the staff and the jar' (*'ek paradoseōs de isōs ho Paulos kai ton rhabdon kai ton stamnon prosethēke'*); for the Apocalypse of Baruch, v. *supra*, note 6.

We cannot summarize here the narratives of the manna and the staff, but merely note that a staff which blossoms is a well-known theme in the folklore of many peoples.[10] It is understandable that in ancient times these relics should be objects of veneration. As for the 'tablets' ('*plakes*' = 'plaques') of the covenant, they were to be found in the Ark according to Exodus 25[16] and especially Deuteronomy 10[1–2]. They were still there at the time of Solomon. They must have disappeared with the Ark. Exactly what prescriptions did they contain? Much more than the Ten Commandments. According to Deuteronomy 9[9] they were of stone and engraved, by the hand of God Himself, with all the words spoken by Him on Sinai, while Moses was present on the mountain. According to some Old Testament scholars, the things in question would be the 'Code of the Covenant' preserved in Exodus 21–23.

9[5]. Of greater importance are the cherubim, that is the representation of two of those winged angelic beings of a very high rank and a slightly animal appearance (*v.* Exodus 25[18–20]; 37[7–9] (LXX 38[6–8]); cf. 1 Kings (LXX 3 Kings) 6[23–28], 8[7]). They were placed in such a way that their wings could overshadow the lid of the Ark. They were therefore not seated on the Ark, but fixed above it in some way. These cherubim acted in some way as a support for the 'Glory' of God, that is for His luminous manifestation in our world. That is why they were called the 'cherubim of glory'.[11]

The '*hilastērion*', usually translated by 'mercy seat', will be spoken about later by the author. 9[5b] states that he will refrain from a more detailed commentary on the contents of the Ark and on the cherubim.[12]

9[6, 7]. Here '*prōtē*' and '*deutera*' clearly refer to the Holy Place and the Holy of Holies. That the priests in general went into the *first*, whilst the *second* was reserved for the High Priest, conforms with the Pentateuch (Exodus 30[10]; Leviticus 16[29–34]), as does the obligation of the High Priest to offer expiatory sacrifices, first for himself and then for the people, and also the indication that he entered there only once a year. Yet this detail seems to contradict 7[27], where he seems to enter daily,[13] as has already been pointed out.

[10] See P. SAINTYVES, *Essais de folklore biblique*, Paris 1923, Chap. II.

[11] '*Cheroubin*' (an Aramaic form or a Hebrew dual?) alternates with '*cheroubim*' (Hebrew plural). The vowel '*i*' is sometimes replaced by '*ei*' but the pronunciation is the same. On the appearance of the Glory, *v.* Exodus 40[34]; Psalm 63[3] (?) = LXX 62[3].

[12] HOSKIER, *op. cit.*, p. 26, thinks that the author omits a more detailed commentary not through lack of space, but through fear of divulging hidden things. But why should these little mysteries be more jealously guarded than the great ones?

[13] There was discussion among the Rabbis to determine whether the High Priest went into the Holy of Holies once only on that day or several times. According to the Yôma Mishna 5.1–4; 7.4 (GOLDSCHMIDT, III, pp. 128f and 194), he seems to have entered four times, but according to another interpretation of Exodus 30[10], twice.

At the end of v. 7 we should expect '*pherei huper tōn heautou kai tou laou agnoēmatōn*' = 'he offers for his own involuntary faults, as well as for those of the people'. In any event, this must be the sense. For in a general way, sacrifices purified only from involuntary transgressions, especially those of a ritual nature, at least in theory (*v.* Leviticus 4¹³⁻²¹; Numbers 15²²⁻²⁹). '*Ou chōris haimatos*' introduces a theme which is developed later, on the need for blood in expiation.[14]

9⁸. Why is the Holy Spirit mentioned here? Presumably because he is supposed to have inspired Moses, when he gave the Commandments. So we see that several conceptions of the origin of the Law are intermingled, without any clear distinction between them by the author: God spoke directly to Moses (8⁵), or through angelic intermediaries (2²), or by inspiring Moses (here). But two serious difficulties are concealed in this verse. What is the exact meaning of '*tēn tōn hagiōn hodon*'? 'The way leading to the sanctuary' ('*hagion*' taken as neuter)? Or 'a way to be travelled by the saints' (masculine), that is by Christians ([*sic*] Peshitta)? We prefer the first interpretation, because '*ta hagia*' in this pericope is taken in the neuter. Yet it is the '*hagioi*' who must travel this road.[15] The separation between the two parts of the sanctuary symbolizes the fact that before the coming of Christ the throne of God in heaven was inaccessible to believers. In order that the way should be open, two conditions must be fulfilled. (1) It is necessary for the earthly sanctuary to lose its 'meaning'. (2) It is necessary for Christ to open the way to the throne of God. The fulfilment of the second condition brings that of the first in its wake.

These reflections put us on the right track for resolving the second difficulty. What is the meaning of '*hē prōtē skēnē*' at the end of v. 8? The majority of scholars have yielded to the temptation of translating these words here as in v. 6 by 'the first part of the earthly sanctuary', i.e. the Holy Place, still separated from the Holy of Holies. This takes no account of the facility with which our author sometimes manipulates expressions with various senses. In fact it is not only the exterior part of the earthly tabernacle which has lost its value, which ceases to 'stand up' ('*echousēs stasin*'), but the whole of the earthly sanctuary. For this reason, together with Eugène Ménégoz (B. du C.), we see the '*prōtē skēnē*' as 'the Tent of the first covenant', contrasted with the heavenly tabernacle. It is true that in the Alexandrian conception of the world, the heavenly tabernacle existed metaphysically from all eternity; but from the religious point of view it comes into the reckoning only in 'our time' ('*ho kairos ho enestēkōs*',

---

[14] In the history of religions blood can also play another rôle, namely that of giving life to the dead or to dead gods. See ALFRED LOISY, *Essai sur le sacrifice*, 1920, the least known and undoubtably the best book by that author.

[15] Cf. Odes of Solomon 33.11: 'I reveal my paths to those who seek me'; *ibid.*, 39.11: 'A path was prepared for those who follow it.'

v. 9), that is in the era inaugurated by the ascension of Christ. That is why the earthly Tent can be called the first, like the old covenant.[16]

9⁹. How exactly was the old sanctuary a 'parable' pointing to our time? It is because the passing of the High Priest into the Holy of Holies is a typological foreshadowing that only a High Priest (much more powerful of course) will be able to enter the Heavenly Holy of Holies, an event which has already taken place. After '*enestēkota*' ('present') there should be a full stop and a new paragraph. For now (v. 9b) a new line of argument begins. No longer is there a simple contrasting in general terms of the two sanctuaries, but a precise statement of the superiority of the Christian religion in comparison with the Jewish. '*Kath' hēn*' (v. 9b) refers to '*parabolē*', that is to the old covenant. According to this (v. 9c), that is according to the old '*skēnē*', taken here as a symbol for the whole of the old covenant, sacrifices were offered and a host of ritual laws (food, drink, washings) were observed; but all this collection of rites suffered one capital shortcoming: it could not give 'a perfect conscience' to those who practised it. It is to be noted that '*latreuōn*' = 'worshipper' has a wide sense here; it does not refer merely to the priest, but includes all those who obey the prescriptions of the Law. No one who practises the Jewish religion, priest or layman, can ever obtain the essential thing, the one thing which matters, viz. the purification of his conscience. We have before us here one of the most important pronouncements of our Epistle and of the whole of the New Testament. It is, indeed, a decisive revelation which is being highlighted, that it is vain to multiply rites, for they cannot give assurance of forgiveness and purification. 'How shall I be assured of my salvation', was the question which preoccupied Luther, whose conscience remained uneasy in spite of observances conscientiously fulfilled. Fundamentally it is the same question which our theologian is answering. And he preaches the same negative attitude with regard to the rites. The word '*suneidēsis*' is not common in the New Testament, but it is found in the same sense ('conscience', moral and religious) in the Apostle Paul, when he enjoins us not to hurt the conscience of the weak.[17]

9¹⁰. In connexion with points raised by the details of this verse, the reader is advised to re-read especially the laws about food in the Book of Leviticus, Chapter 11; Deuteronomy 14; Leviticus 17¹⁰⁻¹⁶ (cf. Haggai 2¹¹⁻¹³). On ablutions ('*baptismoi*'), many texts are to be found in the Pentateuch, notably Exodus 29⁴; Leviticus 11²⁸, ³²,⁴⁰ and 14¹⁻⁹; Numbers 8⁷; and 19 *passim*. To these can be added indications

---

[16] We can glimpse here the author's faithfulness to the Jewish conception of the two successive ages, which time and again shines through despite his Alexandrine metaphysics. His thought is often Greek, but his sensibility remains constantly Hebrew.

[17] See 1 Corinthians 8⁷⁻¹³ and 10²⁵⁻²⁹. Cf. the studies mentioned below, note 6, p. 86.

(11) *But Christ presented Himself as High Priest of the good things
now arriving. And it was through the more sublime and perfect Tent
(erected not by the hand of man; I mean, not belonging to the creation
here below) (12) that He entered—once and for all—into the Sanctuary.
And this not by means of the blood of goats and of bulls, but by means
of His own blood; and it was thus that He obtained an eternal redemption.*

on the extra complications introduced by the Rabbis, according to
Mark 7[31] par., which are also preserved in the Talmud (*v.* the texts
mentioned by Strack-Billerbeck I, pp. 695–715). *'Epikeimena'* =
'concerning' (Robinson, *Moffatt Commentary*: 'they relate to . . .').

All these laws are termed *'dikaiōmata sarkos'* by the author, that
is 'commandments concerning bodily life'.[18] It may be surprising
that the sacrifices are viewed only (*'monon'*) from the standpoint of
food, drink and ablutions. The author presumably had in mind
primarily sacrifices which were 'eaten', whether preceded or not by
washing; *'kairo diorthōseōs'* = 'the time of restoration' (Spicq:
'of reformation'); *'diorthōsis'* is not found elsewhere in the Bible.
But the verb *'diorthoō'* is found in Isaiah 62[7] in the sense of 're-
establish', and the synonym *'diorthōma'* in Acts 24[2]. The point in
question is that of putting right a situation compromised by sin.

9[11–12]. Here it would be more readily acceptable to read with some
witnesses,[19] *'archiereus tōn mellontōn agathōn'* = 'High Priest of the
good things to come', that is to say the good things expected by the
faithful at the end of time. But the reading *'genomenōn'* adopted by
Nestlé is the more difficult and would be hard to explain if it were not
original. Once more we must understand the aorist participle as
inceptive or 'ingressive'. The good things have begun to come into
existence; for in the opinion of the author, as in the whole of the
New Testament, the Christian who has received the Holy Spirit
participates from that moment, in some degree, in the good things of
the new world. *'Dia tēs meizonos'* connects very well with *'eisēlthen'*
in v. 12: 'He went through a heavenly tabernacle'. It is another way
of expressing the idea that He crosses the heavens to reach the throne
of God.[20]

This higher tabernacle is distinguished from the *'hagia'*. The Tent
is presented here as the way; the sanctuary (*'hagia'*) is the objective.
This rather suprising distinction can mean only one thing: He passes
through the Holy Place (the heavenly one) identified with heaven, in

[18] Instead of *'dikaiōmata'*, some witnesses, especially the Vulgate and the
Byzantine Text, read *'dikaiōmasin'*, which would then be in apposition to *'pomasin'*.
But it would be necessary to make this dative agree with the nominatives *'dōra
kai thusiai'*, which is awkward.
[19] See especially the Vulgate, the Textus Receptus and S, A.
[20] Is there an allusion here to the image which compares the heavens to a tent?
Cf. the work cited *ad* 1[11–12] by R. EISLER. The allusion is possible.

(13) *For if the blood of goats and bulls and the ashes of a heifer scattered over defiled persons sanctifies so that the flesh is purified,* (14) *how much superior is the power of the blood of Christ, who offered Himself as a victim without blemish to God, with the help of the eternal Spirit; He purifies our conscience in order to free us from dead works and to [permit] us to serve the living God.*

order to enter into the Holy of Holies. This heavenly sanctuary is superior (*'meizōn'*) and more perfect (*'teleiotera'*) than the earthly Temple. This is a first feature which shows the superiority of our High Priest.[21] A second point is the quality of the sacrifice. He offers His own blood, not that of animals. Thirdly, He offers the sacrifice once only, once for all, as 7 has already emphasized. Fourthly, the salvation of the faithful is assured for eternity.

But the objection will be raised that the sacrifice was accomplished at Golgotha and not in heaven. Yet that event had a supernatural effect; it opened the way which leads to the heavenly Holy of Holies; there Christ brings as the offering before the supernatural altar His own life, which He gives to ensure the salvation of believers. The principle of the theology of blood will be discussed later.

9[12]. *'Hagia'* is again a synonym for *'hagia tōn hagiōn'* = 'Holy of Holies' (these two words are added by the manuscript P).

9[13]. *'Aiōnia lutrōsis'* (= 'eternal redemption') contains as often with our author, some degree of metonymy. It is not the redemption (*'lutrōsis'*) which is eternal, but the salvation.[22] *'Heuramenos* = 'having obtained' can be explained here from the fact that the author is placing himself at the present time, when the obtaining is already an accomplished fact, although the final salvation is not yet bestowed on the faithful.[23]

---

[21] Many interpreters have sought to overcome the difficulty by thinking that *'skēnē'* in v. 11 (as in 2 Corinthians 5[4] and 2 Peter 1[13–14]) could refer to the earthly body of Jesus, by the sacrifice of which (instrumental *'dia'*) He entered into heaven. [Sic] CHRYSOSTOM: 'here He speaks of the flesh' (*'tēn sarka entautha legei'*), MPG 63, col. 119; likewise THEODORET, MPG 82, col. 741; Calvin, Westcott and many others. But it is difficult to think that such an antimonophysite as our author would be able to deny that Christ's body belonged to our creation.

[22] For the word *'lutrōsis'*, cf. Luke 1[68]; 2[38]. The feminine form *'aiōnia'* is unusual. Normally *'aiōnios'* is used (cf. the expression *'zōē aiōnios'*). On the different senses of *'lutron'*, *'lutrōsis'* and cognate words, see TWNT IV, pp. 341ff. p 46 reads *'eis ta hagia aiōnia, lutrōsin heuramenos'* (not mentioned by Nestlé). See HOSKIER, op. cit., p. 44.

[23] The use here of the aorist participle is somewhat reminiscent of that in Philippians 2[6ff], where the participles seem to express a progression in the action; it is an Aramaism, as Lohmeyer believes. See P. BONNARD, *L'épître de saint Paul aux Philippiens*, Neuchâtel and Paris, ad loc. The correct form would of course be *'heuromenos'*. But bastard forms of the aorist (with *'a'* and without *'s'*) had already achieved general acceptance in the Koiné. Cf. the forms *'eipa'*, *'eipas'*, etc. which are quite common in the N.T.; BLASS-DEBRUNNER, §81.

Vv. 13 and 14 again make use of an argument *a minore ad maius*. If animal blood had a certain effect, how much greater must be the effect of the blood of Christ. The idea that the blood of the old covenant would be able to bring about a bodily cleansing only is surprising. Does it not assure forgiveness of sins? That was certainly the idea that the Jews had about it. But according to our Epistle, this concept was also of the flesh. For they thought of sin as an outward defilement which could be washed away by outward ritual.

Here the author breaks with the magical conception of religion, which can have no effect on the *conscience* of the believer. What holds all his attention is the sense of guilt which crushes the conscience of the sinner. In this way the Epistle implicitly puts us on our guard also against the magical interpretation of the death of Christ. He did not set a magic mechanism in motion. It was a wholly personal work which He carried out on earth and in heaven. And the author strives to provide some enlightenment of this mystery, which constitutes a kind of gnosis for Christians who are no longer beginners. So far as details of vv. 13 and 14 are concerned, the reference to the heifer ('*damalis*') alludes to the red heifer (Numbers 19), the ashes ('*spodos*') of which played a part in some rites of purification.[24] '*Koinoun*' = 'to make common', 'to defile'. '*Dia pneumatos aiōniou*' (= 'by the eternal spirit') is much better attested than the easier reading '*dia pneumatos hagiou*' ('by the holy spirit').[25] Some scholars, as Robinson, take '*aiōniou*' as a masculine noun and translate 'in the spirit of the Eternal'. But such a use of '*aiōnios*' is unknown elsewhere (except as the French 'Eternel'). We must turn rather to the Pauline thesis in which the second Adam possesses a spirit of eternal life. It is thanks to this that He remains pure ('*amōmos*') and that He was able to conquer death. On the '*erga nekra*' ('dead works'), see above at 6¹.

In v. 14 we read with Nestlé '*tēn suneidēsin hēmōn*' ('our conscience').[26] The expression '*ho theos ho zōn*' ('the living God') implies not only that God is alive, but also that He acts. This turn of phrase is characteristic of a dynamic conception of the deity, and is poles apart from the Aristotelian conception.

From v. 15 onwards it might seem that '*diathēkē*' assumes the sense of 'testament', but in v. 15 itself, this sense seems to be very doubtful. For again Christ is called '*mesitēs*' = 'mediator', which is better applied to the idea of covenant, the more so since there is

[24] According to Numbers 19 the heifer was to be burned, and then cedar wood, crimson wool and hyssop were to be thrown into the flames; finally the ashes were to be mixed with the water of purification. Crimson wool, hyssop and cedar wood also play a part in the purification of lepers (Leviticus 14⁴), but they are not mentioned in Exodus 24 in connexion with the ratification of the covenant.

[25] '*Pneuma hagion*' is given by D, P and the Latin versions. DANIELUS EUGENIUS SCHERDLIN identifies '*pneuma aiōnion*' with the divine nature of Christ in his dissertation *Specimen Hermeneuticum in locum ad Hebr.* 9¹³⁻¹⁴, Strasbourg 1859, p. 33.

[26] '*Humōn*' is scarcely attested except in S and the Textus Receptus.

(15) *And since His death took place for the purification of trans-*
gressions under the old covenant, He is the mediator of a new covenant,
so that the beneficiaries of the call may come into possession of the
eternal heritage which was promised them. (16) *For where a will is*
involved, the death of the testator must be made public. (17) *For a will*
takes effect only on condition that someone has died. Can it ever come
into force while the testator is still alive? (18) *That is why the first*
covenant was not inaugurated without [the shedding of] blood. (19)
Indeed, when Moses had read to the people the complete list of directives
in keeping with the Law, he took the blood of bulls and goats, mixing
it with water and using crimson wool and hyssop, and sprinkled the
book itself and all the people with it. (20) *And he said: 'This is the blood*
of the covenant which God has prescribed for you.' (21) *In the same*
way he sprinkled the Tent and all the cultic objects. (22) *And it is with*
blood that almost all the purifications are made according to the Law.
And without shedding of blood, there is no forgiveness. (23) *It is*
necessary then that the copies of heavenly things should be purified
by these operations. But the heavenly things themselves must be
purified by more excellent sacrifices than these. (24) *For Christ did not*
enter a sanctuary made by human hands, which would be only a copy
of the real one, but heaven itself, in order to appear now before the face
of God, for our benefit. (25) *And it was not in order to offer Himself*
repeatedly, as [we might be led to believe by analogy with] the High
Priest going each year into the sanctuary with blood not his own. (26)
For then Christ would have had to suffer many times since the creation
of the world. No, in fact He revealed Himself once for all at the con-
summation of the ages to abolish sin by His sacrifice.

express reference to the '*prōtē diathēkē*', which there is no reason to
translate otherwise than by 'first covenant'. The death of Christ is
necessary for the reason indicated in v 14: His blood seals the
covenant. '*Dia touto*' precedes '*hopōs*' = 'for the following reason',
'in order that' (Moffatt: 'a forward reference').

9¹⁵. '*Aiōnios*' (here in the masculine) '*klēronomia*' is the 'eternal
inheritance' which no one will be able to take from us; the expression
occurs also in the Odes of Solomon 33¹⁰ and in Slavonic Enoch
66⁶. With Calvin, we link the genitive ('*tēs aiōniou klēronomias*')
to '*tēn epanggelian*': the point is of receiving 'the promise' (i.e. the
fulfilment of the promise) of this inheritance. The genitive could of
course also be linked to '*keklēmenoi*' = 'those who have received the
call of an inheritance' or 'the call to an inheritance', but the Greek
genitive would be just as strange.

9¹⁶⁻¹⁸. It is here only that the sense of 'testament' for '*diathēkē*'
becomes necessary. For we are told that the '*diathēkē*' can become

effective only after the death of the testator.[27] Perhaps the author's
mind turned to the last meal of Jesus recorded in Luke 22[29], in
which He seems to leave a testament. '*Mēpote*' instead of '*oupote*'
deserves explanation. We conclude that a question is being asked:
'Can it ever . . . ?'

But 9[18] speaks of a 'first' ('*prōtē*'; '*diathēkē*' being understood),
which can only be the 'first covenant'. For no one has ever looked on
the Law as a testament of Moses, and moreover his death has no
theological significance. It was oxen and goats that were killed when
the first covenant was ratified. '*Hothen*' = 'that is why' must link
v. 17 to v. 18 and is rather awkward. Riggenbach thinks that God is
obviously the testator; but as God does not die, animals were sub-
stituted for Him. We do not think that this great scholar could
have felt very satisfied with this explanation, which could at most
(and still) be valid for religions with a totemic basis, and the Jewish
religion could certainly not be counted among these. Windisch
adroitly avoids it by speaking in both cases of '*Stiftung*' ('pious
bequest') which only serves to mask the problem. Lohmeyer[28]
thinks that '*diathēkē*' means 'decree'. Even if this sense were able to
bridge the gap between the two usual meanings, the translator will
have to opt, in each case, for one or the other.

9[19] recalls the origins of the covenant concluded through the intermediary of Moses between the God of Sinai and the people; the
words of consecration of the covenant (v. 20) drawn from Exodus 24
are quoted. The writer adds details not found in that chapter, once
more following rabbinical traditions. Indeed, Exodus 24 speaks at
this point neither of water, nor of crimson wool, nor hyssop, nor of
the sprinkling of the book, although the book is mentioned at 24[7]
under the name of '*biblion tēs diathēkēs*' ('book of the covenant').
The sprinkling of the people is mentioned however (24[8]). The exact
rôle of the animals and of their blood is less clear than our theologian
seems to admit. In some cases the animal was cut into two (Genesis
15[9-21]) and the contracting parties passed between the two pieces.
But there is no question of that here. According to the Rabbis the
question at issue was of the consecration and purification of the
people in order to make them capable of receiving the covenant and
to bind them to it.[29] Note that in v. 20 the writer replaces '*idou*'
(= 'behold' i.e. 'here is') from the formula in Exodus 24[8] by '*touto*'
(= 'this' is the blood), presumably through remembering the formula

---

[27] We do not say that the writer made conscious play on the two senses of the
word '*diathēkē*' (though it is not impossible). Do we not also use the word
'Testament' for a collection of books, without always realizing clearly that we are
giving the word a sense quite different from its original meaning?

[28] In his work *Diatheke*, 1913.

[29] In the Mechilta of Rabbi Ishmael, Tractate Babodash, Chap. 3, concerning
Exodus 24[8], Moses said to the people after the sprinkling: 'Now you are bound,
held and secured.' See the edition of JACOB Z. LAUTERBACH with English translation, vol. 2, Philadelphia 1935, p. 211.

'*touto esti to haima*', recorded in Mark 14²⁴—though it does not mean that he knew it through that Gospel.

9²¹⁻²² add the sprinkling of the tabernacle and of the cultic objects. However, the tabernacle did not yet exist; at least, the account of its being made came later. Also Exodus 24 mentions the altar only. Josephus, however, speaks of a sprinkling of the tabernacle.³⁰

9²² states a general thesis: without shedding of blood ('*chōris haimatekchusias*') there is no purification.³¹ This dogma is not explained, but taken as self-evident. It is based on a belief universally held in antiquity which saw the blood as the seat of life, the soul in some degree, the latter being regarded as the life-principle (*v.* Leviticus 17¹¹).

So far as the application of this doctrine of the blood to the death of Christ is concerned, it will always run into one major difficulty, because that death did not, strictly speaking, involve blood-shedding. In spite of reminders of the wounds caused by the nails and the thrust of the lance, and assertions like those of Rudolf Steiner that a single drop of His blood falling to the ground was sufficient to change the destiny of the planet,³² this explanation will always seem rather strained. On the other hand, we cannot agree with Riggenbach in thinking that for our Epistle 'blood' is simply a synonym for 'life'. For the writer insists too seriously on the analogy with the blood in the Old Testament for this way of thinking to be ascribed to him. It is none the less true that if we wish to distil from this passage its essential religious idea, which is presented under the imagery of shed blood, that idea is the gift of life, in conformity with the Gospel texts such as John 10¹¹⁻¹⁵; 15¹³; Mark 10⁴⁵ par.; and Matthew 26²⁸ par.³³

But how is it to be understood that the sacrifice had supernatural effects, by cancelling sins and gaining a victory over the devil? Here is a mystery which no New Testament author explains to us. Here we are in the presence of a miracle, perhaps the greatest of the whole Bible, which even the Apostles could do no more than put on record—if they did not find themselves obliged to remain silent (cf. 2 Corinthians 12⁴ᵇ).

³⁰ *Antiquities*, III, §206 (8.6).
³¹ '*Schedon*' goes with '*panta*' despite Chrysostom and others, who link it with '*katharizetai*'; it would then mean: everything is almost purified by blood. The idea that purification lacks effectiveness is indeed claimed by our author. But can the adverb '*schedon*' be linked with a verb? The noun '*haimatekchusia*' in v. 22 is quite unknown elsewhere. It may be of the writer's own coining. But Windisch thinks that its absence from Greek literature is mere chance.
³² RUDOLF STEINER, *Johannes Evangelium*, Chap. 7 (Lectures of 1908 published in 1925) and *Lucas Evangelium*, p. 19 of the 9th Lecture (published in 2nd edn 1923).
³³ On the doctrine of atonement through the death of Christ, notable information and analyses can be found in the books by VINCENT TAYLOR, especially *The Atonement in New Testament Teaching*, 1941; and also in H. H. FARMER, *The Healing Cross*, 1939.

9²³. *'Hupodeigma'* = 'the copy'. We understand the necessity for purifying earthly things, which are copies of heavenly things. But why the purifying of the heavenly things themselves? Luther and Calvin think that basically the verb *'katharizesthai'* governs *'hupodeigmata'* only; in this case we should have before us what grammarians call a zeugma (an ill-assorted pair). But it is difficult to see what other verb could be adduced for v. 23b. Moffatt declares that the author's thought takes on a strange twist ('almost fantastic'), but without giving any explanation. As a suggestion, we think that the purification of the lower reaches of heaven is implied in the victory over Satan which is asserted in 2¹⁴. Where was Satan and where was he to be driven from? According to 1 Peter 3¹⁹ᶠᶠ (the descent into hell by the usual interpretation) he could be located in hell, and the expression 'master of death' (2¹⁴) might tempt us to read the same idea into our Epistle. But it must be noted that there is no mention of a *descensus ad infernos*. Consequently, it is more valuable to recall that according to Pauline thought the powers of evil (except probably death itself) were to be found in the heavens (Ephesians 6¹² *'en tois epouraniois'*) and that the *'archontes'* ('rulers') conquered by the cross are astral spirits (1 Corinthians 2⁸; Colossians 2¹⁵). Traces of this idea can also be found elsewhere, for example in Psalm 68¹⁹ (LXX 67¹⁹) and in the Odes of Solomon (38) in which the Saviour on his return to heaven overthrows the hostile powers. According to the Ascension of Isaiah, Satan and his host reside between the earth and the firmament.[34]

If we look at our text from this standpoint, the purification of heaven is necessary merely because the hostile powers had settled there, in order to oppress men and to separate them from God. It is good to recall also Romans 8³⁸, which at bottom asserts nothing other than the removal of this barrier. Cf. also Revelation 12¹³.[35]

The supreme sacrifice (9²³) is of course the sacrifice of His life which Christ offered and which, followed by His ascension, had the effect of decisive upheavals in the supernatural world.

9²⁴. This verse makes it clear that Christ had to enter the heavenly sanctuary in order to appear before God. The verb *'emphanizein'* = 'to show', in the middle voice = 'to show oneself', 'to appear', cf. Wisdom 1²; John 14²¹⁻²². *'Prospherein'* ('to offer gifts') has a double sense here. Christ offered Himself in order to sacrifice Himself, but He also presented to God (in heaven) gifts, and He did it once only, in contrast with the earthly High Priest.[36] At the end of v. 25 the thought is rather clumsily expressed. If these few words are taken literally, it might be thought that Christ also offered blood other

---

[34] Ascension of Isaiah, Chap. 7, cf. the rulers of the spheres in Gnosticism.

[35] The Christological hymn preserved in 1 Timothy 3¹⁶ may contain a covert reference to this event: 'He appeared to angels . . . was taken up into glory.'

[36] In v. 25, several witnesses have again added *'tōn hagiōn'* after *'ta hagia'*; this is superfluous, since in that case it could only mean the Holy of Holies.

(27) *And just as it is appointed for men to die once only—after which comes the judgement—*(28) *so Christ Himself, having offered Himself once to take away the sins of many, will appear a second time, without there being any question of sin, to those who are waiting for Him, for their salvation.*

than His own. In reality the author is simply taking advantage of the opportunity in order to remind us of another capital difference between the two sacrifices, viz. Christ alone offered His own blood.

9²⁶. More than one entry by Christ is unnecessary, not only because it has been accomplished for all time but also because such a thing would presume a repetition of the passion. The expression '*apo kataboles kosmou*' (= 'from the creation of the world') even conveys the idea that in that case the passion at Golgotha would not be the first.[37] Here is a clear statement of what is called linear time, as opposed to time according to the Stoics and the mystery religions for whom time was cyclic.[38] Note also the repetition of the adverb '*hapax*' = 'once for all' which appears three times: vv. 26, 27, 28.

9²⁶ᶠᶠ. '*Sunteleia tōn aiōnōn*' is synonymous with the expression 'the end of time'. Time ('*aiōnes*') here is the totality of the centuries which in another terminology form the present aeon ('*ho aiōn houtos*').[39] Strictly speaking our aeon is not ended. But people were conscious of living in the last days. '*Hapax pephanerōtai*' = 'He appeared once for all', recalls the uniqueness of the incarnation,[40] the second coming of Christ in glory not being considered as an incarnation. '*Athetēsis hamartias*' as in 7¹⁸ above asserts the cancelling or expiation of sins.

9²⁷⁻²⁸. '*Kath' hoson*' naturally corresponds to '*houtōs*', a stylistic device dear to the author. Fundamentally, however, there is no question of similar things, but only of events which depend on one

[37] The idea of such a repetition of the passion is so profoundly repugnant to Christian thought and sensibility that even ORIGEN who believes in a succession of worlds in time, rebuts this possibility in a very categorical manner. See *Contra Celsum, GCS*, ed. KOETSCHAU, IV, 67–68, pp. 337f and V, 20–21, pp. 21f.

[38] See especially O. CULLMANN, *Christ and Time*, ET London 1951. But Cullmann will certainly not contradict us if we recall that the so-called linear conception is not an invention of the Bible, for it was a presupposition of Zoroastrianism.

In fact the expression 'linear time' must be taken *cum grano salis*. It is the disposition of certain events which may take one or other of these forms. Time itself never returns, unless it be in the memory of men. On the Christian conception of time, see also the remarkable book by H. CONRAD-MARTIUS, *Die Zeit*, Munich 1953, especially the last chapter.

[39] For '*aiōnes*' with a plural (not dual) sense, cf. Luke 1³³; 1 Corinthians 2⁷; 10¹¹; Ephesians 3⁹, ¹¹; Colossians 1²⁶; I Timothy 1¹⁹ and elsewhere. '*Aiōnes*' in 1 of this Epistle has a different sense.

[40] The verb '*phanerousthai*' is used for the appearing before men, as in John 3⁵, ⁸; 1 Peter 1²⁰.

another. There is, it is true, a certain similarity between the unique-
ness of Christ's death and that of men.[41] But the analogy ends there.
Men are making their way to judgement. Christ will reappear to
His own, that is to those who receive Him and accept Him as
Saviour, at the parousia of course, or at the time of their meeting in
heaven.[42]

9^{28} presents us with a play on words between '*prosenengkein*' (Latin:
'*offere*') and '*anenengkein*' (Latin: '*au-ferre*' or '*tollere*'). But what is
the meaning of 'without sin' ('*chōris hamartias*'), an expression which
must characterize the second coming of the Lord? The witnesses are
unanimous in giving this rather difficult reading. Now was not Christ
always without sin? Might the author be drawing a distinction between the absence of sin (first coming of Christ) and the impossibility
of sin (second coming)? But would it be necessary to insist on the
impeccability of the glorious Lord and could the expression really
have this sense? Or alternatively should '*chōris hamartias*' signify
'without atoning sacrifices for sins'? Strictly speaking this is not the
sense of '*hamartia*'. Nevertheless, this interpretation may suggest the
right explanation. The author means that Christ will no longer have
to combat sins and sinners, and Moffatt rightly refers us back to
7^{26}. It is not for the atonement of sins that He will return. Some,
Grotius among them,[43] have sought to take these two words with
'*apekdechomenois*': the Christians will be without sin. But all other
considerations apart, to construe in this way would be a pure
'hyperbaton' and seems to us to be grammatically impossible.

At the end of v. 28, some witnesses, notably A and P, add '*dia
pisteōs*' = 'through faith' an addition which does no harm, but
which we do not think should be inserted into the text.

---

[41] Some subtle theologians have made the point that Lazarus and some other
people have died twice. Calvin replies that it is the ordinary human condition
which is in question here ('*de ordinaria hominum conditione*').

[42] The expression 'after that (i.e. after death) the judgement' could give rise to
the idea that the Epistle places the latter immediately after death. But this is not
certain. The judgement of men could take place during the parousia of Christ,
that is at the end. If early Christianity did not elaborate any clear doctrine on this
subject, it is partly due to the fact that the end and the judgement were thought to
be very close at hand. Moreover, it is almost superfluous to recall that 'judgement'
is almost a *vox media*, since the ordeal may just as well end in acquittal as in
condemnation. An interesting interpretation of the judgement is to be found in
1 Corinthians 3^{12-15}: believers will be saved by faith, but they will be judged
according to their works; and from these their place in the Kingdom will be
allocated.

[43] See GROTIUS, *ad loc*.

CHAPTER X

WHILST THE earlier chapters have developed the theme of the superiority of the New High Priest over the former ones, **10** insists especially on the superiority of the new sacrifice of Jesus over the Mosaic rites. It does not expressly contest the legitimacy of the Jewish cult in pre-Christian times, but it proclaims (1) its spiritual ineffectiveness even under the old régime, and (2) its abolition by the coming of Christianity. The decisive point is that the conscience of sinners has never been eased by the Mosaic sacrifices.

(1) *The Law, indeed, was possessed only of the shadow of the good things to come and not of the perfect form of the realities. That is why, through ever the same sacrifices unceasingly offered year by year, it could not give perfection to those who offered them.* (2) *If it were otherwise, would they not have ceased offering them, since the worshippers, purified once for all, would no longer have been conscious of their sins?* (3) *But in fact by these very sacrifices there is an annual reminder of sin.* (4) *For it is impossible for the blood of bulls and goats to take away sins.*

10¹. The rites sketched in only the shadow (*'skia'*) and not the true form (*'eikōn'*) nor essence of salvation. One might think of the shadow which future events cast into the present, in the form of a prefiguration. But the dominant idea of this pericope is not that of the bond which can exist between the shadow and the reality, but on the contrary that of the abyss which separates them. The shadow is never anything but an illusion; and thus the Mosaic sacrifices could at the most create the illusion of salvation. What is curious is that the very reality of salvation is called an *'eikōn'* = 'image', i.e. a sculpted image. But we must not conclude from this that the new religion itself is only the imperfect copy of things, that is of the heavenly realities. *'Eikōn'* must simply indicate the solidity and perfection of the new things,[1] in contrast with the fleeting and unreal nature of the redemption according to the ancient rite.[2]

---

[1] The difficulty disappears if we read with p 46 *'kai tēn eikona'* instead of *'ouk autēn tēn eikona'*. The sense would then be: the Law was only the shadow and image of the heavenly realities. The reading is not listed by Nestlé. HOSKIER says (*op. cit.*, p. 30) it 'looks the best to me'.

[2] It will occasion no surprise that the contrast between *'skia'* = 'shadow', on the one hand, and *'paradeigma'* or *'archetupos'* = 'model', on the other, is to be found frequently in Philo. For him the cult according to the letter is a pale copy of certain heavenly realities (though he never envisages the abolition of the Jewish cult). To this end he develops a strange and far from clear opposition between Bezalel (Exodus 31²) and Moses. The former is the earthly architect

Should the three words '*eis to diēnekes*' (= 'for ever', 'unceasingly')
be taken with what precedes (oblations which are continually
offered)? Or with what follows (salvation which it is impossible to
acquire in this way)? The placing of the words in the sentence makes
us select the first of these ways of construing them.

A serious difficulty in the exegesis of the text is raised by the clash
of two readings, namely '*dunatai*' (= 'it can', i.e. the Law can) and
'*dunantai*' (= 'they can', i.e. the priests can). The second reading is
slightly better attested,[3] but is syntactically impossible for '*nomos*'
would be without a predicate. '*Teleiōsai*' as often = 'to make perfect',
'to give perfection' ('*teleios*', Heb. '*tāmîm*').[4] This perfection shows
itself primarily through a purified conscience. We are reminded of
this in v. 2.[5] The Jewish cult cannot ease the conscience; sacrifices
must be continually repeated, not only because man continues to sin,
but also because he can never be sure of having obtained pardon.
This is exactly what Luther held against indulgences: the more you
buy of them, he thought, the less sure you are of salvation.[6]

That is why **10**[3] teaches us that 'each year' sins are recalled and made
a present reality in the cultic acts, whether at the time of the great
annual sacrifice by the High Priest, or of the sacrifices offered by the
faithful on the occasion of an annual pilgrimage. There may even be
(according to Windisch and others) a slight allusion to a very un-
reassuring text, namely Numbers 5[15], according to which a consequence of sacrifices is to recall to God the sins which He ought to
punish.[7]

---

who builds the tabernacle. Moses had had in addition dealings with the heavenly
tabernacle. See *De Somniis*, I, §206, Chap. 35; *De Plantatione Noe*, §27, Chap. 6;
Legum Allegoriae, III, §102, Chap. 33. In the second reference the expression
'*pragmata*' can also be found to denote heavenly realities.

[3] As supporters it has not only the Byzantine Text, but S, A, C also, and it was
adopted by von Soden. (B stops, as is known, at 9[14], the remainder being completed by an unknown hand in the 15th century). But the other reading which is
virtually unknown except in the Western text (D, old Latin versions and the
Vulgate), has just received strong support through p 46. It is, moreover, the
only one grammatically possible. The plural '*dunantai*' could, it is true, presuppose
'they' as subject, i.e. the priests, but the subject '*nomos*' is then without a verb.
Therefore, with Riggenbach and Spicq, we opt for the singular.

[4] It is thus that according to Matthew 5[48], man should be or become perfect,
as God has always been perfect. But there the analogy ends, divine perfection
and human perfection being manifestly incommensurable.

[5] p 46 reads '*kan*' for '*ouk an*', and other witnesses simply '*an*'. In this case we
are of course not confronted by a question but by a statement: the cult would have
ceased, if . . .

[6] On '*suneidēsis*' see also PHILO, *Quod Deterius*, §146, Chap. 40. BOUILLON, *op.
cit.*, II, pp. 756ff, explains '*suneidēsis hamartiōn*' as 'a mentality which induces
evil actions'. Interesting, but dubious.
For the meaning of '*suneidēsis*' in the N.T., see HENRI CLAVIER, ' "*Hē suneidēsis*", *une pierre de touche de l'hellénisme paulinien*', in the Jubilee volume of the
1,900th anniversary of St Paul's visit to Greece (Athens 1953), also EDMOND
GRIN, 'Morale de la conscience et morale de la grâce', *Cahiers de la Faculté de
théologie de l'Université de Lausanne*, VI, 1934, pp. 35–53.

[7] PHILO, *De Plantatione Noe*, §108, Chap. 25, says, 'these sacrifices do but put

(5) *And so He said, on coming into the world:* '*Sacrifice and offering, You have not desired. But You have prepared for me a body.* (6) *Burnt offerings and sin-offerings have given You no pleasure.* (7) *Then I declared: Here I come—in the roll of the book there is reference to me—to do Your will, O God.*'

10⁴ gives, in the form of a dictum, the basis of the author's thought. The blood of animals, even when offered with the maximum of devoutness, cannot wash away sin. It cannot even be said that sacrifices were a second-best, they are ineffective. By this the author aligns himself with the anti-ritualist tendencies which can be glimpsed in certain prophets and Psalmists (cf. vv. 5, 6), amongst the Essenes, in John the Baptist who wishes to save by baptism alone, as well as in Stephen, the great predecessor of our theologian.

How then does the author come to terms with the general belief that the Mosaic cult was instituted by God? We are of the opinion that from the different hypotheses about the origins of the Jewish cult, he gives preference to the one which attributes the Law to the angels, just as Stephen did. See **2¹** and Acts **7⁵²**, also Galatians **3¹⁹**. At first sight therefore the Law of Moses could in no way claim to have absolute divine authority.

10⁵⁻⁷ quote Psalm 40 (vv. 7–9) = LXX Psalm 39. This text stresses precisely the uselessness of the sacrificial cult, which God neither ordained nor approved. But the Psalmist (perhaps a prophet?) also makes a curious statement about himself: he asserts his willingness to do the will of God and declares that his mission is foretold in a book of Scripture. For the author *ad Hebraeos* this Psalm has undoubtedly Christological meaning. It is Jesus speaking at the moment of His entry into the world, and He refers to a scriptural prediction. One curious detail is that whilst the Masoretic text says (Psalm 40⁷) 'You have given me ears' (i.e. in order to listen to your orders) our Epistle has: 'You have prepared for me a body' (*'sōma'*), which might be an allusion to the incarnation of Christ, and even to the sacrifice of His own body, which is to replace the Jewish sacrifices (cf. 1 Corinthians 11²⁴; Luke 22¹⁹). *'Sōma'* also appears in the

---

Him in remembrance of the ignorance and offences of the several offerers' (*'thusiai hupomimnēskousai tas hekastōn agnoias kai hamartias'*); and *De Vita Mosis*, II, §107, Chap. 22 says about sacrifices: 'it is not a remission but a reminder of past sins which they effect' (*'ou lusin hamartēmatōn, all' hupomnēsin ergazontai'*).

But in both texts, the Rabbi of Alexandria is speaking of the sacrifices of the wicked. In the Gospel of the Ebionites, on the other hand, *all* sacrifices provoke the anger of God: 'I am come to do away with sacrifices, and if ye cease not from sacrificing, the wrath of God will not cease from you' (*'ēlthon katalusai tas thusias kai ean mē pausēsthe tou thuein, ou pausetai aph' humōn hē orgē'* (LIETZMANN, *Kleine Texte*, no. 8, p. 11, according to EPIPHANIUS, *Haeresis* 30.14; translation: E. HENNECKE, *N.T. Apocrypha*, vol. 1, ET London 1963).

(8) *Having therefore first announced 'You have neither desired nor been well-pleased with sacrifices, offerings, burnt-offerings, nor sin-offerings' which, however, are offered according to the Law, (9) He then declares: 'Here I come to do Your will.' Thus He abolishes the first cult, in order to establish a new one. (10) And it is because of that will that we are sanctified once for all, by the offering of the body of Jesus Christ. (11) Now every priest stands each day to perform his duties and many times offers the same sacrifices, which yet can never cancel sins. (12) But He, having offered for sins a single sacrifice of everlasting effectiveness, has sat down at the right hand of God, (13) waiting henceforward until His enemies lie before Him as a footstool for His feet. (14) For by one single oblation He has made perfect for ever those whom He sanctifies.*

majority of the LXX manuscripts (Psalm 39[7]), but it is not known whether it is the original reading.[8]

Among the various Jewish sacrifices listed '*thusia*' (= 'blood sacrifice') = '*zebah*'; '*prosphora*' (= 'offering') = '*minhah*; '*hōlokautōma*' (= 'whole burnt offering') = ' '*ôlāh*'; '*peri hamartias*' (= 'sin offering') = '*hattā't*'.

10[7]. '*Kephalis*' means literally: the head of the rod around which a manuscript is rolled, and perhaps also the roll itself. '*Kephalis bibliou*' = 'the roll of the book' or 'a book in the form of a roll'.[9]

10[8], [9a] add nothing new. But v. 9b gives a terse summary of the situation: no compromise is possible between the Jewish cult and that of the new High Priest. The Jewish religion is abolished in order that Christianity may be established.

---

[8] The other Greek translations (Theodotion, Aquila, Symmachus) have '*ōtia*' (= 'ears'), which is the correct translation of ' '*oznayim*', v. ORIGEN, *Hexapla*, ed F. FIELD, II, 1875, p. 151. Some rare manuscripts of the LXX also read '*ōtia*'. The *Vulgate implies the reading* '*sōma*'. Is this the result of corruption due to the carelessness of a copyist who may have repeated the final C of the preceding word '*ēthelēsas*', which would have given CΩTIA, finally emended to CΩMA? Or alternatively, as is claimed by Theodoret of Cyrrhos, could it be the writer of the Epistle to the Hebrews who changed '*ōtia*' to '*sōma*', a reading which may then have slipped into the LXX manuscripts through a concern for harmonization? The question cannot be answered in the present state of our knowledge. But in our Epistle the reading is in no doubt; it is not only attested by all the witnesses, but the author makes it the pivot of his Christological argument. For Theodoret, see *MPG* 82, col. 748 and 83, col. 57.

[9] The expression is almost pleonastic, because all books were in the form of rolls. It may be asked whether '*kephalis*' here is synonymous with '*kephalaion*' (cf. 8[1]), which means the summary of a chapter and finally a chapter. In that case it would be possible to translate: 'in a chapter of the Book'. But whatever the interpretation may be, the identity of the book is unknown (a book of the Torah?). If our author knew the tradition recorded in Luke 4[16ff], it would then be the Book of Isaiah, in which indeed Jesus found predictions concerning Himself. See Isaiah 61[1f]; cf. 58[6].

(15) *The Holy Spirit also bears witness of this to us. For after having said* (16) *'this is the covenant which I shall make with them', the Lord adds 'after those days I shall place my laws in their heart and I shall write them in their minds;* (17) *and never more shall I remember their sins and their transgressions'.* (18) *Now where there has been remission of sins, there is no further sacrifice for sin.*

10¹⁰ confirms our interpretation. Christ offered His body ('*sōma*') in accordance with the will of God ('*thelēma*', v. 7b), in order to consecrate us ('*hagiazein*'), that is to bind us to the body of Christ, as the Apostle Paul would say. As for the last word of v. 10 namely '*ephapax*' (= 'once only', 'once for all'), its importance must not be minimized, for it is considerable. Through it, the author once more underlines the uniqueness of Christ's sacrifice in comparison with those of the old covenant. But more than this. In texts like these Christianity becomes aware of its profound originality, which distinguishes it from the mystery religions, in which the sacrifice of the god is repeated from year to year.

10¹¹, ¹² insist again on the uniqueness and on the effectiveness of the new cult in comparison with the old, but add a curious detail: the priests of the old covenant *stood* before the altar which in a way represents the deity; Christ, in contrast, is *seated* at the right hand of God—an enormous privilege and scandalous to Jewish ears (cf. Mark 14⁶³) and one which even the angels and archangels did not possess.[10]

What will happen between the ascension of Christ and the end of the world? The successive submission of all enemies, according to Psalm 110 already quoted, in which there is precise reference to a High Priest after the order of Melchizedek. Moreover, we know also that this Psalm is quoted by Paul in 1 Corinthians 15²⁸, and for him the Messianic reign of Christ, which prepares the kingdom of the Father through the submission of enemies, becomes effective between the ascension and the parousia.

10¹⁴. '*Teteleiōken*', as always = 'has made perfect', has relieved of the defilement of sin and of bad conscience. '*Hagiazomenoi*' (= 'those who are sanctified') is a synonym for Christians.[11]

10¹⁵⁻¹⁸ give the statute of the new order in the words already quoted from the prophet Jeremiah (31³³);[12] cf. 8¹⁰⁻¹². In the first place the new covenant will be written in our hearts and in our understanding. Consequently, we shall be able to distinguish good and evil, the will of God and the will of the devil, without having recourse to

[10] See 1 and 2 Enoch *passim*.
[11] Only p 46 has '*anasōzomenous*' = 'those who are on the way to salvation'.
[12] '*Marturei hēmin*' = 'bears witness for us', for our instruction (*dativus commodi*). There is no reason to translate as 'to bear witness *with* us', which would require '*sum-marturei hēmin*'.

(19) *Therefore, my brothers, with complete confidence we can enter the approach to the sanctuary by the blood of Jesus.* (20) *This way which is newness and life, He opened for us by permitting us to pass through the veil, I mean the way which has been opened by His flesh.* (21) *And we have a High Priest who has authority in the house of God.* (22) *Let us approach then with a true heart and in full assurance of faith, our hearts purified by sprinkling from an evil conscience and our bodies washed with pure water.*

stringent laws like the Mosaic Law. In the second place, God will remember our sins no more, they will be cancelled. But what is to be thought about sins committed after conversion? Will they be all cancelled? This question is broached, at least partially, in the parenetical passage which begins at v. 19.

The general idea of 10^{19-25} is that since Christians have access to the heavenly sanctuary, they would be wrong not to appreciate this enormous privilege which is bestowed upon them.

10^{19}. '*Parrhēsia eis tēn eisodon*' (lit. 'boldness for entering') is a little strange; '*parrhēsia*' usually connotes an attitude composed of assurance and courage, and is rather strained to be followed by '*eis*'. Either the word must be taken in the intellectual sense, i.e. the certainty of having access, or, more probably, 'the possibility of making our own way confidently along the path opened by Christ'. This path leads to the sanctuary ('*ta hagia*'), the heavenly sanctuary of course. The Christian can present himself before God without the intermediary of the priests or any intercessor other than Christ; His rôle is not only unique, it is qualitatively superior also, because He makes free men of us, relieved of the feeling of guilt, as v. 22 a little further on explains. This way is called '*prosphatos*' ('recent')[13] and '*zōn*' (living'). The first adjective stresses the newness of the Christian solution. If the way is also called living, it is by metonomy, because Christ is the principle of life. So the writer does not go as far as the Gospel of John, which teaches us that Christ Himself is the way, the truth and the life (John 14^6). But in a certain way he has reiterated the same truth.

This way was opened through the veil ('*katapetasma*'), which separated the faithful from the sanctuary. Here a difficulty arises: is it one of the two curtains of the earthly sanctuary that is under discussion or another curtain closing the entry to heaven? The two aspects of the question cannot be separated. It goes without saying that the point here primarily concerns access to the heavenly sanctuary. But the impossibility of access under the old covenant was

---

[13] The derivation of '*prosphatos*' is uncertain. Beware of attempts to turn the word into a verbal adjective from '*pro-sphattō*' (to kill recently?), which would require double 't'. The meaning of '*prosphatos*' is, however, quite clearly 'recent', *v.* ESTIENNE, *Thesaurus, ad verbum.* Theodoret explains '*prosphatēn*' [*sic*] as '*tote prōton phaneisan*' (what first appeared then).

symbolized by the curtains of the Temple, notably by the inner curtain which closed off the Holy of Holies. The writer may have been thinking about the tearing of the veil in the Temple at the moment of Jesus' death, as in Mark 15³⁸ par. It is on these verses that Olaf Moe¹⁴ mainly relies to emphasize, quite rightly, the development in our Epistle of the idea of the universal priesthood. For indeed, all believers have access to the throne of God.

10²⁰. In all the manuscripts the end of v. 20 includes these words: '*tout' estin tēs sarkos autou*' (= 'that is, of His flesh'). They seem to be in apposition to '*katapetasmatos*' as if the flesh were the curtain; this is difficult to accept; for the curtain is a barrier, whilst the earthly life and death of Jesus have bridged the abyss between men and God. It is vain to explain as Riggenbach does (pp. 314f) that the flesh was even so an obstacle between Christ and God; this thinking is foreign to our Epistle. Should we then join this phrase to the verb '*enekainisen*' and translate: 'He opened by His flesh', i.e. by His death ([*sic*] Spicq, p. 316, and many others)? But then it would be necessary to read the dative '*tē sarki*' or at least '*dia tēs sarkos*'. If one is unwilling to admit, as Holsten¹⁵ thinks, that an awkward gloss has entered the text, the genitive '*tēs sarkos autou*' must be taken with '*hodon*'; the author wishes to make it clear that the way was opened and travelled by Christ Himself.

10²¹. Christ has authority in the house of God, understanding by this the heavenly house, whilst Moses (see 3) was merely at the head of the earthly sanctuary.

10²². Exhortations begin here. First of all it is necessary to keep full awareness of the privileges and to behave with the maximum of faith and worthiness fitting to those who hold these privileges. They have and must have an upright heart ('*kardia alēthinē*').¹⁶ '*Plēro-phoria*' is the 'fulness' of faith, which engenders good works in abundance, like a tree which bears much fruit. '*Rhantizō*' = 'to sprinkle', here 'to purify'. Once again the stress is on the good conscience of Christians. But why mention physical purification ('*lelous-menoi to sōma*') by water? It is true that it is not just any sort of water that is meant, but pure and purifying water ('*hudati katharō*'), a kind of holy water, and this seems to constitute an allusion to baptism. But then the reference to the washing of bodies is still more surprising, especially in the light of 1 Peter 3²¹ which rebuts the association of ideas between baptism and physical purification. To overcome the difficulty, we must postulate with Spicq (and at the

¹⁴ *TZ*, 1949, pp. 161ff.

¹⁵ HOLSTEN, *Exegetische Untersuchungen über Hebräer* 10.20, Berne 1875, pp. 11–15.

¹⁶ This expression may contain an allusion to Isaiah 38³, according to RIG-GENBACH, p. 316, note 73. At the beginning of v. 22 we read '*proserchōmetha*', as does Nestlé; '*proserchometha*' is less well attested; among the ancient manuscripts only D gives this reading. In p 46 the indicative is corrected to the subjunctive.

HEH

(23) Let us hold with unyielding attachment to the religion of hope. For He who made promise to us is faithful. (24) Let us watch over one another in order to bring our charity to white heat and to foster our good works. (25) Let us not desert our own assemblies, as is the habit of some, but let us encourage one another, the more so as you see the day draw near. (26) For if we sin deliberately, after we have received knowledge of the truth, there remains no further sacrifice for sin, but only a kind of terrible prospect of judgement, (27) as well as [the approach of] burning anger which must consume the rebels. (28) Suppose that someone flouts the Law of Moses; he will be put to death without pity, on the testimony of two or three witnesses. (29) Then he who has trampled on the Son of God, who has held as of no account the blood of the Covenant by which he was sanctified, who has outraged the spirit of grace, do you not think that he will be judged as deserving a still more severe punishment? (30) For we know who said: 'Vengeance is mine, I will repay', and again 'the Lord will judge His people'. (31) It is a terrible thing to fall into the hands of the living God. (32) But remember the earlier days when after being enlightened you endured a hard struggle accompanied by sufferings; (33) on the one hand, inflicted by insults and persecutions and through them made into a spectacle before the world, and on the other becoming fellow-sufferers with those who were undergoing such treatment. (34) For you also shared in the suffering of the prisoners, and you accepted with joy the spoliation of your belongings, knowing that you were in possession of a better and a lasting heritage. (35) Therefore do not lose your assurance which brings a great reward with it. (36) Indeed you have need of perseverance, in order that after you have done the will of God, you may obtain the object of that promise; for it is a question only of 'a little, of how little time; (37) he who must come will come and will not delay. (38) And my righteous one will live by faithfulness. But if he shrink back, my soul will take no delight in him.' (39) Now, we are not of those who shrink back to perdition, but of those who have faith unto the obtaining of life.

risk of saddening Markus Barth)[17] that the author presumes some spiritual effect from this physical bath. But why does he not say so? Otherwise one might suppose with Riggenbach that the total renewal of the Christian should extend into his physical life. We opt for this explanation which seems to contradict 1 Peter 3[21], but which is in accord with the general tendency of early Christianity, which considered the whole man as the object of the saving providence of God. We are not putting it forward, however, as certain, and we are doubtful whether any completely satisfactory explanation of this passage could be provided.

10[23] and the following verses give more concrete counsel and orders. We must maintain as 'inflexible' ('*aklinē*') the confession of our hope.

[17] See his very interesting work, *Die Taufe ein Sakrament?*, Zurich 1952, and the critical studies in *RTP*, 1953, pp. 20ff (MASSON) and in *RHPR*, 1953, pp. 255ff (HÉRING).

We have already seen that 'our hope' is a way of saying 'our religion'. The 'confession' indicates the content of what we proclaim. We must therefore remain unflinchingly bound to the principles of the Christian hope. It is not a vain hope, for God is faithful to His promises. Cf. 1 Corinthians 10^{13} for the assertion of God's faithfulness, and 3^6 and 3^1 for the meaning of '*elpis*' and of '*homologia*'.

10^{24}. But the Christian should not confine himself to the personal enjoyment of his salvation (as some mystics teach). The faithful show communal responsibility and have a duty to be concerned about the salvation of others. Further, a healthy rivalry should reign in the field of charity and good works.[18]

10^{25}. 'Do not forsake the assemblies, as some do.' We do not know whether it is through fear of the Jews ('*dia ton phobon tōn Ioudaiōn*') or of the pagans or simply through culpable negligence. At first the assemblies took place daily (Acts 2^{46}), later weekly (Acts 20^7).[19] '*Episunagōgē*' means the whole group of Christians met together in assembly. Desertion of the assembly implies also desertion of the Church as such. The expression 'the day' naturally refers to the day of judgement. Christians must not forget that it is near. For the use of '*hēmera*' = 'the day' in the absolute sense and with the same meaning, cf. I Thessalonians 5^4; 1 Corinthians 3^{13}. This usage goes back to the Old Testament; see for example Ezekiel 7$^{10-12}$; 30$^{3-9}$. In the New Testament, the expression '*ekeinē hē hēmera*' = 'that day' is sometimes found, e.g. Matthew 7^{22}; 13^1; 24^{36}.

10^{26}. Exhortations are followed by threats. To a certain category of bad Christians, judgement is announced (v. 27) in the form of a consuming fire, as in Isaiah 26^{11} according to the LXX text,[20] which is an image intended to show how terrible is the wrath. But who are the people so threatened? Modern commentators generally admit that they are apostates, that is to say those who deny Christianity after adhering to it, in full knowledge of what they were doing. At first sight, there is nothing to justify this interpretation. For it is simply a question of those who sin wilfully and not through weakness (as for example the Apostle Peter at the time of his denial). And that is also what was said by Numbers 15^{30}: those who sin 'with a high hand', that is with deliberate intent, are excluded from

[18] '*Parozusmos*' is difficult to translate. This very inflammatory term is rarely used in a good sense as here. It is as if a fever for doing good should infect the faithful (see translation).

[19] It is interesting to note that even PHILO, for whom the cult had primarily an esoteric meaning, nevertheless exhorts the cultured Jews whom he is addressing to be conscientious attenders at synagogue worship, *v. De Migratione Abraham*, §90–92, Chap. 16.

[20] Cf. Deuteronomy 4^{24}; Ezekiel 38^{19}; Zephaniah 1^{18}; Psalm 79^5 (LXX 78^5). Those who have sinned wilfully must be cut off, according to Numbers 15^{30}. But two or three witnesses are necessary, according to Numbers 35^{30} and Deuteronomy 17^6.

the community. In general the Fathers interpreted this text in this
way. Yet on closer examination, the above exegesis can indeed be
supported. The mention of those who desert the assemblies is the
first argument in its favour. For such people are in the process of
turning their backs on Christianity. Then the expression '*hupenan-
tioi*' (= 'opponents', v. 27) confirms that rebels are under discussion.
Similarly in v. 29 the people who hold in contempt the precious blood
of the Eucharist, who insult the Holy Spirit, bring us closer to this
explanation. Finally the parallel with the situation described in
3[7ff] and in 3[15ff], where some rebel like the people in the wilderness,
must not be forgotten. Thus, finally, we come to think that it is
apostasy which is under discussion, and we then understand why the
punishment is so terrible. Such people are not condemned by an
arbitrary decree of God; by excluding themselves from the Christian
community they lose *ipso facto* the benefit of the sacrifice of Christ,
who forgives and atones for sin. Notice also that it is not an opinion
peculiar to our author; some Synoptic texts going back to Jesus
Himself say substantially the same thing. See Mark 8[38] par.[21] The
mortal sin of 1 John 5[16f] also seems to have defection in view.

What happens if the apostate repents? The author does not en-
visage this possibility, because as we saw in **6**, he thinks that in this
case repentance is not possible.

Some details in this passage still require clarification. (V. 26a)
'*Epignōsis*' (= 'knowledge') reminds us that we are not thinking of
people who adhered to Christianity without due consideration and
knowledge. (V. 26b) Why is there no sacrifice left for apostates
('*ouketi apoleipetai thusia*')? It goes without saying that they can no
longer profit from the Jewish sacrifices, which are ineffective any-
way. But our author means something else: he who has excluded
himself from fellowship with Christ, can no longer profit from the
benefits of that sacrifice ('*thusia*' in the singular).

10[27]. '*Ekdochē*' = 'expectation'. Spicq translates this very well by
'prospect'; the question is less of a psychological fact than of an
objective future which is drawing nearer.

10[28-29]. If rebellion against the Law of Moses entailed in certain cases
capital punishment,[22] those who show contempt for Christ must
expect the worst for stronger reasons. It is another example of the
well-known argument *a minore ad maius*, very much in vogue among
the Rabbis, and which had already been used in **2[2]** in order to give
an almost identical proof. The reference to the two or three witnesses
is made as very much of an afterthought, because they figure in the

[21] Remember nevertheless that Jesus forgave Peter his denial, because he
sinned through weakness; he was not guilty of real apostasy.
[22] Idolaters (Deuteronomy 17[2-7]), blasphemers (Leviticus 24[10-16]) and false
prophets (Deuteronomy 18[20]) are those specifically mentioned.

verses in Numbers and Deuteronomy which speak of the execution of a sinner. The expression '*haima tēs diathēkēs*' (= 'blood of the covenant') was of course used in the Old Testament, e.g. Exodus 24[8]. According to Paul (1 Corinthians 11[25]) and Luke (22[20]) Jesus alludes to it. (See our commentary on *The First Epistle of Saint Paul to the Corinthians*, ET London 1962).[23]

10[30] endorses the preceding arguments with two further quotations from Scripture. The first is taken from Deuteronomy 32[35]; but it corresponds to the Masoretic text and not to the LXX, which the author normally quotes.[24] The second text, taken from Deuteronomy 32[36] (= Psalm 135[14] = LXX 134[14]) agrees word for word with the LXX as well as with the Hebrew text.

10[31]. The conclusion given in v. 31 also has the ring of a quotation and is somewhat reminiscent of a word of King David recorded in 2 Samuel 24[14] (LXX 2 Kings): 'let us fall into the hand of the Lord, for his mercy is great; but let me not fall into the hand of man' (likewise 1 Chronicles 21[13], cf. Ecclesiasticus 2[18]). But David had faith in the Lord (Bengel: 'It is a good thing to fall in faith'). Here they are traitors and we can almost hear their cry of anguish.[25]

10[32–34]. Perhaps afraid that he has frightened his readers too much, the author decides to praise them for their conduct in the past and to show them that they can perfectly well expect the heavenly reward, on condition of course that they persevere. '*Tas proteron hēmeras*' gives a rather vague indication of time, viz. 'the past days', in which the recipients of the letter fought a good fight ('*athlēsin*'). They feared neither the persecutions nor the shame with which they themselves were afflicted, nor the reprisals to which they might expose themselves because of the care given to Christian prisoners. Moreover, they accepted not only with resignation but with joy

---

[23] '*En hō hēgiasthē*' is absent from A, but seems necessary for the development of the thought. This remark indicates how the Christian has been bound to the Church. Yet there is no need to see in it an allusion to the Eucharist.

[24] The Hebrew text says 'vengeance is mine, I will repay' (as here). The LXX texts give '*en hēmera ekdikēseōs antapodōsō*' ('in a day of vengeance I will repay'). The text as read in our Epistle can also be found in the Samaritan Pentateuch, see BENJAMIN BLAYNEY, *Pentateuchus Hebraeo-Samaritanus*, Oxford 1790, p. 529 (*ad* Genesis 32[35]). The Apostle Paul (Romans 12[19]) also quotes like our author. The Hebrew text is quoted too exactly for us to think of it as a quotation 'from memory' from the LXX. So the impression takes shape that at this point the author had the Hebrew text before him (an unusual thing), or that he quoted from a Greek version other than the LXX. Furthermore, it would be *a priori* quite astonishing if all Jews in the whole Roman Empire (and beyond) should have always had for all the books of the Old Testament the same version, as is often rather thoughtlessly assumed. Even Philo's text is far from agreeing always with our text of the LXX. See PETER KATZ, *Philo's Bible*, Cambridge University Press 1950. Moreover, PHILO also uses the expression 'day of vengeance', see *Legum Allegoriae*, III, §35, Chap. 34.

[25] In connexion with v. 31, Slavonic Enoch 39.8 should be compared.

('*meta charas*') the loss of their possessions; the spoliation of the goods of condemned people, which threw their families into want, was a common thing among the Romans and perhaps also among the Jews. But Christians know that the eternal good things cannot be taken from them, as Luther's hymn restates at a later date: '*Das Reich muss uns doch bleiben*'.

Details: '*Phōtisthentes*' = 'after having been enlightened', seems to be an allusion to baptism, but especially to its effect, namely the giving of the Holy Spirit. '*Athlēsis*' ('struggle', v. 32) recalls the description of the Christian as an athlete of the faith, which gradually became widespread in the Church. '*Theatrizomenoi*' (v. 33) can be compared with '*theatron egenēthēmen*' in 1 Corinthians 4⁹, 'to be made a public spectacle', but this does not necessarily imply an allusion to a violent death in the arena. At all events the victims must have felt as though they were being pilloried.[26] '*Anastrephomai*' (v. 33), a passive form with middle sense = 'to conduct oneself'. '*Thlipsis*' = 'persecution' (v. 33), as in John 16³³; Acts 20²³; 2 Corinthians 1⁴, ⁸; 6⁴; Revelation 7¹⁴. '*Huparxis*' like '*huparchonta*' = 'goods' (v. 34).

10³⁵, ³⁶. The need for endurance ('*hupomonē*'), which is one of the cardinal Christian virtues; cf. James 1²⁻⁴ and 2 Peter 1⁵⁻⁷. How can the Christian 'lose' ('*apoballō*') assurance ('*parrhēsia*')? In many ways. By being lukewarm (see v. 24 above), and in a general way by a refusal to persevere in the right attitude. The author implicitly gives his addressees some grounds for thinking that they still have this assurance.

10³⁷⁻³⁹ quote words which are essentially promises and words of comfort, see Isaiah 26²⁰; Habakkuk 2³⁻⁴. The coming of God will not therefore be a cause for fear but of hope for those who persevere. And according to Habakkuk 2⁴: 'My righteous one shall live by faithfulness.'[27] It is probable that the author was thinking not about

---

[26] D alone gives '*oneidizomenoi*' ('insulted') for '*theatrizomenoi*'. In v. 34 it is necessary to choose between several readings: (a) '*desmois*', p 46, the ψ manuscript of the LXX, and Origen; (b) '*desmiois*', the Western Text, as well as A and 33; (c) '*desmois mou*', S, Byzantine Text; (d) '*desmois autōn*', two MSS of the old Latin. Nestlé, whom we have followed, adopted (b). But (a) is equally well attested.

[27] Must we read '*dikaios mou ek pisteōs zēsetai*' as Nestlé does, along with p 46, the so-called Alexandrine text and the Clementine Vulgate? Or '*dikaios ek pisteōs mou zēsetai*', as in D and the Syriac versions? Or '*ho dikaios ek pisteōs zēsetai*', with p 13 and the Byzantine Text? Or even '*ho dikaios ek pisteōs autou zēsetai*' as does TERTULLIAN, who gives '*vivit fide sua*' (*v. De exhortatione castitatis* 7, *CSEL* 70, p. 138)? The LXX of Habakkuk 2⁴ (at least in the Rahlfs edition, which follows the B manuscript) gives '*ho dikaios ek pisteōs mou zēsetai*'. On the other hand the Hebrew text reads like Tertullian 'by *his* faithfulness ('*be'emûnāṭô*'). The Apostle Paul in Romans 1¹⁷ says '*ho dikaios ek pisteōs zēsetai*'. We have accepted the Nestlé text, but we would make no issue of it.

the faithfulness of God, but about that of 'the men of faith' (*'esmen ... pisteōs'*). They will inherit life (*'psuchē'*), that is eternal life.[28]

Having arrived at the end of this fine chapter, we cannot but admire the exemplary skill with which the author manages, we will not say to juxtapose, but to link into an organic whole the theoretical and the parenetical parts of his homily. He seems to have understood that a purely dogmatic sermon runs the risk of wearying his congregation, whilst a purely moralizing homily runs the risk of boring them and, a rather more serious point, of concealing from them the fundamental facts of the revelation from which the principles and power of the new life derive.

---

[28] As nearly always, *'psuchē'* has the sense of 'life' (cf. RIGGENBACH); see also XENOPHON, *Cyropaedia*, IV, 4.10: *'tas psuchas peripoiēsasthe'* = 'you have saved your lives' (ed TEUBNER, 1912, p. 191); ISOCRATES, Letter 2, To Philip, I, Chap. 7: *'dia to peripoiēsai tēn hautou psuchēn'* = 'because he preserved his life' (Loeb ed); cf. also Luke 21[19] and 1 Thessalonians 5[9].

CHAPTER XI

THIS CHAPTER is certainly the most popular of the whole Epistle. It has been the inspiration of innumerable sermons. In it, faith is exalted not as one virtue among others, but as the cardinal Christian virtue, or to put it in a better way, as an orientation of our whole life which will give a new purpose, and which alone can obtain, if not miracles like those granted to the people of old, at least certain entrance into the promised land. It should be noted, however, that we must not presuppose here some aspects assumed by the notion of faith in the work of the Apostle Paul. Here it is not contrasted with works, nor, in a general way, intended to make 'justification' possible. Indeed, *'pistis'* in this Epistle is turned less to the past (*faith* in the work performed by Jesus Christ) than to the future, and comes very close to what is elsewhere called hope (*'elpis'*). If we wish to look for parallels in the Pauline Epistles, it is the faith of Abraham which provides them rather than that of the Christian. Sometimes, however, *'pistis'* assumes still another shade of meaning; it can signify a *belief*, for example the belief that God exists and that He is the creator.

As for the examples of men of faith, the author draws them from the Bible, that is from the history of Israel. All this does not mean that the sermon is the writer's own free composition. Semitisms are quite numerous and can give rise to the supposition that he used a Jewish Midrash which eulogized the devout men of the past. For the sake of comparison Ecclesiasticus 44–50 may be cited. But by giving particular stress to the rôle of faith, he gives a Christian tone to the whole panegyric.

(1) *Faith is the guarantee of the good things hoped for, the proof of the existence of invisible realities.* (2) *Through this faith the men of old received a good reputation.* (3) *By faith [alone] we understand that the worlds were fashioned by the Word of God, so that creation did not come forth from the world of appearances.* (4) *It was because he had faith that the sacrifice offered by Abel took on a greater value than*

11¹. *'Hupostasis'*, as in **1³** = 'essence', 'substance'.[1] In hyperbolic language, which highlights the Christian's absolute certainty that

---

[1] JEROME: *'possessio'*, *MPL* 26, col. 420. Peshitta: 'assurance' (*'pîsâ'*). Riggenbach: 'steadfast expectation'. Erasmus, Zwingli, E. Ménégoz: 'solid confidence'. In what matters, these renderings amount to the same thing. THEODORET, however, takes *'hupostasis'* in the sense of *'opsis'*, i.e. visual anticipation, *MPG* 82, col. 757. Cf. also R. E. WITT, *'Hupostasis'*, in *Amicitiae Corolla, Essays presented to Rendel Harris*, 1933, pp. 319–343. The commentators are agreed on the sense of *'elengchos'* as 'proof' or 'demonstration'.

Cain's. Because of it he received the reputation of being a righteous man. It was God Himself who gave favourable approval of his offerings, and it is through his faith that he still speaks even though he is dead. (5) Through faith Enoch was carried away [to heaven] so that he did not see death, and he was not found, because God had carried him away. For even before he was taken he had gained the reputation that he pleased God. (6) Now, without faith it is impossible to please [God]; for anyone who approaches God must believe that He exists and that He rewards those who seek Him with perseverance. (7) Through faith, Noah after receiving a warning about events still hidden, was seized with a holy fear, and built an ark for the saving of his household. And by his faith, he condemned the world and became heir of the righteousness which comes through faith. (8) Through faith Abraham obeyed the call to set out towards a country which he should receive as an inheritance and he went out not knowing whither he was going. (9) Because of his faith he settled in the promised land like a foreigner, living in tents, with Isaac and Jacob, joint heirs of the same promise. (10) For he was waiting for a city which has true foundations, whose architect and builder is God. (11) It was also through faith that Sarah herself, who was barren, received power to give birth to offspring, and this when she had passed the age; for she believed the one who had promised was faithful. (12) Therefore from one man—and from a man on the threshold of death—descendants were born 'as numerous as the stars in heaven or the countless grains of sand on the seashore'.

the divine promises will be fulfilled, the writer declares that faith already grasps the substance of what is promised. '*Elengchos*' = 'demonstration'. Faith takes the place of a proof of 'things' ('*pragmata*'), that is, as always, invisible realities which are not rationally demonstrable. The parallelism of this short strophe is yet not quite perfect. The '*elpizomena*' (= 'things hoped for') do not yet exist, whereas the '*ou blepomena*' (= 'things not seen') are the invisible world which is present in the beyond. The opposition between the visible and the invisible worlds, taken up again in v. 3, is in keeping with Platonism and Philonism. But what is totally lacking in these latter philosophical conceptions is the hope of the world 'to come', upon which our writer lays such particular stress.

11². The verb '*emarturēthēsan*' has, of course, the passive sense = 'they received attestation'.

11³. Before proceeding to the list of the heroes of ancient times, the Epistle states a very interesting theological thesis: if we did not have faith, we might believe that the visible world is eternal, and that the world of appearances (again a Platonic expression!) could in some degree be explained by itself. It is exactly the position of St Thomas Aquinas, who decides for the doctrine of a non-eternal world only because it is shown by revelation, that is to say by faith, as our writer says.

11⁴. Here begins the impressive review of the men of faith. They could be called martyrs, not only because they bore witness to the truth, but also because, by their faith and way of life, they often became the victims of God's enemies. The first 'martyr' (cf. Matthew 23³⁵) was Abel (Genesis 4⁴ff). Why did his sacrifice please God in contrast with that of his brother? Because he had faith. The idea that his blood still speaks after his death, is drawn from Genesis 4¹⁰. Analogous ideas about the blood of the martyrs 'accusing' can be found also in Revelation 6¹⁰ and Enoch 47¹.²

11⁵⁻⁶. Enoch was a figure who is known to have inspired a whole literature in late Judaism. There are notably several books which glorify him and which were even in part attributed to him.³ Together with the prophet Elijah, he is the only case in sacred history of a man who did not die. Our Epistle does not stray from the sober statements of Genesis 5. '*Misthapodotēs*' = 'he who grants a suitable reward'. '*Metatithēmi*' here is a technical term for raising to heaven. '*Euareskō*' = 'to please', 'to be approved'.

11⁷. Noah gave heed to the divine warnings (Genesis 6¹³⁻²²), at a time when nothing foreshadowed the catastrophe. '*Chrēmatistheis*' again has the passive sense of 'having received an oracle', i.e. a message or warning (cf. 8⁵). '*Eulabeia*' does not have the same meaning as in 5. Here the word is used in a good sense as 'fear of the Lord', 'holy fear'. But how can it be declared that he condemned the world? He condemned it morally by highlighting its lack of faith. But were the others warned? In any event the building of the ark should have attracted their attention. But there is more to it than that. According to a tradition apparently referred to in 2 Peter 2⁵ ('*Nōe dikaiosunēs kēruka*'), Noah preached to his contemporaries, who did not listen to him and who, therefore, had no excuse.⁴

---

² NAIRNE, *The Epistle of Priesthood*, 1913, recalls at this point the following passage from PHILO: *Quod deterius potiori insidiari soleat*, §48, Chap. 70. But we have been unable to find anything characteristic there. BLASS emends '*pleiona*' to '*hēdiona*' in 11⁴.

Instead of '*marturountos epi tois dōrois tou theou*' (the Nestlé text, which we have retained), S*, A and P* read '*marturountos epi tois dōrois autou tō theō*'. This would mean: 'because he (Abel) bore witness to God by (?) his gifts'. An interesting reading, but one which implies an unusual sense for the preposition '*epi*'.

³ Apart from the books called 1 Enoch and 2 Enoch (see Bibliography), mention must also be made of the book published by H. ODEBERG under the title *3rd Enoch*, Cambridge 1928. In it the patriarch is identified with a remarkable emanation from God called Metatron.

⁴ Some scholars even see a reference to Noah's preaching in the well-known but difficult text of 1 Peter 3¹⁹, holding that it was the pre-existing Christ who preached through the mouth of Noah. On this subject, see the commentary by JEAN MONNIER on the 1st Epistle of Peter, Paris 1899, and that of E. G. SELWYN, London 1946.

Noah obtains here what Paul allows to Abraham, namely righteousness through faith. The phrase '*mēdepō blepomena*' ('things
not yet seen'), which the writer uses here must refer, not to future
aeons but to earthly events which are yet to take place.

11⁸. Abraham is again one of the greatest heroes of faith, namely of
faith in the future and more exactly in the divine promises which
concern him. They relate first of all to the promised land, and secondly
to the patriarch's innumerable posterity. '*Exelthein*' = 'to go out',
to leave one's native land, could be taken with '*hupēkousen*' = 'he
obeyed' so as to set out. But it is more natural to take this infinitive
with '*kaloumenos*': he was called to go out. 'A man is never greater
than when he knows not whither he goeth,' as Oliver Cromwell
might have said.⁵ Abraham went out into the unknown ('the land
which I will show you'), because he trusted the divine promises. Yet
the notion of the promised land remains ambiguous. In the first place,
it is Palestine, and from some definite time Abraham knew this (*v.*
Genesis 13¹⁵; 15¹⁸). He lived there modestly as a stranger and as a
wanderer; '*paroikeō*' = 'to live on the fringe of the population', as
an immigrant in some respects. But the promised land is also the
heavenly homeland, as v. 10 shows. The first is obviously a prefiguration of the second. The heavenly city lasts; it has foundations, that
is to say foundations which really deserve the name ('*tous themelious*'),
because it was built by God.⁶

11¹¹. A cross which is frankly too heavy for expositors to bear is
presented in this verse. Sarah is abruptly introduced only to disappear again to leave the ground clear for Abraham alone. But what
is much more curious and even inconceivable is that she is credited,
thanks to her faith, with an act which is specifically masculine,
namely '*katabolē spermatos*' ('*emissio seminis*'). It is unhelpful to say
that the medical thinking of some Rabbis ascribed to the woman a
relatively active rôle in conception;⁷ this is one of those happy
refuges which H. J. Holtzmann called 'a nice little discovery of the
exegetes', for the Greek expression is only used of men. The simplest

---

⁵ SIR CHARLES FIRTH, 'Oliver Cromwell and the rule of the Puritans in England', *The World's Classics*, no. 536, p. 471.
⁶ See Isaiah 33²⁰; Psalm 87¹ (LXX 86¹); Revelation 21¹⁴, ¹⁹; 4 Esdras 10²⁷.
PHILO, *De Praemiis*, §150, Chap. 6, speaks of the frailty of earthly cities, following
the contemplation of the ruins of ancient cities, from which one might doubt
whether they had ever been inhabited.
⁷ Talmud Nidda, 31a (GOLDSCHMIDT, XII, 442) speaks only of the woman's
part in the forming of a child. The texts of Lactantius and Theophylact which are
sometimes quoted (*v.* SPICQ, p. 349), prove nothing so far as Judaism is concerned.
The Vulgate translates it '*conceptionem seminis*', which is a false meaning if one
sticks to the text. CHRYSOSTOM, *MPG* 63, col. 162, rightly says '*nenekrōmenou*',
but explains '*eis katabolēn*' thus: '*eis to kataschein eis sperma, eis hupodochēn
dunamin elaben hē nenekrōmenē, hē steira*' ('to gain seed, she who was dead, the
barren woman, received power for its reception').

(13) *All these died under the rule of faith, not having received the fulfilment of the promises, but seeing them and greeting them from afar, confessing that they were only strangers and travellers on the earth.* (14) *Indeed, those who speak thus show thereby that they are [still] in search of a country.* (15) *And if they had intended to refer to the one they had left, they would have had time to return to it.* (16) *But in fact they are longing for a better country, that is a heavenly one. Therefore God is not ashamed to be called* their God: *for He has prepared for them a city.* (17) *Thanks to his faith Abraham, when put to the test, offered up Isaac and was thus going to sacrifice his only son, and yet he had taken the promises seriously and to him it had been said: 'Through Isaac a posterity shall be raised up for you.'* (18) *For he said to himself that God is powerful enough to resurrect someone even from the dead.* (19) *That is why he brought him back from the dead, as a prefiguration.* (20) *It was also through faith that Isaac gave a blessing to Jacob and Esau about the future.* (21) *By faith Jacob, before he died, blessed each of the sons of Joseph and bowed himself [as he leaned] on the top of his staff.* (22) *Through faith Joseph, at the end of his life, made mention of the exodus of the children of Israel and gave instructions about what to do with his bones.* (23) *By faith, Moses was hidden for three months after his birth by his parents. For they saw that he was a fine child, and they did not fear the king's edict.* (24) *By faith Moses, when he was grown up, refused to be called the son of Pharaoh's daughter,* (25) *preferring to be ill-treated with the people of God rather than enjoy a life of sin for a time.* (26) *He valued the reproach of Christ more than the treasures of Egypt; for he had his eyes fixed on the reward.* (27) *By faith he left Egypt without fear of*

solution would be to strike out the name of Sarah as an interpolation. A perfectly coherent text would then be obtained: Abraham, who received the power to beget, is the same who had received the promises mentioned in v. 12. He it was who was close to death and who, in a general way, is the subject of the whole section 11⁸⁻²⁰. But if one is unwilling to subscribe to this severing of the Gordian knot, another sense must be given to '*katabolē*', something like 'to create a posterity'. One might also consider emending '*katabolē*' to '*katalabē*', a noun which might signify 'reception' or 'conception'. But it is doubtful whether this noun, rare in any case, ever in fact assumed this sense (*v.* Estienne's *Thesaurus*).

11¹². '*Nenekrōmenos*' = lit. 'someone who had died', a hyperbole here for someone who was near to death. The end of v. 12 contains a quotation from Genesis 22¹⁷; cf. Genesis 15⁵; 32¹³; Exodus 32¹³ and Deuteronomy 3³⁶ (LXX only).

11¹³. '*Kata pistin apethanon*' does not mean of course that they died because of their faith; this would have required '*pistei*' or better '*dia pisteōs*', but 'in a state of faith', 'under the rule of faith', which

*the king's anger, and held firm like a man who could see the Invisible
One. (28) By faith he observed the Passover and performed the sprinkling of the blood, so that the destroyer should not touch their firstborn.
(29) By faith they crossed the Red Sea as on dry land—whilst the
Egyptians in their attempt were engulfed. (30) By faith the walls of
Jericho crumbled after they had been encircled on seven consecutive
days. (31) By faith Rahab the harlot did not perish with the unbelievers;
because she had welcomed the spies peaceably. (32) And what shall I
say more? For I should not have time, if I wished to tell about Gideon,
Barak, Samson, Jephthah, David, Samuel and the prophets, (33) who,
through faith, fought victoriously against kingdoms, and exercised
justice, obtained the fulfilment of promises, stopped the mouths of
lions, (34) quenched the power of fire, escaped the edge of the sword,
regained vigour after sickness, became strong in battle, and put to
flight enemy armies. (35) Women received back their dead through
resurrection. Others suffered the torture of the wheel, spurning deliver-
ance, in order to obtain a better resurrection. (36) Others underwent the
trial of indignities and of scourgings, of chains and imprisonment. (37)
They were stoned; sawn in pieces; put to death by the sword. They
went from place to place clothed in sheepskins and goatskins. They
were despoiled, persecuted, ill-treated. (38) The world was not worthy
of them. (39) They wandered about [taking refuge] in deserts, in mountains, in caves and holes in the ground; and yet all of them, while
receiving a good reputation because of their faith, did not harvest the
fulfilment of the promises. (40) For God foresaw something finer for
us, so that they should not enter into perfection without us.*

hopes without having seen or touched. The expression 'to see and
greet from afar' echoes the text of Deuteronomy 3^{25-27}, where Moses
sees the promised land from the summit of a mountain.[8]

11^{14-15} drop the form of prefiguration and openly assert that the
patriarchs were seeking the heavenly Jerusalem as in v. 16.

11^{16}. '*Epaischunomai*' = lit. 'to be ashamed'. Why should God have
hesitated to have Himself called 'their God'? Undoubtedly because
He is the one universal God. But it goes without saying that as in the
Apostle Paul's writings, Christians of every nation are all heirs to the
promises made to 'the people'.

---

[8] PHILO, *De Specialibus Legibus*, IV, 17, refers to mariners who shouted a
greeting to the land which was in sight (according to SPICQ, II, p. 350, to whom
we owe the reference). In *De Migratione Abraham*, §43, Chap. 9, PHILO extols the
patient hope of Abraham as a sign of faith, just as this Epistle does. But in other
passages, too long to be quoted here, it can be clearly seen that for him, the
heavenly country is the suprasensible world, the dwelling place of the soul in its
pre-existence—an idea which does not figure in the Epistle to the Hebrews. See
De Confusione Linguarum, §76–82, Chap. 17; *De Agricultura*, §64f, Chap. 14;
Quis Rerum, etc., §267, Chap. 54.

11¹⁷⁻¹⁸. The sacrifice of Isaac. What is most terrible in the eyes of the ancients, is not so much the obligation to violate a father's affection, although this point is strikingly made in Genesis 22⁷⁻⁸, as the prospect of losing one's posterity and of seeing the collapse of the faith in God, who would have gone back on His promises.

11¹⁹ can be interpreted in two ways. '*Ek nekrōn egeirein*' can (and it is the universally accepted exegesis) allude to the hope of a resurrection for Isaac. But it is possible that the idea is even more paradoxical and grandiose. He knew that God can raise up a posterity even from the dead ('*sperma*' = 'posterity' here). According to Matthew 3⁸ par., God can even raise up children for Abraham 'from these stones' ('*ek tōn lithōn toutōn*'). This is what makes us incline towards the above explanation, although we do not claim it as proven. The imperfect '*prospheren*' (v. 17) simply expresses intention. Abraham was preparing to ... was going to ...; this sense is quite suitable here. '*Komizein*' is used for 'to receive', hence 'to bring back' a dead person. '*En parabolē*' = 'through' or 'in a likeness', which means that the story is a prefiguration, probably of the death and resurrection of Christ.

11²⁰. Cf. Genesis 27²⁸⁻²⁹. According to this narrative, the blessing of Jacob by Isaac was the result of Jacob's trickery. But the writer of Genesis 27 records it with satisfaction, because he believes it to be in accordance with God's will. Our writer takes into account Jacob's faith, presumably because that is what ensured the effectiveness of the blessing.

11²¹ deals with the blessing of Ephraim and Manasseh by Jacob, see Genesis 48¹⁴⁻¹⁶. The quotation is from the LXX, but it is probably the result of a translator's error and gives a slightly unacceptable sense. Before whom did Jacob prostrate himself? Before God, of course. The mention of the top of the staff ('*epi to akron tēs rhabdou autou*') could only mean that he was leaning on it, but the sense is quite awkward. One might at a pinch think of a pilgrim's staff, or of an invalid's stick, upon the head of which a man might lean,⁹ but can '*proskuneō*' have this meaning?

11²². Cf. Genesis 50²⁴⁻²⁵. Joseph trusted the divine promises which assigned Palestine to his descendants; he had no doubts about their returning there. Therefore he was able to give instructions about moving his bones.¹⁰

⁹ The Masoretic text says that he prostrated himself on the head of his bed. This is not very clear either. But it might be supposed that he did it through weakness. The Hebrew text gives '*hammiṭṭāh*' = 'the bed', but the LXX seems to have read '*hammaṭṭeh*' = 'the staff'.
¹⁰ The moving of bones is in no way surprising. When decomposition was complete, it was usual to collect the bones in order to give them final burial. See K. BORNHÄUSER, *Die Gebeine der Toten*, Gütersloh 1921.

11²³. The examples drawn from the story of Moses begin here. This verse, however, deals rather with the faith of his parents. Exodus 2²⁻³ speaks only of the mother, but Josephus also speaks of both parents.[11] '*Pateres*' = '*goneis*' = 'parents'. '*Paidion*' here = 'a very young child', a 'baby' (Spicq). '*Asteios*' = 'beautiful', 'pretty', presumably has the natural sense, without our being obliged to think of his intellectual or moral qualities.

11²⁴⁻²⁶. These and the following verses deal with an act of faith of Moses himself. After his adoption by a daughter of the Pharaoh, who had found him (Exodus 2¹⁰), he could have led a distinguished carefree life, on condition that he renounced his people and his religion. But he preferred fellowship with his own ill-treated people to the treasures of Egypt. '*Sunkakoucheisthai*' occurs here only in biblical literature, though there is no difficulty about the sense, viz. 'to be ill-treated along with'. The expression 'the reproach of Christ' ('*ton oneidismon tou Christou*') is set in heavy type by Nestlé, as though it were a quotation. But it does not occur in the Old Testament, which is aware only of the reproach incurred by the people. The reference to Christ is, of course, due to the pen of our author, who sees in the suffering of the people a prefiguration of or an allusion to the suffering of Christ.[12]

11²⁷. Through faith he left Egypt. Siding with Calvin against Luther (*Gloses*), we hold that this deals with the Exodus and not with his flight to the land of Midian (Exodus 2¹⁵), which was motivated by fear alone, a contradiction of what this verse affirms.[13] By what right can it be said that he saw '*ton aoraton*' = 'the Invisible One', i.e. God? It is presumably an allusion to the revelation of the deity in the Burning Bush (Exodus 3²). It is true that the text speaks only of the appearance of 'the angel of the Lord'; but from v. 4 onwards it is indeed the Lord who is present and who speaks to Moses. As this appearance, which confirmed his faith, occurred before the Exodus, it can support Calvin's interpretation. '*Kartereō*' is intransitive, = 'he persevered', 'he held firm'. If a transitive force could be supported, a possible translation would be 'he remained firmly bound to God'; he clung in some way to Him.

[11] PHILO, *De Vita Mosis*, I, §9, Chap. 2, makes a passing reference to the parents. Similarly JOSEPHUS, *Antiquities of the Jews*, II, §217f, Chap. 9.4. According to the Priestly Code (Exodus 6²⁰), his parents were called Amram and Jochebed.

[12] Psalm 89⁵¹ (LXX 88⁵¹) speaks of 'the reproach of Thy servants'. Our author may have seen in all the servants of God, and not merely in the one of Isaiah 53, a prefiguration of Christ. But this is doubtful.

[13] Luther has none the less some eminent predecessors and successors among exegetes. CHRYSOSTOM had already remarked: 'So even his flight was an act of faith' ('*hōste kai to phugein pisteōs ēn*'). His great temptation would have been to plunge headlong into danger and say, 'I will see if God saves me' ('*idō ei sōzei me ho theos*', *MPG* 63, col. 181f). Cf. Bengel, Moffatt, Windisch, Michel. On the other hand, Calvin's interpretation is accepted by Grotius, who says so in connexion with Exodus 10²⁸ᶠ, and also by Bleek, Riggenbach, Bonsirven, etc.

11²⁸. The celebration of the Passover took place before the departure from Egypt. This creates a slight inversion, which should not, however, disturb us. Later Gideon is likewise named before Barak. '*Poiein to pascha*' (lit. = 'to make the Passover') is another Semitism, a literal rendering of the Aramaic verb ' '*aḇaḏ*'; the usual Greek expression is '*thuein to pascha*' (lit. = 'to sacrifice the Passover'). The rite is described in Exodus 12⁵⁻²⁴. '*Ho olothreuōn*' = 'the destroyer': often it is an angel of death, as for example in 2 Samuel (LXX 2 Kings) 24¹⁵⁻¹⁷; 1 Chronicles 21¹⁴⁻¹⁷; cf. the angels of destruction in Revelation 14¹⁷ᶠ and 16. However, according to Exodus 12²³ the Lord Himself struck down the first-born of Egypt.

11²⁹. The crossing of the Red Sea, v. Exodus 14²¹ᶠᶠ. '*Peiran lambanein*' = 'to make an attempt'. It is known that the Egyptians too attempted the crossing, but were 'engulfed' ('*katepothēsan*'). Cf. the triumph song of Miriam, Exodus 15¹⁻²¹. God performed the miracle, but the faith of Israel was shown in its courage.

11³⁰. The walls of Jericho (cf. Joshua 6) did not fall by pure magic. The faith of Israel played a decisive part in the event, according to our Epistle.

11³¹. Rahab (Joshua 2) welcomed the spies because apparently she had faith in the future of the Israelite people. '*Pornē*' can mean hardly anything other than 'harlot', and there is no point in weakening the sense of the word as do the Talmud and Nicholas of Lyre, who call her an 'innkeeper'.[14] Faith, therefore, can save even pagans and persons of evil reputation. In fact Rahab has even been regarded as an ancestor of Jesus Christ according to Matthew 1⁵. According to St Augustine,[15] Rahab was a prefiguration of the salvation of pagans. '*Met' eirēnēs*' (= 'peaceably') implies that she could have denounced the spies, if not killed them.

In **11³²⁻³⁴**, rather than weary his readers, the writer limits himself to listing the heroes and speaks of them all together. For Gideon, see Judges 6–8, for Barak, Judges 4–5, for Samson, Judges 13–16, for Jephthah, Judges 11–12. Texts concerning David and Samuel are too numerous to be given. The reference to the 'prophets' is presumably aimed primarily at Elijah, Elisha, Jeremiah and perhaps Amos, Hosea and still others.

---

[14] For Nicolas, see vol. VI, p. 157, Bâle 1506. For legends concerning Rahab, cf. GINZBERG, *The Legends of the Jews*, Philadelphia 1946, vol. 4, p. 5 and vol. 6, p. 171, note 12. According to some Talmudic texts, Joshua even married Rahab, see Talmud Meggilah 14b (GOLDSCHMIDT, IV, p. 60). But according to Matthew 1⁵, her husband was called Salmon.

[15] *MPL* 49, col. 540.

11³³. Who conquered kings? Certainly the Judges, and David; Samuel too, perhaps, for he condemned Saul and thus instigated his downfall. 'Exercised justice' ('*ergazesthai*' is another Semitism arising from ' '*abad*') is a very general expression, which could apply not only to the Judges, but to David and Samuel also, as well as to all the dutiful kings. The phrase 'to obtain the fulfilment of promises' may bring Joshua 21⁴¹⁻⁴³ to mind, but it is a reminder too of the providential help received by prophets such as Elijah, according to 1 Kings (LXX 3 Kings) 17⁴,⁹; 18¹ and elsewhere. The lions are probably an allusion to Samson in Judges 14⁶ and to David in 1 Samuel (LXX 1 Kings) 17³⁴⁻³⁷; to Benaiah in 2 Samuel (LXX 2 Kings) 23²⁰ and to Daniel in Daniel 6²³ and 1 Maccabees 2⁶⁰.

11³⁴. The fire reminds us of the three young Jews in the burning fiery furnace, of Daniel 3⁴⁹ᶠ (LXX) and I Maccabees 2⁵⁹. People saved from the sword are many; but perhaps we should think of the story told in the Book of Esther, in which the whole Jewish people living in Persia was saved from extermination. For miraculous cures, see the illness of King Hezekiah in Isaiah 38. If '*astheneia*' is taken as referring in a more general way to 'weaklings', to whom God gave strength, we may also think of Judith (Judith 13⁷ᶠ) or of David's combat with Goliath (1 Samuel [LXX 1 Kings] 17). '*Parembolē*' can mean any kind of 'entrenchment', but sometimes quite simply an army. Texts on this subject can be found in Judges 4¹⁵ᶠ and in the Books of Maccabees. '*Allotrioi*' = 'enemies'; '*klinein*' = 'to cause to bend' or 'to put to flight'. These few words could be applied to the cases of many of the Judges and Kings and notably also to the Maccabees in their struggles against the Syrians. In any case it can be seen that faith can work miracles even in the military realm.

11³⁵ᵃ must remind us of the resurrection of the son of the widow of Zarephath by Elijah, in 1 Kings (LXX 3 Kings) 17¹⁷⁻²⁴, and that of the Shunnamite's son by Elisha in 2 Kings (LXX 4 Kings) 4³²⁻³⁷. In **11³⁵ᵇ** we find examples more especially selected from the history of the persecutions by Antiochus Epiphanes. Thus Eleazar (2 Maccabees 6¹⁹) could have avoided death, if he had consented to be a traitor. '*Tumpanon*' lit. = 'drum', suggests something like torture on the wheel.[16] '*Anastasis kreittōn*' = 'a better resurrection' in contrast with fleeing from death, which would have allowed the martyrs to 'return to life'. Their resurrection was certain and better.

11³⁶. For insults and tortures, see the story of Jeremiah (Jeremiah 20; 37¹⁵, LXX: 44¹⁵), of Michaiah (1 Kings [LXX 3 Kings] 22²⁴⁻²⁷), of Hanani (2 Chronicles 16¹⁰), and again the persecutions in Seleucid times.

As is well known, stoning was a punishment inflicted by the Jewish authorities. The case of the prophet Zechariah, 2 Chronicles

[16] See Wetstein, II, p. 430.

24^{20f} can be cited, and perhaps that of Jeremiah according to a tradition recorded by Tertullian.[17] Torture by the saw was inflicted on the prophet Isaiah by King Manasseh according to several Jewish sources, notably the Babylonian Talmud,[18] and also the Ascension of Isaiah, a Jewish writing re-edited by Christians (5^{1-14}).[19]

In connexion with 'death by the sword' (lit. 'by the mouth of the sword', which is a Semitism derived from '*lepi ḥereḇ*'), it is not out of place to think of some of the prophets. The death of Uriah, according to Jeremiah 26^{23}, could especially be cited. We do not think that the author intended a reference to John the Baptist (whom he never mentions elsewhere)—even if the writer of the Epistle were Apollos.

11[37]. Who were the hunted people, who clothed themselves in animal skins, hiding in deserts and caves? First and foremost, Elijah and Elisha; to some extent David also, who according to 1 Samuel 21–27 had to 'go underground' and live in caves; also, no doubt, the resistance groups of the Maccabean period who lived in the same way.

11[38]. The statement '*hōn ouk ēn axios ho kosmos*', which means 'of whom the world was not worthy', deserves a comment. For a long time Semitists, Bolten[20] among them, have, in connexion with Matthew $10^{11, 13}$, called attention to the fact that the rendering of '*axios*' by 'worthy' is a mis-translation; it would carry the suggestion that the disciples should lodge only with 'good' families, who would be worthy of them. In fact '*axios*' seems to be a mistaken translation of '*zākāh*' which sometimes means 'worthy', but sometimes 'generous' or 'hospitable'. Obviously the second sense is the one suitable in the Matthaean text, the disciples having to find out whether anyone

---

[17] *Adv. Gnosticos Sconpiace* 1.8; *MPL* 2, col. 137 and *CSEL* 20, p. 161.

[18] See Talmud Yebamoth 49b (GOLDSCHMIDT, IV, p. 481); *Martyrium Jesaiae*, a work extant in Ethiopic, edited by CHARLES with a Latin translation (1900), to quote only the most ancient sources.

Before '*epristhēsan*' Nestlé gives '*epeirasthēsan*', (= 'they were tested'), a very pale expression alongside the others. But it seems that this reading was a correction of '*episthēsan*', a correction mistakenly inserted into the text of some manuscripts in addition to '*epristhēsan*'. p 13, A, the Textus Receptus and also the Latin versions give '*epristhēsan*' before '*epeirasthēsan*'. p 46 and the Peshitta have '*epristhēsan*' only. '*Epeirasthēsan*' only is given in the Clementine edition of the Vulgate. One minuscule gives '*eprēsthēsan*' (= 'they were burned'), which could be a corruption of '*epristhēsan*' (same pronunciation) unless '*eprēsthēsan*' is the original reading. Nestlé's text is based especially on S and B. CLEMENT OF ALEXANDRIA reads '*epeirasthēsan*' in the 4th Book of the *Stromateis*, §102, 1, Chap. 16 (ed STAHLIN, *GCS* 2, p. 293).

[19] On the subject of the violent deaths of the prophets, readers are referred to the monograph by H. J. SCHOEPS, *Die jüdischen Propheten-Morde* (in Symbolae Biblicae Upsalienses, Uppsala 1943, II).

[20] See JOHANN ADRIAN BOLTEN, *Das Neue Testament*, Altona 1792, and DALMAN, *Aramäisch-Neuhebräisches Wörterbuch*, I, 1897, p. 211, who gives 'merciful' as one meaning of '*zākāh*'; cf. BUXTORF (*v.* Bibliography) on the verb '*zākāh*'.

was willing to receive them. Our verse 11[38] could be similarly explained; for the world expelled these people, so that they had to wander in the desert. In this way the ideas of vv. 37–38 are very closely linked. But the statement that the world was not worthy of them is almost a truism. '*Opai tēs gēs*' = 'openings in the earth', i.e. underground caves.

11[39]. All these men of faith were yet unable to share in the Christian salvation; '*marturēthentes*' is again a passive = 'have received a good testimony'. It is not until 12[1] that they themselves are called witnesses.

11[40]. This verse, however, gives us a hint that they will inherit the promised land together with the Christians. If God has put back 'the great day', it is for our good, so that we may share in salvation. The fact that the Epistle mentions no Christian martyr may be confirmation of the hypothesis that the writer used a Jewish source here.

In dealing with the rôle of faith in the believer's life, this chapter brings us face to face with a paradox: sometimes faith assures him of victory, but sometimes it leads him to martyrdom. St Paul and the Fourth Gospel resolved this difficulty, by showing through the example of the Passion of Jesus, that martyrdom also constitutes a victory, namely over the invisible powers.[21]

[21] See Colossians 2[14f], and C. H. DODD's reflexions on the Johannine account of the Passion, in his book *The Interpretation of the Fourth Gospel* 1953, especially from p. 432. On the idea of martyrdom in Judaism, see LOHMEYER, *RHPR* 1927, pp. 316ff.

CHAPTER XII

(1) *Behold! A great cloud of witnesses surrounding us. Let us there-fore rid ourselves of all that could weigh us down [and especially] of sin which handicaps us so easily, and let us run with endurance the race set before us;* (2) *fixing our gaze on the head of our faith, who leads us to perfection—on Jesus, who in exchange for the joy which was available to Him, endured the cross, braving the shame; after which He sat down at the right of God's throne.* (3) *For you must fasten your thoughts on Him who, for the sake of sinners, endured such bitter opposition, so that you may not tire in your souls by losing heart.* (4) *In your struggles you have not yet resisted sin to the extent of shedding your blood.* (5) *And you have forgotten the exhortation which is addressed to you as to sons: 'My Son, do not take lightly the Lord's correction. But on the other hand, being rebuked by Him, do not be discouraged.* (6) *For Him whom the Lord loves, He corrects, and He chastises every son whom he adopts.'* (7) *It is for your education that you endure this. God treats you like sons. For what son is there who is not corrected by his father?* (8) *But if indeed you are left without correction, of which all have had their share, assuredly you are il-legitimate children and not sons.*

12¹. Here for the first time the heroes put forward as examples in **11** are expressly called martyrs (in the sense of witnesses of God). It is as though these men of old time were following the struggles of Christians from above, and we might remind the reader of the very widespread belief in Greece and elsewhere, that the heroes of old, as for example the Dioscuroi among the Greeks, sometimes appeared over battlefields to encourage those fighting in a righteous war. The word 'cloud' ('*nephos*') is therefore particularly well chosen. The first effect of this heartening presence should be to rid us of 'im-pedimenta' ('*ongkos*'), i.e. of all that would encumber the con-testants. '*Ongkos*' means a 'weight'. And just as athletes must shed their superfluous weight by a slimming procedure, champions in the Christian race will have to rid themselves of all that weighs them down, notably sin ('*hamartia*'), which binds them to the world, and prevents them from reaching the goal.[1]

Sin is here called '*euperistatos*', an adjective which, to the best of our knowledge, is unknown elsewhere. It appears to be derived

[1] It is almost needless to observe how frequently in ancient Christian literature the Christian's similarity to an athlete is used. For the New Testament see: **10**[32]; Philippians 3[12]; 1 Timothy 6[12]; 2 Timothy 2[5]; and especially 1 Corinthians 9[24-27]; Cf. PHILO, *Legum Allegoriae*, III, §47, Chap. 5, where he exhorts the mind ('*dianoia*') to rid itself of the 'heavy encumbrances of the body' ('*ongkoi sōmati-koi*').

from *'peri-istēmi'* = 'to surround', *'eu'* signifying that sin has a clear understanding of the advantage which it can take of the situation in causing the Christian to fall.[2]

Now that the somewhat negative conditions have been stated, a call is issued for the cardinal virtue needed for victory, namely endurance (*'hupomonē'*) (see above **10**[36]). The contest (*'agōn'*) is qualified as *'prokeimenos'* = 'what is set before us', what is proposed for us. It is possible that the writer was thinking of imminent persecution. But is not the whole of the Christian's life a contest?

12[2] at last adds Jesus Himself to the cloud of witnesses of the old covenant. He is the head or leader (*'archēgos'*) of faith (*'tēs pisteōs'*), which means that He is something like the team-captain of Christians. He is also called *'teleiōtēs'*, because He perfects us in our religion. This word is another *hapax*, unknown elsewhere in sacred or secular literature. There is no doubt about the sense; for the verb *'teleioun'* means 'to make perfect'. It should not therefore be translated by 'author' as does the Preuschen-Bauer Lexicon.

12[2b] provides a striking summary of the way in which Jesus understood and accomplished His mission. At first sight it is much in keeping with Philippians 2[6ff]. Jesus willingly chose the cross and shame in order to be subsequently raised up by God. But there is no question here of any equality with God which He might have seized. It is not even certain that the joy (*'chara'*) which was 'before Him' refers to the heavenly bliss of pre-existence which He had surrendered. Jesus could also have enjoyed earthly glory, if He had agreed to be the king of Israel (see Matthew 4[8]; Mark 8[29–33] par.;[3] John 6[15]). *'Kataphronein'* here does not mean to despise something in order to shun it, but 'to despise' (suffering) by submitting to it.

12[3]. This verse brings forward a new idea. Christians should think about Jesus Christ and meditate on His person and destiny. *'Analogizesthai'* = lit. 'to count up'. The passion was something He endured all His life because of the resistance (*'antilogia'* = 'contradiction') of sinners. Judas and the Sanhedrin are not the only ones to come to mind, but the Pharisees too, and perhaps also the lack of understanding which He met even among His immediate followers. The example of Christ should preserve Christians from discouragement, *'kamnein'* meaning 'to be weary' and *'ekluesthai'* 'to relax', 'to be faint' (cf. Mark 8[3] par.; Galatians 6[9]).

---

[2] As this verse conjures up contests on the running track, the verb *'periistēmi'* might be compared with *'huperbainō'*, which is a technical term from wrestling, meaning 'to bestride' or to encircle the legs. See DAREMBERG and SAGLIO, *Dictionnaire des antiquités grecques et romaines*, III, 2, p. 1340. Cf. PHILO, *Quod Deterius*, etc., §27, Chap. 8. PREUSCHEN-BAUER translates *'euperistatos'* by 'easily ensnaring', but offers no justification.

[3] For the interpretation of this passage, see our *Royaume de Dieu*, Chap. 6.

12⁴. There has so far been no bloody persecution; and **10³⁴** spoke only of prison and sequestration. But reference to the struggle against sin leads us towards another explanation: the writer wants to remind his readers that they have not yet shown their full potentialities in the contest with sin. We may agree with Father Spicq that there is also here an allusion to the pancratium, the most dangerous part of which was a bout with armoured fists.⁴

12⁵. These trials should not be looked on as a sign of divine malevolence; they are chastenings which have the education of a man as their aim. The writer is admirably served by the Greek language (and Greek ethics) which expresses the two ideas in one word *'paideia'*. The Wisdom literature frequently develops this theme (see Proverbs 13; 22; 23; Ecclesiasticus 22; 30; 42 and elsewhere). It is its sons whom God educates in this way—a point made clear with the help of a quotation from Proverbs (3¹¹⁻¹²), which reproduces exactly the Septuagint text. *'Kai eklelēsthe'* may be either a question ('have you forgotten?') or a statement ('you have forgotten'). *'Oligōreō'* = 'to minimize', to give too little importance to, to despise.⁵ For the sense of *'ekluō'*, see above, v. 3. *'Elengchomai'* = 'to be disciplined', 'be punished'.

12⁶ could be summarized by the famous Greek proverb formerly held in high esteem among some pedagogues: *'ho mē dareis anthrōpos ou paideuetai'*—if you have not been flayed, you will never be a gentleman. *'Paradechomai'* = 'to accept'. God accepts the faithful as one adopts a son or a pupil, but He uses the whip (*'mastix'*, hence *'mastigoō'*) if necessary.

12⁷. *'Prospheromai tini'* = 'to behave' in relation to someone; with *'hōs'* = to treat someone 'as' or 'like' . . . God treats us like sons. But earthly fathers must correct their children; the heavenly Father even more.⁶

12⁸. If you had been spared the *'paideia'*, you could not consider yourselves as true sons, but merely as illegitimate children (*'nothoi'*).

---

⁴ If indeed the wrists and hands were armed with leather thongs covered with lead and studded with nails, it can be well understood that blood would flow. See DAREMBERG and SAGLIO, *op. cit.*, IV, 1, pp. 754f.

⁵ The first part of this word contains of course the root *'oligos'* ('few', 'little'), the second (according to Boisacq) the root *'ōra'* = 'care'. So the sense should be 'to care too little'. The word is a *hapax* in the Bible and rare outside it.

⁶ In vv. 6–7, papyrus p 46 provides a good example of haplography (or homoioteleuton).

(9) *Besides, we have had our earthly fathers to discipline us, and we submitted [to them]. Shall we not therefore with more reason submit to the Father of spirits in order to live?* (10) *They indeed disciplined us for a short time to the best of their lights, but He disciplines us with a view to what is suitable for us, in order that we may share in His holiness.*

(11) *For every correction seems to us at the time to be accompanied not by joy but by sorrow. But later it yields in return the fruit, which gives peace and uprightness to those who have profited from the training.* (12) *Therefore brace again your weary hands and your failing knees* (13) *and make straight paths for your feet, so that the faltering limb may not be put out of joint, but rather be healed.* (14) *Strive for peace with all, and for the sanctification without which no one will see the Lord.* (15) *Take good care that no man by losing the grace of God, and that no bitter root by growing in height, hamper or infect the community.* (16) *Take good care that no fornicator or profane person [be among you] like Esau, who gave away his birthright in exchange for a single meal.* (17) *For you know that when he later wished to be the heir to the blessing he was rejected. For he found it impossible to make [his father] revoke his decision, although he made his request with tears.*

12[9–10] develop the idea which underlies v. 7b. We must submit to divine correction with even more readiness than to that of earthly fathers, for it has our eternal good as its purpose. *'Entrepomai'* = *'hupotassomai'* = 'to submit oneself'. For the phrase 'father of spirits' (*'patēr tōn pneumatōn'*), cf. Numbers 16[22]; 27[16]; Revelation 22[6]; Enoch 37[2]; 59[2].

12[11]. Nevertheless, the writer does not go so far as to think that this education is a matter for rejoicing. At the time (*'pros to paron'*) it causes sadness (*'lupē'*), but in the long run it obtains for us a great benefit which is here called the peaceful fruit of righteousness. The word fruit (*'karpos'*) must arouse the sense of how fertile this education is for it produces two virtues especially, namely inward peace (*'eirēnikon karpon'*) and moral rectitude (*'dikaiosunēs'* is an explicative genitive). Finally, another borrowing from the language of sport: the education which divine Providence gives is a gymnastic of the soul (*'gegumnasmenois'*).[7]

12[12]. Conclusion: straighten yourselves up. *'Pariēmi'* = 'to be exhausted'; *'paraluomai'* = 'to be paralysed' or 'weakened'. This verse is reminiscent of Isaiah 35[3], perhaps also of Ecclesiasticus 25[23].

[7] It is well known that this group of ideas on the divine education is one of the main themes developed in the ethics of Clement of Alexandria; see D. FAYE, *Clément d'Alexandrie*, 2nd edn, 1906, *passim*, and selected texts in BARDY, *Clément d'Alexandrie*, in the series 'Les moralistes chrétiens', 1926, pp. 91f and pp. 104f.

12¹³. The first part of this verse as far as *'humōn'* is a borrowing from Proverbs 4²⁶. *'Trochia'* = 'rut', 'track' of wheels, here = 'path'. The verse seems a little out of keeping because it seems to try to make the task easier for the champions. But in the moral sense, it is a matter of the straight path which alone is in conformity with God's will and the only one able to heal the sick. *'Ektrepomai'* = 'to turn aside', can be used of a lame (*'cholos'*) limb which becomes dislocated, again therefore an allusion to the running track. Nothing precise is said about the exact nature of the trials. What is involved may be the misfortunes which crush every man and in which the believer can discern the intentions of providence. But the writer is probably thinking primarily about specifically Christian trials, namely the opposition (*'antilogia'*) of enemies of Christianity. The sequel will speak of misfortunes of a very different type, viz. those which must be regarded as true punishments.

12¹⁴. *'Eirēnēn diōkete meta pantōn'* = 'pursue after peace with all men', could be a quotation from Psalm 34¹⁵ (LXX 33¹⁵). The verse is also reminiscent of Romans 12¹⁸. At any rate the Apostle Paul speaks of peace with all men, and therefore with outsiders also, which compels him to add *'ei dunaton, to ex humōn'* ('if it is possible, in as far as it depends on you'). Here only dealings with other Christians are in question. And so it may be asked whether the *'hagiasmos'* (= 'sanctification') is not a social virtue here, something like the sanctification of the relations between members of the Church.

12¹⁵. The verb *'enochlein'* (for exact sense, see below) goes with two subjects: (a) *'husterōn'* and (b) *'rhiza'*. *'Husterōn'* = 'to be deficient', 'to have lost' does not allege that there are people who have already lost grace; but they are in danger of so doing. Grace is therefore not something which cannot be lost. *'Rhiza pikrias'* = 'root of bitterness' as in Deuteronomy 29¹⁷. *'Pikria'* may perhaps allude to the scene of bitterness and rebellion in the desert (see 2⁸, ¹⁵). *'Enochleō'* = 'to cause trouble' or 'scandal'.[8]

12¹⁶. This verse gives definite examples of the evil roots which spread poison. *'Pornos'* = 'fornicator'. Esau had this reputation among the Rabbis. *'Bebēlos'* more difficult to explain (= 'weak'?), seems to be placed in contrast with what is sacred and may mean something like 'unclean'. This sense is attested elsewhere, and it is Esau again who is so designated, because he had in some degree profaned his birthright, as v. 16b reminds us (cf. Genesis 25³³); *'brōsis'* lit. = 'food'.[9]

---

[8] *'Ochlos'* does not mean 'crowd' only, but also 'trouble'.

[9] For the juxtaposition of *'pornos'* and *'bebēlos'*, cf. also PHILO, *De Specialibus Legibus*, I, §102, Chap. 14 and IV, §40, Chap. 7. Philo also sees Esau as a glutton: *De Virtutibus*, §208. H. LEISEGANG lists other texts too (in his Index of Philo's works) which it is useless to quote here. The Midrash Genesis Rabba 65.1 (FREEDMANN, II, p. 581) calls Esau a debauched person and likens him to a pig, referring to Psalm 80¹⁴ (LXX 79¹⁴).

(18) *Now you have not come into contact with material displays
[of the divine power]: neither with burning fire, nor thick darkness,
nor whirlwind,* (19) *nor with a trumpet blast, nor with the sound of
words, of which those hearing refused to hear one word more.* (20) *For
they could not bear the command: 'If even an animal sets foot upon
the mountain, it shall be stoned.'* (21) *And—so terrifying was the
manifestation—even Moses declared: 'I am filled with fear and trembling.'* (22) *On the contrary, you have come to Mount Zion, which is
also the city of the living God, to the heavenly Jerusalem and the myriads
of angels, the solemn assembly* (23) *and gathering of the first-born
who are enrolled in heaven, and to God the Judge of the universe, and
to the spirits of the righteous who have attained perfection,* (24) *and to
Jesus, mediator of the new covenant, and to the blood of sprinkling
which speaks otherwise and more powerfully than that of Abel.* (25)
*Take good care not to refuse [the offer of] Him who speaks [to you].
For if they did not escape [punishment] after rejecting the one who gave
them decrees on earth, with how much more reason shall we be unable*

12¹⁷. The refusal to bless Jacob's brother by his father is here linked
with his renunciation of his rights. '*Apodokimazō*' = 'to reject as
unworthy'. It will be noticed that our writer's position is signifi-
cantly different from that of the Apostle Paul in the Epistle to the
Romans (9¹¹⁻¹³); for Paul the divine decision is independent of
merits or demerits. In dealing with the whole of this verse, Genesis
27³⁰⁻³⁹ must be compared; there Esau tries vainly to bring about a
change of decision in his father who had already blessed Jacob.
'*Iste*' is probably an indicative = 'you know'. '*Metanoia*' here =
'change of mind', namely by Isaac, which Esau had failed to induce.
'*Autēn*' could be taken with '*eulogia*' (= 'blessing'), but the construction of the sentence links it more closely with '*metanoia*'.
Tears are mentioned in Genesis 27³⁸ᵇ. If '*metanoia*' is taken in the
sense of 'conversion', as do a very great number of commentators,
including Chrysostom,[10] Calvin, Bengel and Moffatt, the reference
would be to a conversion of Esau which the latter did not 'find'. And
then it would be necessary to admit that the ancestor of Edom is
regarded as the prototype of those who relinquish faith and who
according to 6⁴ᶠᶠ cannot afterwards repent. But the Epistle does not
say that.

12¹⁸. Probably to add further encouragement for his readers, the
writer contrasts the earthly revelation of the old covenant with the
more reassuring one of the new. To this end the writer chooses as

---

[10] *MPG* 63, col. 215. Esau did not really repent, he wept not from contrition,
but from rage ('*ta gar dakrua ouk ēn metanoias, alla epēreias, kai thumou mallon*').

Kᴇʜ

to escape, if we turn away from Him who speaks [to us] from the height of heaven; (26) Him whose voice then shook the earth, but who now announces saying: 'Yet once more I shall shake not the earth only, but also the heaven.' (27) The words 'once more' indicate the removal of what can be shaken, because it is created, in order that what cannot be shaken may remain. (28) Therefore, by receiving an unshakeable kingdom, we enter into possession of a privilege. Let us use it to serve God in a way which is pleasing to Him, with religious fear. (29) For our God is also a consuming fire.

the culminating point of the old revelation that of God on Mount Sinai, and sets, in contrast to it, the peaceful, serene image of the heavenly Zion.

12$^{18-21}$. These verses emphasize the terror caused by the volcanic eruption of Sinai, in which God manifested Himself. The contrast between the two mountains is of course also stressed in Galatians 4$^{24-26}$.[11]

'Psēlaphōmenon' = 'what was touchable' or 'solid', emphasizing the material nature of the phenomena. We add the dative *'orei'* after the participle; it is quite well attested by P, K, D and a section of the Syriac texts.[12] *'Kekaumenon pur'* is not a relatively harmless fire like that of the burning bush, but a 'fire which devours'. *'Gnophos'* and *'zophos'* are synonyms = 'darkness, gloom'. *'Thuella'* = 'the whirlwind' which whips up a column of fire or smoke. The sound of the war trumpet (*'ēchos'* = 'noise') which must in some degree herald the coming of a king, made a 'deafening din' (Spicq). The most curious manifestation is kept till last—the words of God Himself (*'theou phōnē'* according to Exodus 19^{19}) causing a terrifying effect. The listeners did not want to hear more (v. 19b); not only the sound of the voice, but the contents of the instructions must have been distressing, that not even an animal had the right to set foot on the mountain.

12^{21}. Moses himself was seized with fear and trembling in the presence of these 'phenomena' (*'phantazomenon'*), cf. Exodus 19; Deuteronomy 4^{11f}; 5^{22}.

[11] It is almost pointless to remind readers of the important part played by mountains in Near Eastern cults. And the eschatological rôle of mountains, and notably of Zion, in Jewish literature, will cause no surprise. The study by JOHANNES JEREMIAS, *Der Gottesberg*, Gütersloh 1919, was unfortunately not accessible to us. See many texts, including Psalm 2^6; Isaiah 2^2; 11^9; 25^{6f}; 4 Esdras 13^2; 6^{35}.

[12] The rationalizing interpretation that the phenomenon was 'nothing but' a volcanic eruption would not have impressed believers. For once it is admitted that God manifests Himself in the whole creation, why should He not also do it in extraordinary phenomena? In any case the story of the prophet Elijah (1 Kings 19$^{9-15}$) teaches that terrifying phenomena are not necessarily the supreme manifestations of deity. On the divine voice, cf. DÖLGER, *'Theou phōnē'*, in *Antike und Christentum*, 1936, p. 218.

12$^{22-23}$ gives impressions of the heavenly Jerusalem (already announced in 11$^{10-16}$) of which the earthly Jerusalem was a mere copy and prefiguration (cf. Revelation 21 and 22). It is inhabited by myriads of angels. In a general way, heaven, or at least the seventh heaven, is the dwelling place of the angels according to the Enoch literature; here the élite of the heavenly host is assembled in the heavenly Zion. The word '*panēguris*' conveys the impression of a joyful cultic assembly (cf. in the LXX Amos 5^{21}; Hosea 9^{5}; Ezekiel 46^{11}). The dative seems to be a '*dativus modi*' = 'assembled in a throng'; it seems to be in apposition to '*muriasin*' (= 'the myraids who are in assembly'). '*Panēgurei*' could also be taken as the second member of the list, and it would then refer to another assembly, namely that of the faithful.[13] But the absence of a '*kai*' makes this interpretation difficult. In any event the comma must go after '*anggelōn*'.

12^{23}. Next comes a problem about the '*ekklēsia (tōn) prōtotokōn*' (= 'the gathering of the first-born'), etc. Is it the assembly of all the elect, enrolled in the book of life.[14] But then the recipients of the letter would be part of the assembly, and it is not clear how they could 'meet' the assembly. So the phrase must refer to the elect under the old covenant, whereas the '*pneumata dikaiōn teteleiōmenōn*' (= 'the souls of the righteous who have reached perfection') could be the Christian martyrs (cf. Revelation 6^{9}).[15]

Why is God mentioned between the '*prōtotokoi*' (= 'first-born') and the '*pneumata*' (= 'spirits')? Perhaps because they surround His throne. God the judge of the universe is an allusion to the last judgement. It is, however, possible that the noun '*kritēs*' has the Hebrew sense of 'one who reigns', perhaps even 'the one who comes with help' (cf. Psalm 68^{6} [LXX 67^{6}], where God is the '*kritēs tōn cherōn*' = 'the support of widows').

12^{24}. '*Iesou*' is of course a dative. He is the '*mesitēs*' (= 'mediator'), in conformity with the Epistle's whole teaching. His blood purifies. It cries out more loudly than Abel's, and it has more far-reaching effects. After these revelations the author returns to exhortation, as is his habit.

[13] This verse probably inspired J. M. MAYFART in his fine hymn 'Jerusalem, die hochgebaute Stadt'; see especially verses 4 and 5.

[14] For the 'book of life', see Exodus 32^{32f}; Psalm 69^{29} (LXX 68^{29}); Isaiah 4^{3}; Daniel 12^{1}; Enoch 47^{3}; 104^{1}; 108^{3}; Philippians 4^{3}; Revelation 3^{5}; 13^{8}; 17^{8}; 21^{27}. Cf. *TWNT*, II, pp. 618f.

[15] St Paul speaks of a single '*prōtotokos*' (= 'first-born'), namely Christ. Here the '*prōtotokoi*' are all those whom He has caused to share in the new birth. Nor is it completely ruled out that they represent a category of angels. But so far as is known they are referred to in this way only in late Gnostic texts; cf. *Excerpta e Theodoto* 27.35: '*prōtoktistoi*' (in CLEMENT OF ALEXANDRIA, ed. STÄHLIN, *GCS* III, p. 116). We are therefore more inclined to identify the '*prōtotokoi*' with the elect, and more especially since they had been already so designated in Judaism. On this subject see the interesting study by PAUL WINTER (in English), 'Monogenes para patros', in *Zeitschrift für Religions- und Geistesgeschichte*, 1953, pp. 335–364.

12²⁵⁻²⁶. *'Paraiteomai'* is a verb with several meanings. The only sense which is suitable here is 'to disparage' or 'decline' (an offer); it is then almost synonymous with the verb *'ameleō'* used in 2³. *'Lalounti'* in v. 24 and *'lalounta'* in v. 25 may allude to the opening of the Epistle (see *'lalēsas'* 1¹ and *'elalēsen'* 1²). **12²⁵ᵇ** again develops an argument *a minore ad maius*, as often happens in the Epistle (cf. 2²ᶠ).Who is the *'chrēmatizōn'* (= 'the one who gives oracles') on earth? It is debatable. We think that the most straightforward interpretation is to take it as being Moses. God Himself spoke at Sinai, yes; but only to Moses who then passed the commandments on to the people. *'Ton ap' ouranōn'*, with *'chrēmatizonta'* understood, means 'the one who gives instructions from the height of heaven', that is, God. Once His voice shook the earth, and it will shake the entire universe. *'Apostrephesthai'* = 'to turn oneself away'. This is a threat, yet also a promise, drawn from the book of the prophet Haggai (2⁶).

12²⁷⁻²⁸. These verses give a commentary on the prophetic passage. The expression *'eti hapax'* is not very clear. The writer seems to be saying that because God will, at some final date, perform this terrible miracle, all that is not shaken by Him (*'ta mē saleuomena'*) will last eternally. *'Metathesis hōs pepoiēmonōn'* means a changing of created things in so far as they are shakeable. But really it is a matter of their destruction and disappearance. Notice that back in 11⁵, the verb *'metatithemai'* already had the sense of 'disappear'. As the city of Antioch was frequently shaken by earth-tremors, Father Spicq (I, p. 252) thinks that the Epistle's recipients may have lived there.

12²⁸. What remains will be the unshakeable kingdom (*'basileia asaleutos'*), that is the Kingdom of God; and we are the ones who will receive it. But what is the exact meaning of *'echōmen charin'* (= 'let us have grace')? It is difficult to see how this privilege could be the object of exhortation. It is better to read the quite well attested *'echomen'* ('we have').[16] Alternatively, *'echōmen'* could be translated 'let us give thanks' = *'gratiam habeamus'*, as do Chrysostom, Riggenbach, Windisch, Moffatt, Michel, and others.

What is the meaning of *'di' hēs'* in v. 28b? It could be expected rather that the cult (*'latreia'*) would be the means of expressing thanks (*'charis'*) than the converse. But grace can give us the possibility of serving God 'acceptably' (*'euarestōs'*). There is no doubt about the *'latreuōmen'* = 'let us serve'; but it could have had an influence on the verb *'echein'* in the first part of the verse.

---

[16] *'Echomen'* is given by p 46, S, P and the Latin versions. This reading is adopted by von Soden. *'Echōmen'*, adopted by Nestlé, is supported by A, E, D and the Byzantine Text.

CHAPTER XIII

THIS CHAPTER gives the clear impression of being an appendix. For (a) the moral injunctions which it contains, in contrast with the rest of the Epistle, are rather clumsily linked together, and do not follow the end of **12** at all well;—(b) it adds nothing new;—(c) it is only in this Chapter that the writer speaks as though he were writing a letter.

It has been thought that **13** is unauthentic. Some have sought to attribute it to the Apostle Paul on account of its vocabulary and general structure, which is somewhat reminiscent of the ending of the first Epistle to the Thessalonians, and because of the reference to Timothy. But at the same time the great themes of **1–12**, and notably the cleavage with Judaism, are either expressly taken up again or presupposed.[1]

If any hypothesis is to be put forward, it could be that the writer, while sending a copy of his homily to a particular congregation, added a letter, viz. **13**$^{1-21}$. **13**$^{22-25}$ form a postscript in any case, and may be from another writer's pen (see below).

(1) *Let brotherly love remain [among you].* (2) *Do not forget hospitality; for through it some have entertained angels unawares.* (3) *Remember those in prison, as though you were imprisoned with them; remember those who are ill-treated, for you live the same bodily life [as they].* (4) *Let marriage be honoured in all its aspects. Let the marriage-bed be undefiled; for God will judge fornicators and adulterers.* (5) *Let your life be free from avarice; be content with what you have at present. For He [God] has said: 'I will not fail you nor forsake you.'* So much so that we can say with every assurance: (6) *'The Lord is my help; I shall not live in fear. What could any man do to me?'* (7) *Remember your leaders, who preached to you the word of God. Meditate upon the outcome of their lives and imitate their faith.* (8) *Jesus Christ is the same yesterday, today and for ever.*

13^{1}. '*Philadelphia*' calls for no philological explanation. This virtue is distinct from the '*agapē*' = 'love', which is available to any neighbour, or to anyone for whom we should be a neighbour (Luke 10^{36f}), whereas '*philadelphia*' is love among Christians, who are brethren by being sons of the same God. And so they are often simply called 'brothers'. In the present day some Christian groups will accept no

---

[1] See SPICQ, 'L'authenticité du chap. 13 de l'Epître aux Hébreux', in *Conjectanea Neotestamentica*, XI, Uppsala 1947, pp. 226ff.

other appellation, for example the 'Moravian Brethren' (*Brüder-gemeinde*) or the 'Plymouth Brethren'. Could this virtue have already weakened among the recipients of the letter? The text does not say so, but perhaps leaves it to be understood, for it may be supposed that moralists rarely make completely superfluous statements. The same considerations must be put forward for what follows.

13². '*Philoxenia*' refers to another aspect of agapé; it is goodwill towards guests and foreigners ('*xenoi*'). Hospitality was so much the more indispensable in antiquity in that even wealthy travellers were generally obliged to lodge with private people on account of the poor state of the inns. At the beginning of their missionary journey, the first disciples that Jesus sent out were able to expect hospitality even from the Jews (Matthew 10[11]); and Christians have a better reason for practising '*philoxenia*' among themselves.[2] Angels were entertained by Abraham (Genesis 18), by Lot (Genesis 19) and by Manoah, though he had guessed who his guest was (Judges 13), and by Tobit (Tobit 12).

13³. The writer speaks of prisoners as though there were some at the time. This Chapter may therefore have been written at a time of persecution, unlike 10[34]. But what is said lacks precision. One should remember prisoners as if one were imprisoned with them. In the phrase '*hōs sundedemenoi*', '*hōs*' seems at first glance to have a purely comparative sense. But '*hōs*' towards the end of the verse seems to take a causal sense. 'Because you also lead a bodily existence, you are exposed to the same trials.' By attraction the first '*hōs*' could have the same force: 'because you are in chains with them', through sympathy in some degree. The idea is only touched on, but it would be quite in line with Pauline conceptions, according to which the whole body participates in the suffering of one member.

13⁴. An injunction concerning the sanctity of marriage. Marriage can be dishonoured by those mentioned in v. 4b, but also, probably, by those who wish to forbid it (see 1 Timothy 4[3]). '*Hē koitē amiantos*': defilement of the marriage-bed need not necessarily make us think of such practices as are condemned in Genesis 38[9]. Any infidelity is a defilement. The nouns '*pornos*' and '*moichos*' are not completely synonymous. The '*pornoi*' are the 'unchaste' in general, that is those who betray their wife for some other woman, whereas the '*moichoi*' commit an act of adultery with a married woman.[3]

---

[2] Hospitality for itinerant brothers had already been held in high regard among the Essenes. See JOSEPHUS, *Jewish War*, II, §124f, Chap. 8.
[3] Cf. J.-J. VON ALLMEN, *Maris et femmes d'après saint Paul*, Neuchâtel and Paris 1951, and H. LEENHARDT, *Le mariage chrétien*, Neuchâtel and Paris 1946.

13⁵. '*A-phil-arguros*' = 'one who is not dominated by love of money'. The Christian should be satisfied with what he has ('*tois parousin*'), and notably with what he earns from honest work. He should avoid two pitfalls: first, the temptation not to work (see 2 Thessalonians 3⁷⁻¹²), secondly, amassing more goods than he needs, through fear of the future, as if Providence did not exist. That is why two reassuring texts are quoted in v. 5b and v. 6. The first is not to be found in the Hebrew Bible nor in the LXX, at least not in so many words. But as Philo knows this text in the same form, it must be allowed once again not that the writer quoted badly, but that he had before him a translation other than that of the LXX.⁴

'*Ou mē*', as always, reinforces the negative (= 'there is no danger that').

13⁶. The quotation, taken from Psalm 118⁶ (LXX 117⁶) does, in this case, agree with the LXX.

13⁷. The word '*hēgoumenoi*' (= 'leaders') is rare in the New Testament (cf. Acts 15²²; Luke 22¹⁶).⁵ The writer chose it to designate any kind of leader, not necessarily Apostles, elders, deacons or bishops. It is said that they preached the word; they are therefore, at least in part, evangelists or teachers ('*didaskaloi*'). They have set an example by their '*ekbasis*' (cf. Ecclesiasticus 2¹⁷), a euphemism for 'death'; probably martyrs are meant.

13⁸. This verse is poorly connected both with what precedes and with what follows. We have here something like a liturgical formula, which must be the end of the first part of this exhortation; which in turn may well have formed originally the ending of the Epistle. As is customary, we have taken '*Christos*' as a proper noun and '*Iēsous Christos*' as the subject; the predicate (understood) is '*estin*' (= 'He is') '*ho autos*' (= 'the same'). It is an affirmation of the unchangeable and eternal character of Christ. The sentence could also be construed '*Iēsous estin Christos*' = 'Jesus is the Christ', etc. That was certainly the early Christian confession.⁶ But '*ho autos*' would then be awkward to place in the structure of the sentence.

---

⁴ Deuteronomy 31⁶: 'he will not by any means forsake you nor desert you' ('*ou mē se anē, oute mē se engkatalipē*'). It is not, however, a word of God, since He is spoken of in the third person. Joshua 1⁵: 'I will not fail you or neglect you' ('*ouk engkataleipsō se oude huperopsomai se*'), where only the first part of the verse agrees with 13⁵ᵇ. PHILO, *De Confusione Linguarum*, §166, Chap. 32: 'I will not by any means forsake you, nor will I desert you' ('*ou mē se anō, oud' ou mē se engkatalipō*').

⁵ See Ecclesiasticus 33¹⁹ (ed. RAHLFS) '*hēgoumenoi ekklēsias*'. The word is used again by Clement of Rome (in the form 'pro-hēgoumenoi') (21⁶). Later it achieved high status, because the Greek Church used it for the heads of monasteries (Igumen = Abbot).

⁶ See O. CULLMANN, *Les premières confessions de foi chrétiennes*, 2nd edn, Paris 1948.

(9) *Do not let yourselves be led astray by various strange doctrines. For it is expedient that the heart should be strengthened by grace and not by foods, from which those who live [by such precepts] have gained no benefit. (10) We have an altar from which those who serve the Tent have no right to eat. (11) For the bodies of the animals whose blood has been offered for sin by the High Priest in the sanctuary, are burned outside the camp. (12) That is why Jesus, in order to sanctify the people by His own blood, suffered His passion outside the gate [of the city]. (13) So then, let us go out to Him, leaving the camp, bearing His reproach. (14) For we have here no permanent city, but we are seeking the city that is to come. (15) Through Him we offer continually a sacrifice of praise to God, I mean the fruit of our lips which make confession of His name.*

13⁹. It is difficult to be precise about the nature of the doctrines against which the writer warns his correspondents. We know from the Epistles of Paul (especially Romans, 1 Corinthians, Galatians, Ephesians, Colossians) as well as from the Catholic Epistles (especially Jude, 2 Peter, 1 and 2 John) and from Revelation, that even in the early days the Church was threatened and sometimes undermined by 'strange' doctrines, of which the majority were essentially Gnostic and incompatible with the evangelical message. It is probable that these doctrines, pre-Christian in origin, infiltrated the Church through the Judaism of the Diaspora.[7] Some Gnostics of ascetic tendencies, especially among the Jewish Christians, expected salvation through the observance of dietary 'taboos'. This is the aspect of the question treated in Romans 14. In **10**, the matter turns on some Mosaic injunctions observed by devotees of the Tabernacle and the Temple. But the expression 'strange doctrines', etc., makes us think here of some sort of Gnostic speculations which had managed to find a place alongside the Mosaic injunctions.

13¹⁰. This verse again takes up the theme of the superiority of the Christian cult over the Jewish one. The Christian '*thusiastērion*' (= 'altar') is inaccessible to Jews. The expression 'to eat from the altar', that is 'to eat what is given in offering' may tempt us to see in this verse an allusion to the Eucharist. However, this sacrament is never expressly mentioned by the writer. The expression '*thusiastērion*' (which Paul uses only for Jewish sacrifices) instead of '*trapeza*' ('table') is strange. Once more we must probably think of the contrast between the sacrifice on the cross and the sacrifices of the Jews. As Jews eat the actual sacrificed flesh ('*dikaiōmata sarkos*', 9¹⁰!), so Christians nourish themselves spiritually on the benefits of the new covenant.

13¹¹⁻¹². A further parallel, and slightly specious, between the sacrifice of Christ and the Jewish sacrifices, following the typological method.

[7] See MORITZ FRIEDLÄNDER, *Der vorchristliche jüdische Gnostizismus*, 1898.

(16) Do not forget to do good and to be generous. For these are the sacrifices with which God is pleased. (17) Listen to your leaders and obey them. For it is they who deprive themselves of sleep for the good of your lives, for which they will have to give an account. Act in such a way that they can perform their task with joy and without grief. For that would be of no advantage to you. (18) Continue to pray for us. For we are persuaded that we have a clear conscience, through striving to show good conduct at all times. (19) I am especially insistent in my request that this be done so that I may be restored to you sooner. (20) May the God of peace, who brought back from the dead the great shepherd of the sheep in the blood of an eternal covenant, (21) namely the Lord Jesus Christ, make you capable for everything that is good so that you may do His will, performing in you what is pleasing to Himself, through Jesus Christ, to whom be the Glory for ever and ever. Amen.

When sacrifices 'for sin' were concerned, only the blood of the animals was to be used according to Leviticus 16^{27}; all the rest was to be burned 'outside the camp'. That is why Christ suffered at Golgotha, outside the city walls.

13^{13f}. This detail also is used for parenetical purposes. We too must 'leave the encampment', that is behave like pilgrims on the earth, like foreigners who must expect to be held in contempt, but always comforted by the hope of the country to come. This idea is quite in line with the arguments developed in preceding Chapters, where Abraham, a wanderer and foreigner in Palestine, is presented as a type of the Christian.[8]

13^{15}. Up to this point nothing but the sacrifice of Jesus for us had ever been under consideration. Yet in a certain way, the Christian can also present offerings, by the 'confession of His name'. From the use of *'homolegein'* = 'to confess' in the LXX, we can infer that it is a matter of publishing our attachment to Christ. In some way, one must proclaim His glory, as Psalm 54^8 (LXX 53^8) and many others proclaim the glory of God.[9] The prefiguration of these Christian sacrifices under the old covenant, was the offering of the fruits of the earth. Hence the reference here to the fruit (*'karpos'*) of the lips.

13^{16-19}. A series of exhortations simply strung together, rather like a catechism.

---

[8] If we were sure that the Epistle was addressed to Jerusalemites, this verse could also have a very mundane sense; it could be an exhortation to leave Jerusalem before catastrophe came, cf. Mark 13^{14} par.

[9] *'Exomologēsomai tō onomati sou'* (in Hebrew ' *'ôdeh'*)—'I will confess thy name'. In the two passages, Psalm 54^8 (LXX 53^8) and 13^{15}, the dative is used, no doubt under the influence of the Hebrew preposition *'le'*.

13¹⁶. '*Eupoiïa*' is a rare noun in Greek literature and unique in the Bible; it is of course formed from '*eu*' and from '*poiein*' in the sense of Mark 14⁷ (= 'to do good'); '*koinōnia*' here = 'generosity', 'alms', 'a collection for charity'.¹⁰ Active charity is also considered as a sacrifice pleasing to God in Philippians 4¹⁸.

13¹⁷. Here there is further reference to the '*hēgoumenoi*' = 'leaders' who go without sleep for our good; '*agrupneō*' = lit. 'to suffer from lack of sleep'.¹¹ Here '*psuchē*' could exceptionally have the sense of 'soul'. But we may also be allowed to think in terms of care for the life of the faithful, that is for their eternal life, for which the leaders are responsible. The parallel with 10³⁹ makes us opt for the second interpretation. 13¹⁷ᵇ gives us a glimpse of the often tragic situation of the local leaders, whose work is sometimes so little appreciated that they do their duty with grief. This cannot do the local congregation any good. The period of enthusiasm seems already to belong rather to the past.

13¹⁸. '*Proseuchesthe*' = 'pray', or more exactly 'continue to pray' (the verb is in the present, as in 1 Thessalonians 5²⁵; 2 Thessalonians 1¹¹; Colossians 4³; Ephesians 6¹⁸; Romans 15³⁰). What is curious is the reason given ('unexpected and mysterious', Spicq). Prayers should be offered for the writer not to sustain him in his human weakness, but on the contrary because he has a clear conscience and is of good conduct. Does he suspect some unfriendliness in the congregation, as did the Apostle Paul when he wrote to the Corinthians? Were there some who judged him unworthy of being upheld by the brethren? Did any bear him a grudge for his anti-Jewish radicalism? It is impossible to say precisely.

13¹⁹ adds another motive: persistent prayer should facilitate the writer's return to those whom he addresses. It is the only verse which hints at a special link with this Church.

13²⁰⁻²¹. Final greetings. From his side the writer expresses his own wishes for his friends. The verses have the ring of a liturgical blessing, filled out a little probably and culminating in a doxology. It is somewhat reminiscent of those in Philippians 4²⁰; Romans 16²⁷; 2 Timothy 4¹⁸; 1 Peter 4¹¹; 2 Peter 3¹⁸. In v. 21 Nestlé reads '*en*

---

¹⁰ See Seesemann, *Der Begriff Koinonia im Neuen Testament*, Giessen 1933. The word is again found in the sense of 'collection' in its use by the Apostle Paul in Romans 15²⁶ and 2 Corinthians 8⁴.
¹¹ Perhaps Cardinal Richelieu who, let us remember, was also a theologian, had this text in mind when he wrote in his political Testament (II, Chap. 4) that the only contentment of those who devote themselves to public administration, is to see 'many people sleeping without fear, under the protection of their wakefulness and living happily through their wretchedness'.

[POSTSCRIPT]

(22) *My brothers, I beg you to put up with this word of exhortation; for I have written briefly to you.* (23) *You know that our brother Timothy has been released. I shall come to see you with him, if he arrives sufficiently soon.* (24) *Greet all your leaders and all Christians. Those of Italy send their greetings.* (25) *May grace be with you all.*

hēmin' (= 'in us'). But the text requires '*en humin*' (= 'in you'), which is moreover quite well attested.[12]

13²². Here there could be an allusion to the homily which occupies the first twelve Chapters, which would contain exhortations to be accepted and endured. But v. 22b speaks of a short letter, which can hardly refer to anything other than **13**, unless our hypothesis (below) is accepted.

13²³. A curious hint: Timothy was imprisoned and then released. It is generally admitted that we may identify him with Paul's companion, who was also known to Apollos. This detail could also be used to strengthen the thesis of a Roman origin for the letter; for it was there that Timothy may have been imprisoned at the same time as the Apostle Paul. The form of greeting is very general: 'all your leaders and all the Christians'. The bonds between the writer of this line and the addressees are therefore not very close, and it is surprising that no one is mentioned by name.

13²⁴. '*Hoi apo Italias*' = 'those of Italy' is ambiguous, as all Introductions to this Epistle make very clear. They could be inhabitants of Italy who are sending greetings to the congregation. But it could also be taken to mean Italians living abroad who are sending greetings to compatriots at home. The first interpretation naturally imposes itself in proportion to one's conviction that the Epistle was written in Rome.

13²⁵. For the use of the noun '*charis*' = 'grace', cf. the greetings at the end of the Epistles to the Corinthians, the Galatians, the Ephesians, the Philippians, the Colossians, the Second Epistle to the Thessalonians, the Pastoral Epistles and the letter to Philemon.

The ending of the manuscript A (5th–6th century A.D.) states that the Epistle was written in Rome. Others have '*apo Italias*' = 'from Italy' or '*apo Athēnōn*' = 'from Athens'. But it is impossible in the present state of knowledge, to know on what traditions these indications are based. The first two could very well have been deduced from v. 24.

[12] The reading '*en humin*' is attested by A, C, the Textus Receptus and the Latin versions. It is true that some more ancient witnesses, namely S and p 46 have the other reading. But as often happens, a dictation error may have crept in through repetition and been emended later.

To sum up: nothing absolutely precludes us from attributing the whole of 13 to the writer of the Epistle, that is to say, probably to Apollos. A postscript following a doxology can also be found in 2 Timothy 4^{19-22} and Philippians 4^{21-23}. Yet this way of looking at it leaves some uneasiness. Is it not a little unexpected to find the writer commending himself and his writings in 13^{22}? Therefore the question arises whether the postscript is from another hand. As there is nothing to prevent our believing that the Epistle could have been written in the 60's, and that 13 could indeed have been written in Rome, may we not think of the Apostle Paul, who might have taken advantage of the opportunity to report the release of Timothy, his faithful companion, and to give a kind of blessing to the writing of his friend and disciple Apollos—rather like the Apostle Peter who probably added the postscript to the First Epistle ascribed to Peter, but which was probably written by Silvanus (see 1 Peter 5^{12-14})? Scholars who have found traces of something Pauline in 13 may therefore be partially right.[13] The hypothesis would in addition explain the antiquity of the tradition in the East which claimed an association of ideas between this Epistle and the name of the Apostle to the Gentiles. The sentence '*dia bracheōn epesteila humin*' then means: 'I am writing briefly to you', and concerns the verses 13^{22-25}.

---

[13] See E. D. JONES, 'The Authorship of Hebrews', *ExT* 46, pp. 562ff; C. R. WILLIAMS, 'A Word Study of Hebrews 13', *JBL* 1911, pp. 129ff. According to F. OVERBECK, 13^{22-25} was added in order to pass the Epistle off as Pauline. See *Zur Geschichte des Kanons*, 2 *Abhandlungen*, Chemnitz 1880, p. 16.

APPENDICES

I

IN HIS very original book *The Epistle to the Hebrews, its Sources and Message*, London, 2nd edn 1936, V. Burch puts forward the idea that the letter-writer may have quoted, among the Old Testament texts, those which played a dominant part in the liturgies of synagogue worship. This seems to be correct in the case of Exodus 19, quoted in **8** and **12**. But so far as the others are concerned, the detailed study of the liturgical texts by H. St John Thackeray, in his work: *The Septuagint and Jewish Worship*, Schweich Lectures, 1920 (published in London in 1921), does not seem to confirm Burch's thesis. Many texts quoted by Thackeray, apart from Exodus 19, viz. especially Leviticus 33; Deuteronomy 16; Ezekiel 1; Psalms 29; 52; 53; 68; 76; 118 (LXX numbering), were not used by the writer to the Hebrews.[1]

II

Since the figure of Melchizedek has nothing specifically Jewish about it, it is not surprising to discover traces of an analogous figure or myth in countries surrounding Palestine. There was for instance the discovery, on the northern slopes of the Taurus Mountains in Asia Minor, near the place called Ywris, of two curious bas-reliefs of considerable size. The one shows a gigantic figure offering ears of corn and grapes, bread and wine, to a king who is humbly prostrated before him. This scene is strangely reminiscent of that in Genesis 14.

Since there was no opportunity of consulting the works by archaeologists on this point, we have had to content ourselves with second-hand evidence, by summarizing an article in the review *Christengemeinschaft* (Stuttgart, October 1931) by Emil Bock, who speaks of the 'magical grandeur of an immensely ancient spiritual life, a breath of which can be caught in this scene carved 3,000 years ago'. An illustration accompanies the article.

III

It is to be expected that attempts will be made to find relationships between either the writer, or his addressees and the Damascus Sect, which according to the documents recently discovered near the

---

[1] See also, on this subject, the instructive article by BÜCHLER in the *Jewish Quarterly Review* 1893, vol. 5, pp. 420ff and 1894, vol. 6, pp. 1ff, entitled 'The reading of the Law and Prophets in a triennial cycle'.

Dead Sea seems to be one and the same as an Essene or para-Essene community. For the idea of the New Covenant has a very important part in it. But this idea is also accepted by Paul (1 Corinthians 11²⁵; 2 Corinthians 3⁶) as well as by the Synoptics (Mark 14²⁴ par.).

Further, our Epistle is silent not only about the famous 'Teacher of Righteousness' (of whom there was perhaps no reason to speak), but also about the 'wicked Priest', whom it would have been tempting to contrast with the new High Priest. In a general way the Jewish priests are certainly treated as inferior to Christ, but never as enemies of righteousness. Nor has there been, to date, any sign of speculation on Melchizedek in any writings which must be taken into consideration.[2]

Was there in the Epistle to the Hebrews a polemic against Jewish Melchizedekians? Such was the thesis of Friedländer (see his study quoted in 7 above). But it remains very hypothetical. A. C. Purdy[3] thinks that the writer to the Hebrews may have caught echoes of rabbinical discussions touched off by the destruction of the Temple. But there is no reference to that event in the letter.

IV

As is well known, since the famous work by C. F. Burney[4] on the Aramaic origins of the Fourth Gospel, which followed the earlier work by A. Schlatter,[5] the question of Semitisms in the language of the Gospels has come again to the fore. Studies such as those by C. C. Torrey[6] and M. Black[7] are proof of this.

The arguments of Hellenistic opponents of Burney's thesis are also well known.[8] In the first place, they stress the disagreement which reigns among the protagonists of Aramaic over a number of details—which proves nothing, since a divergence between two scholars in no way proves that both are wrong. The second argument is more telling: it has been shown that a great number of supposed Aramaisms in the New Testament can also be found in the Greek of the papyri, notably the unexpected use of some prepositions and conjunctions, as well as other peculiarities of syntax. What was involved then, at least to a large extent, was a shift of the Greek language inherent in the Koiné. At this point, Egyptologists intervened in the debate and propounded a quite different thesis. After

[2] On the connexions between the Damascus Sect and the Dead Sea Sect, see the excellent study by H. H. ROWLEY, 'The covenanters of Damascus and the Dead Sea Scrolls', *Bulletin of the J. Rylands Library*, Manchester, vol. 53, 1952, no. 1.

[3] 'The Purpose of the Epistle to the Hebrews' in *Amicitiae Corolla presented to J. Rendel Harris*, London 1933, pp. 253–264.

[4] *The Aramaic Origin of the Fourth Gospel*, Oxford 1922.

[5] *Sprache und Heimat des vierten Evangelisten*, Gütersloh 1902.

[6] *The Four Gospels*, London 1933.

[7] *An Aramaic Approach to the Gospels and Acts*, Oxford 1946.

[8] See especially the outline of the question in J. H. MOULTON, *A Grammar of New Testament Greek*, Edinburgh 1908.

reminding that all the papyri of the Koiné are of Egyptian origin, they set to work to explain the peculiarities through the influence of Coptic. Two studies are noteworthy in setting the direction of enquiry: a short article in the form of a balance-sheet by L. Lefort[9] and a detailed essay by J. Vergotte.[10] If this view is confirmed the principal weapon of those opposing the supporters of Aramaisms in the New Testament will fall to the ground. For the comparisons made by them would prove or confirm quite simply similarities of syntax between Egyptian dialects on the one side and Semitic languages on the other.

Semitisms in the epistolary literature of the New Testament have been much less studied. Much research remains to be done. But so far as the Epistle to the Hebrews is concerned, a curious question could be posed: supposing that the writer were the Egyptian Jew Apollos, who can say whether some Semitisms in this work may not be Coptisms? This would weaken the hypothesis of Biesenthal, who believed that the original document was Semitic. The ball is in the court of the Coptic scholars.

[9] 'Pour une grammaire des LXX', in the review *Museon*, 1928, pp. 152ff.
[10] See his remarkable article on 'Grec biblique' in PIROT, supplement to the *Dictionnaire de la Bible* of VIGOUROUX, vol. III. The question at issue is dealt with from p. 1354.